ANNUALS

WITH STYLE

design ideas *from* classic to cutting edge

ANNUALS
WITH STYLE

MICHAEL A. RUGGIERO *and* TOM CHRISTOPHER

The Taunton Press

Front cover photos: (large) Judi Rutz, © The Taunton Press, Inc.; (top, left to right) Judi Rutz, © The Taunton Press, Inc.; Michael A. Ruggiero; Michael A. Ruggiero; Michael A. Ruggiero; Michael A. Ruggiero; Mobee Weinstein; Judi Rutz, © The Taunton Press, Inc.; Michael A. Ruggiero

Spine photo: Michael A. Ruggiero

Back cover photo: Michael A. Ruggiero

Photos p. i: Michael A. Ruggiero; p. ii: Judi Rutz, © The Taunton Press, Inc.; p. iii: Michael A. Ruggiero (left and right) and © Michael Gertley (center); p. vi: Michael A. Ruggiero; p. 1: Michael A. Ruggiero (top and bottom) and Judi Rutz, © The Taunton Press, Inc. (center); p. 6: © Derek Fell; p. 7: © Michael Gertley; p. 106: © Michael Gertley; p. 107: Judi Rutz, © The Taunton Press, Inc.; p. 150: © Michael Gertley; p. 151: Michael A. Ruggiero

PUBLISHER: Jim Childs

EDITOR: Anne Halpin White

EDITORIAL ASSISTANT: Meredith DeSousa

COPY EDITOR: Marjorie Wexler

INDEXER: Harriet Hodges

COVER DESIGNER: Carol Singer

INTERIOR DESIGNERS: Margery Cantor and Lori Wendin

LAYOUT ARTIST: Lori Wendin

ILLUSTRATOR: Christine Erickson

Taunton
BOOKS & VIDEOS
for fellow enthusiasts

Printed in Singapore
10 9 8 7 6 5 4 3 2 1

The Taunton Press, Inc.,
63 South Main Street, PO Box 5506, Newtown, CT 06470-5506
e-mail: tp@taunton.com

Distributed by Publishers Group West

Library of Congress Cataloging-in-Publication Data
Ruggiero, Michael, 1946-
   Annuals with style: design ideas from classic to cutting edge / Michael A. Ruggiero & Tom Christopher.
     p.   cm.
   ISBN 1-56158-201-8
   1. Annuals (Plants). I. Christopher, Thomas. II. Title.
     SB422.R85   2000
     635.9'312—dc21   99-047133

For T. H. Everett, Miss Hall, Bridie McSweeney,
and Lou Politi, whose standard was excellence
and who always had time to teach.

ACKNOWLEDGMENTS

MANY PEOPLE HELPED with the creation of this book. We owe a special debt to the following. Lynden Miller, whose design with annuals is an inspiration; Mobee Weinstein, who generously shared photographs; Jane Whippo, a great gardener skilled in the ways of annual flowers and vegetables; Matt Horn, nurseryman extraordinaire; and Peggy Cornett Newcomb, whose book Popular Annuals is the source for information about the history of annual flowers in American gardens. In addition, we want to thank Lou Scarlino, who hosted our conferences (and provided the fishing boat); Brad Roeller (who helped us catch the trout); Matthew, who has a talent for marigolds; Suzanne, who remembers to water; and Cindy, Bob, Edward, William, Josephine, and Ann.

CONTENTS

INTRODUCTION

ANNUALS ARE THE EASIEST FLOWERS to grow—and the easiest to enjoy. The investment you make to start a display of annuals is minimal. For the price of a couple of packets of seeds, and few minutes of attention daily, you can fill a tub, a bed, or a whole yard with color. Best of all, you get this payoff quickly, for as the name suggests, annual flowers are fast-growing. Annuals are plants that complete their life cycle within one growing season; Nature has programmed annual flowers to sprout, mature, and blossom all in a matter of weeks. The fact is, annuals come as close as any garden plant does to providing instant gratification.

Ironically, this quick payoff is a large part of what has given annual flowers such an enduring appeal. Too-busy weekend gardeners, people who haven't time to cultivate elaborate effects, still manage to find time for a splash of annuals. Drive through any American neighborhood, urban, suburban, or rural, and annuals are what you find sprouting from the window boxes, whitewashed tires, and old kettles.

Annuals bring color to the landscape all summer long. (Photo by Michael A. Ruggiero.)

Annuals are the perfect plants for the way we live today. Planting a tree to shade future generations is certainly a noble act. But these days, few of us stay put long enough to watch those branches spread. A planting of shrubs or even perennial flowers needs several years to take hold and fill out. Plant a flat of petunias, scarlet sage, or impatiens—or any other annuals—and you'll have your color that same summer.

What's more, annual color is lasting color. Perennial flowers and most flowering shrubs each have a fairly brief season of bloom. Within a couple of weeks, their blossoms wither and the show is over until next year. Once an annual begins to bloom, though, it typically continues to

bear new flowers all summer long, carrying on often until frost cuts down the plant in autumn.

Annuals are far more, however, than plants for the impatient. They are also the ideal plants for self-expression. Sooner or later any arrangement of flowers loses its appeal. You walk outside one day and realize that suddenly, you long for casual instead of elegant, or for hot colors rather than cool. If you've invested several years in perfecting a display of perennials, then sudden inspirations of this sort are not something you can afford to indulge. Starting over with perennials isn't easy.

(above) Tall *Nicotiana sylvestris* adds height to the garden, as well as slender, drooping white trumpet flowers. (Photo © Michael Gertley.)

(left) Dahlias frame an inviting bench with color well into autumn. (Photo © Michael Gertley.)

A garden of annuals can provide buckets of cut flowers, like this assortment of sunflowers. (Photo © Michael Gertley.)

But it's not a problem if you tire of an annual planting. You just pull up the flowers and replant.

Indeed, because annual flowers grow so quickly, in most regions of the United States it is possible to create a whole new seasonal display for spring, summer, and fall. In the South, in USDA Zones 8 to 11, you can plant a winter garden, too. In those mild-climate regions, winter actually offers the best conditions for growing many of the hardy annuals, such as pansies, snapdragons, and flowering cabbage.

Because they demand such a small investment of trouble and time, annuals encourage spontaneity and playfulness. Try a window box full of red and green lettuces for a city apartment or a giant's border of 7-ft.-tall sunflowers and red-leaved castor beans for the front yard of a tiny weekend cottage. When the joke grows stale, try something else.

The conventional rules of garden design say that blue and orange clash, but you think that combination might be eye-catching, so try it. Mix cosmos 'Bright Lights' with larkspur 'Blue Spire' and see how it works. If you don't like the results, try something else.

This flexibility has made annual flowers the newest "discovery" of sophisticated garden designers. These days, the flowers that were once dismissed as too common are appearing in the most elegant settings. Likewise, plant connoisseurs, those gardeners who collect plants like stamps or coins, are taking up annuals because these plants allow them to indulge more thoroughly their lust for novelty. In a single summer, the collector can experience the whole life cycle of a night-blooming flowering tobacco. The next year, he can use same patch to try out a California sky lupine or a Texas bluebell.

In most gardens, though, annual flowers earn their spot with their ability to solve problems. When some hard-to-please perennial dies, you can plug the gap with an annual. Or suppose you've planted daffodils that bloom in April and roses that bloom in June; what do you do for color in the intervening weeks? Plant annuals. Do you want cut flowers for the house? Sow a few rows of zinnias, annual phlox, and baby's breath at one end of the vegetable garden and you'll have the makings of summer bouquets. Broadcast portulaca seed under the rose bushes and you create both a weed-suppressing, living mulch and a second level of bloom. Annual flowers are unsurpassed as problem solvers.

Of course, as perennial fanciers complain, any solution that annuals provide is only temporary. That's the basis for the most common criticism of annual flowers: that replanting them every year involves too much work. It's true that perennial flowers may return year after year from a single planting, if you nurse them through their infancy, blanket them with a protective mulch through the winter, and then lift and divide them every few years. With annuals you start anew every spring. But in many respects, that's an advantage.

If you change the type of annuals you plant in a bed each year, you accomplish the same thing that farmers do by rotating their crops. Changing the planting every year, or better yet every season, prevents any one type of disease or pest from becoming entrenched in your beds. That means you have far less need of toxic insecticides and fungicides. When you pull up last season's annuals, you can take the opportunity to root out at the same time any perennial weeds that have found their way into your bed. Actually, when you garden with annuals, you can get the garden off to a fresh new start several times a year.

There are lots of reasons to grow these flowers. Undoubtedly, though, the best is this: Anyone

can succeed with annuals. Choose from the hundreds of reliable, easily cultivated types profiled in this book, follow the simple procedures outlined in the following pages, and you are guaranteed a garden full of color. You'll have a garden that can change with your mood and with the season. You'll be on the cutting edge of garden design. And most important, you'll have fun.

Blue salvia and yellow marigolds, with an edging of silvery dusty miller, create a vibrant blue-and-yellow combination. (Photo by Michael A. Ruggiero.)

5

*From Classic
to Cutting Edge:*
DESIGNING WITH

PART ONE

ANNUALS

THE STORY of ANNUALS

WHAT EXACTLY ARE ANNUALS? Where do these plants come from, and what sets them apart from the other plants all around them?

When you're anxious to get out and get planting, these questions may seem nothing more than a distraction. Yet to grow any kind of plant successfully, you need to know its background. How can you water your cactus properly if you don't understand that it is a desert plant? And if you aren't aware that your maidenhair fern is a plant of the moist woodlands, and you set it out

in the blazing sun in sandy soil beside your cactus, undoubtedly the fern will die. Learning where a plant comes from and how it grows is fundamental to understanding what it needs to succeed in your garden.

Getting to know a bit about annuals before you

(opposite) The red of *Cosmos bipinnatus* leaps out from a cool background of blue *Salvia farinacea* 'Victoria' and white *Ammi visnaga* 'Green Mist'. (Photo by Judi Rutz; © The Taunton Press, Inc.)

(left) The fan-shaped, blue flowers of scaevola combine beautifully with the tiny honey-scented blossoms of sweet alyssum and the pink bells of fuchsia. (Photo by Michael A. Ruggiero.)

What Is an Annual? The Botanist's Answer

To botanists, the scientists who created this term, an annual is a plant such as an African marigold (Tagetes erecta) or a common sunflower (Helianthus annuus) that is genetically programmed to complete its full life cycle within one year. An annual's seed germinates, the seedling expands, and then it grows into a mature plant that blooms, sets seeds, and afterward dies, all within 12 months.

Understanding the growth patterns of annuals is a key to growing them successfully.

In most cases, true annuals do not survive even for a full calendar year. Instead, their life spans generally last just a single growing season. This means that throughout most of North America, annuals begin their life with the arrival of spring and complete it in the summer or fall.

In the southwestern states, where the most significant difference between seasons is wet and dry rather than cold and warm, an annual may begin its life with the arrival of the annual rains and complete it with the onset of the dry season. In the extreme Southeast, annuals often find summer heat more of a challenge than winter

Though botanically poppies (foreground) are perennials, many gardeners prefer to treat these short-lived plants as annuals. (Photo by M. C. Pindar.)

start sowing seed or buying seedlings is especially important. That's because annuals are an unusually varied group of garden plants. In fact, the term itself, annual, means quite different things to different people.

(left) Lovely nicotiana is a tender perennial that thrives in warm summer weather. (Photo by M. C. Pindar.)

(below) Pansies and sweet alyssum start blooming in spring in the North and in winter in warm climates. (Photo by Michael A. Ruggiero.)

cold. There, annuals are commonly plants that begin their lives after the summer heat subsides in the fall and complete them during the more temperate weather of winter.

Understanding these growth patterns is important because they largely determine the role that annuals can play in your garden. For example, the common pattern of a spring-to-fall life span in the northern states explains why gardeners in that part of the country regard annuals primarily as a source of summertime color. These gardeners set themselves up for trouble, though, if they take this attitude with them on a transfer to the Sunbelt. The smart gardeners in that

(opposite) *Phlox drummundii,* a hardy true annual, is lovely massed in informal gardens. (Photo by Mobee Weinstein.)

(left) Annual blossoms take many forms. The dangling bells of fuchsias tumble from hanging baskets in shady spots. This cultivar has delicately ruffled petals. (Photo by Michael A. Ruggiero.)

region are more likely to regard annuals as plants for any season but summer.

The annual's calendar

Regardless of the type of calendar an annual follows, you cannot change its basic schedule, at least not if it is a true annual, a botanist's annual. Once such a plant begins making seeds, it is going to direct all its energy to that process. When seed production starts, the plant stops adding new stems, leaves, and flower buds, and soon its overall vigor drains away.

This habit also explains the exceptional color of an annual's floral display. The true annual can expend all of its stored energy on the production of flowers and seeds. An annual can (and usually does) bloom itself to death. A perennial cannot afford such extravagance. It must budget its

The versatile snapdragon (a tender perennial) has a host of uses; its spiky form brings vertical line to the garden, and it now comes in a range of sizes, from dwarf to tall, plus in many colors, from pastels to brights. (Photo by Richard Shiell.)

PROLONGING BLOOM

With a few types of annuals, plant breeders have provided a less troublesome way of achieving the same effect, prolonged blossoming without seed production. By crossing closely related but genetically incompatible types of flowers, they have created hybrids that are healthy and flower normally but are sterile, incapable of bearing seed. Catalogs usually describe such flowers as "mules"; their advantage is that they are, effectively, self-deadheading.

energy more sparingly, so that enough remains in the dormant roots over the winter to produce the next spring's new shoots.

Understanding the true annual's calendar can save you much wasted work and much disappointment, for no matter how you nurture such a plant after seed production has begun, it is still going to deteriorate. Often, a thrifty gardener will try to preserve a favorite annual through the winter by bringing the plant indoors in the fall. This may work if the refugee is one of the tropical perennials that we grow as annuals in our gardens. But if the plant is a true annual, a botanist's annual, such rescue operations are doomed to failure. That plant has completed its allotted life

span, and it will not survive to flourish again the following year, no matter how well it is nurtured.

Although you can't stop an annual's internal calendar, you can delay it somewhat. If you remove an annual's flowers before the seeds start to form (signaled by withering blossoms), you stall the natural progression to the last phase of the annual's life cycle. This is why deadheading, pinching off the flowers as they age and start to wither, is an essential part of the maintenance routine for most annuals. Frustrating the annuals by preventing them from setting seeds is the secret of their prolonged period of bloom.

What Is an Annual?
The Gardener's Answer

Botanists group plants according to their natural characteristics. Gardeners are practical people. We categorize plants by their uses, and so we let annuals define themselves. We don't care if a plant is genetically programmed for an annual

The familiar zonal geranium (*Pelargonium* x *hortorum*) is a tender perennial, not a true annual. (Photo by Judi Rutz; © The Taunton Press, Inc.)

life cycle or not: If a plant behaves like an annual in our gardens, then that's what we call it. For this reason, gardeners have, over the years, included in this category many plants that botanists would not call annuals.

Tender perennials

American gardeners classify as annuals many fast-growing, frost-sensitive perennials. These are plants like the New Guinea impatiens that survive from year to year in their tropical or subtropical homelands, but that die when exposed to the cold weather they encounter during most North American winters. Because New Guinea impatiens is so quick to mature, reaching a blooming size within a few months of sowing its seeds, we use it as an annual. And so we call it an annual.

> ## CLASSIC TENDER PERENNIALS
>
> * Zonal geranium (Pelargonium x hortorum)
> * Sweet alyssum (Lobularia maritima)
> * Garden verbena (Verbena x hybrida)
> * Snapdragon (Antirrhinum majus)
> * Impatiens (Impatiens spp.)

This group of cold-sensitive, or tender, perennials includes many of the most popular "annuals." Not surprisingly, this list expands as you move northward and the severity of the winter weather increases. Even hybrid tea roses should be treated as annuals throughout much of Canada, according to Trevor Cole, an Ontario horticulturist and the former director of the Dominion Arboretum in Ottawa.

The delicate ivory flower of *Corydalis ophiocarpa,* a biennial, blooms with tulips in spring. (Photo by Steve Silk; © The Taunton Press, Inc.)

Biennials

Another type of plant that most gardeners grow as annuals today is the biennial. These are plants such as pansies (Viola x wittrockiana) that normally have a two-year life cycle. The first year they produce only greenery; they bear flowers and seeds in their second year of growth, and after that, like annuals, they die.

A few demanding gardeners still start their own biennials, so that they may have access to all

OUR PARENTS' BIENNIALS

A generation ago, the common practice was to sow biennials in mid to late summer, and then to hold the seedlings over the winter in a cold frame or protected nursery bed. The following spring, the ready-to-bloom plants were moved out into the garden. But this process requires more time and resources than most contemporary gardeners have at their disposal. To spend eight or nine months preparing for a six-week-long display of pansy flowers is not feasible today.

the cultivars that are available only as seed. But they trick the biennials into flowering in their first season of growth by sowing the seeds in late winter or very early in the spring. Most of us are content to buy biennials as packs of young plants at the garden center and plant them directly into the garden. Either way, though, we count on the plants blooming that year, and they have become, for all practical purposes, just another sort of annual.

In many cases, this treatment has expanded the ranges of these plants into regions where,

BIENNIALS TO GROW

- ✻ Hollyhock (Alcea rosea)
- ✻ Canterbury bells (Campanula medium)
- ✻ Bachelor's button (Centaurea cyanus)
- ✻ China pink (Dianthus chinensis)
- ✻ Stock (Matthiola incana)

previously, growing them successfully was impossible. The Southeast, in particular, has benefited, because many biennials are plants such as pansies that prefer cool and temperate weather. These flowers won't survive a southern summer, and if cultivated on a biennial schedule, they cannot be successfully grown in that region. But these same plants often do flourish in the mild, moist weather of a southern winter. If purchased

The selection of impatiens hybrids continues to expand. The example here combines double flowers with variegated leaves. (Photo by Michael A. Ruggiero.)

If you love cut flowers, your annual garden can provide them by the bucketful. (Photo © Michael Gertley.)

as ready-to-flower transplants and set out in the garden in the fall, these "annuals" may bloom happily for months. Pansies, in particular, have become a staple of wintertime gardening in the Southeast and in the mild-winter areas of the Southwest.

What Is an Annual for You?

Ultimately, the choice of what plants to classify as annuals is largely personal. The only real requirement is that the plant must reach a visually effective size in one growing season. Aside from that, anything goes.

Vegetables and herbs

Increasingly, contemporary designers are mixing vegetables and herbs into plantings of annual flowers. What could make a cooler foil to the bright, hot colors of the blossoms than a lush green mound of 'Spicy Globe' basil or an edging of the lacy-leaved Japanese mustard, mizuna?

Flowering kales and flowering cabbages have long been popular as early spring or fall plantings in annual beds and in containers, so why not include some of their striking (and better-tasting) relatives, the red heading cabbages? Nothing makes a more arresting foliage plant than the scarlet-stemmed 'Ruby' chard (Beta vulgaris). Unless, maybe, cardoon (Cynara cardunculus). This Italian relative of the artichoke is normally grown for its edible stalks, which taste like artichoke hearts. But in the annual garden you can admire the 6-ft. tufts of toothed gray-green leaves and the 3-in. blue blossoms that make cardoon look like thistles on steroids.

Ornamental grasses

Over the last decade, ornamental grasses have won an ever-bigger role in American gardens; unfortunately, some of the most spectacular grasses won't tolerate cold weather. The burgundy-leaved Pennisetum setaceum 'Rubrum', for instance, won't overwinter north of USDA Zone 9. This restricts the use of this wonderful

Pansies and lobelia keep company with basil in this garden. (Photo © Michael Gertley.)

⎯ GIVING YOUR ANNUAL GARDEN A FRENCH TWIST ⎯

A geometric bed of lettuce edged with sweet alyssum and parsley. (Photo © Michael Gertley.)

It should come as no surprise that a nation as devoted to the pleasures of the table as the French would understand that food should be beautiful as well as savory. And if it is beautiful, why not enjoy that beauty in the garden as well as in the dining room? This simple reasoning inspired the potager, a centuries-old French style of decorative vegetable gardening that in recent years has become popular in North America.

The only absolute rule of potager making is that everything you plant there must produce some sort of edible crop. A potager shrub, for example,

might be Rosa gallica 'Officinalis', the apothecary's rose, whose perfumed petals are a traditional ingredient of herbal remedies. Likewise, any annuals you plant in the potager should provide food for the pot as well as color— nasturtiums, whose buds, leaves, and blossoms are all edible, are an obvious choice.

Classically, the potager is a hidden garden, shielded from the outside's view by a high fence or wall. This, of course, serves to protect the plantings from hungry wildlife, but it also ensures that the transition from the surrounding landscape into the gourmet fantasy

within is an abrupt surprise. Inside the enclosure, the style may be any that suits you, though you'll find that a formal arrangement of raised beds simplifies the organization of vegetable crops with their carefully scheduled planting times. And formality suits the potager; the concept seems to work best when its vegetables appear as well garnished as a plate of nouvelle cuisine.

In a traditional potager, you'll find pea and bean vines trained up an obelisk-shaped frame, and red and green lettuces alternated in a checker, and hedges of 'Ruby' and green-stemmed chards woven into an embroidery-like "knot." There might be a tufted carpet of dwarf basils, a screen of 'Burgundy' okra along the wall, or a meticulously arranged pattern of many-colored peppers. And certainly, scattered over the vegetables like a dusting of paprika, there will be flowers.

Generally, most of the flowers are annuals, which are cleared in fall and replanted in spring along with the vegetables. The most outstanding flower for a potager is undoubtedly the sunflower (Helianthus annuus), with its edible seeds and petals and its decorative, dramatic tall flowers. Other good choices include French marigolds, pansies, and calendulas.

Cardoon is a dramatic, sculptural focal point in a bed or border. (Photo by Chris Curless; © The Taunton Press, Inc.)

plant to the Gulf Coast, southern Florida, and the coastal areas of southern California—if you try to grow it as a perennial. Farther north, this grass makes an outstanding summer annual, its fountains of wine-dark leaves providing the perfect punctuation mark in a border of blue, mauve, and violet annuals, or perhaps among lower-growing red and purple blossoms and foliages.

Houseplants in the garden

Do you move your dracaena and philodendron outside for the summer? They can furnish a note of tropical exuberance to the flower bed. But bring them inside again before the first fall frost, or they will die like any other annual. Or transplant an "annual" tree into your garden: The variegated calamondin (x Citrofortunella mitis 'Variegata'), a dwarf citrus tree with white-, gray-, and green-mottled leaves and white-striped

PLANTING A VACATION

The huge leaves of *Colocasia* bring a taste of the tropics to northern back yards. (Photo by Michael A. Ruggiero.)

Who hasn't, at some point, dreamed of running away to a tropical paradise? This dream can easily become reality for annual gardeners. They can use their versatile, fast-growing plants to give a convincing, if temporary, tropical look to their plantings. For a few months, at least, escape will be as easy as a trip to the backyard.

Because so many of the popular annuals are actually tropical plants, this project is a simple one, even in our northernmost zones. Really, the only stumbling block for most North American gardeners lies in the change of perspective needed. We are used to mimicking our native meadows and woodlands in our garden design. To make a convincing counterfeit of a tropical landscape, you have to think jungle.

Forget quiet good taste, subtle effects, and delicate color contrasts. That's all temperate climate stuff. For your jungle what you want is oversized foliage—huge leaves—and lurid colors. In fact, this is your chance to indulge in those annuals that you like but have never found the right spot for. This is your chance to savor the gaudy and loud.

The first step in jungle-making is finding the right spot. To be convincing, your jungle has to be more or less self-contained; to look up from the banana tree to a vista of conifers spoils the illusion. A backyard terrace makes an ideal spot for the do-it-yourself tropics, if you enclose it with a hedge of tropical greenery. The corner of a fenced-in yard also works well, or you can create your jungle on a deck by setting long planting boxes around the perimeter.

Tall, large-leaved annuals are the most efficient at creating an enclosure, and the most tropical of these are the com-

pact banana trees Musa acuminata 'Dwarf Cavendish,' 'Dwarf Lady Finger', and 'Dwarf Jamaican Red'. These may be purchased as dormant crowns in early spring. Once planted into large tubs (half whiskey barrels are ideal) of loose, organic-rich potting soil and watered, these annuals soon sprout leaves that may measure 4 ft. long and a foot across. The red-leaved banana Ensete ventricosum 'Maurellii' is especially spectacular. Bananas hate cold, but they are safe outside when spring has advanced to the point that nighttime temperatures don't drop below 50°F, and once the soil

has warmed, you can even transplant the bananas from the tubs right into your beds.

Another excellent enclosure plant is elephant's ear (Colocasia esculenta), which reaches a height of 4 ft. and bears heart-shaped leaves as long as 3 ft. This plant may be purchased inexpensively as dormant tubers in mid spring, started in pots indoors, and then planted out when the soil has warmed to 60°F. Intermingle these with the taller-growing cannas such as the green-leaved 'Los Angeles', the bronze-leaved 'Black Knight', and the reddish-leaved 'Red King Humbert' to create an authentic tropical tangle. As a bonus, the cannas also bear colorful flowers.

For additional color, there are countless good cultivars of coleus, impatiens, caladiums, and Madagascar periwinkles. Tuck these in around the feet of your elephant's ear, cannas, and bananas. Don't worry about blending colors harmoniously—the more flamboyant the clash of foliages and flowers, the better. Remember, what you are aiming for is the kind of space where you lounge in a shirt decorated with parrots.

Move a wrought-iron table and chairs into the center of your newly created clearing, and surround the setup with houseplants, the philodendrons, begonias, and sago palm that have been gathering dust inside all winter. These plants will thrive, as long as you keep them watered and don't set them out in

full sun. Angel's trumpets (Brugmansia spp.) also thrive in tubs. These tropical shrubs will die with the first fall frost, but can reach a height of 4 ft. in a single summer's growth, and their 8-in.-long, trumpet-shaped flowers are night-fragrant, releasing their perfume at dusk. These blossoms are especially attractive in the flickering light of tall, bamboo "tiki" torches; fill these with citronella-scented oil, and they'll keep the mosquitoes away as you pass the long summer evenings sipping one of those parasol-decorated fruit punches.

SOME ANNUALS
FOR A TROPICAL PARADISE

- Compact banana trees (Musa acuminata 'Dwarf Cavendish', 'Dwarf Lady Finger', 'Dwarf Jamaican Red') for enclosure
- Red-leaved banana (Ensete ventricosum 'Maurellii')
- Elephant's ear (Colocasia esculenta)
- Cannas ('Los Angeles', 'Black Knight', 'Red King Humbert')

Cannas offer both dramatic foliage and bold, hot-colored flowers. (Photo by Michael A. Ruggiero.)

Coleus foliage is available in many colors and combinations and in a host of sizes and shapes. (Photo by Michael A. Ruggiero.)

Ornamental grasses such as *Pennisetum* add color, texture, and movement to the garden when their flower plumes sway in the breeze. (Photo © Michael Gertley.)

fruits, lends an air of exotic elegance to the garden. It, too, will overwinter happily indoors, in a pot by a sunny window.

Use your imagination and keep expanding your personal list of annuals. As you do this, remember that a spice of surprise is one of the most effective ways to bring a garden to life. If you live in Wisconsin, planting banana trees and elephant ears in your front yard flower bed is guaranteed to startle passersby and make the local garden club wake up and take notice. Maybe next year you can mix clusters of giant sunflow-

ers with hills of vividly kerneled Indian corn to develop an authentically native American theme.

Annuals in Retrospect

One of the best ways to understand the visual impact that annuals can have on your garden is to imagine how it would look without them. That may seem difficult: Who could imagine a garden without petunias, marigolds, zinnias, scarlet sage, pansies, wax begonias, and impatiens? Is it possible to garden without them?

Indeed it is. Once upon a time, we did.

Before about 1840, American gardeners made very little use of annual flowers, at least for decorative purposes. This is why, for much of the summer then, the most colorful part of the landscape was the vegetable garden. There you would find the blossoms of runner beans and squashes and, at the homes of those with a taste for spicy foods, a blaze of nasturtiums (Tropaeolum spp.). Nasturtiums were regarded as a gourmet item in the days of self-sufficiency—their flower buds and seeds were pickled, to be served as a condiment with meat, and the peppery leaves were added to salads. In the 1850s, even their flowers were grown to be eaten, not for viewing.

Gardens without annuals

Otherwise, our ancestors had little more than a few primitive and unspectacular versions of the balsam impatiens (Impatiens balsamina), China aster (Callistephus chinensis), marigold (Tagetes spp.), and mignonette (Reseda odorata). To these they might have added two more annuals that were more often grown as curiosities: the cockscomb (Celosia argentea var. cristata), which bore grotesque blossoms of red, pink, orange, and yellow in the shape of a rooster's crest, and Gomphrena globosa, which earned its common name of globe amaranth (bachelor's button is the traditional southern name) with abundant crops of small, button-shaped flowers in unremarkable shades of pink, purple, and white.

Annuals in the wild

Our ancestors didn't cultivate more annual flowers because they didn't have them. Back then, most of the annuals we treasure today were still growing undiscovered in exotic and inaccessible places such as Peru and California. Lewis and Clark brought back the first clarkias (Clarkia spp.), a monkey flower (Mimulus lewisii), and a blanket flower (Gaillardia aristata) in 1806.

But Lewis and Clark were collecting for the benefit of botanists, and their finds and those of other contemporary explorers stayed in the gardens of a handful of collectors, unchanged from their wild state. It wasn't until a generation later that the introduction of new annuals into ordinary yards began.

European influences

Until then, American gardens remained largely fields of green. Colonists of Spanish descent had

Nasturtiums were among the first annuals grown in gardens because they're edible. (Photo by Michael A. Ruggiero.)

This gardener paired old-fashioned globe amaranth (foreground) with the modern-looking bronze foliage of the dramatic copper-tone mallow. (Photo by Michael A. Ruggiero.)

introduced the courtyard into the Southeast and the Southwest; fountains and arbors were the focus of their gardens, with color contributed mostly by brightly glazed tiles. French and English planters had brought plans for parterres, elaborate interwoven patterns of evergreen hedges. In the interstices of these living embroideries, an especially ambitious gardener might plant spring bulbs, but the more lasting color, the color that carried the garden through the rest of the year, was liable to come from mulches of different colored gravels or crushed brick.

Flowers for the wealthy

There were flowers, but these for the most part were perennials and shrubs that blossomed in intermittent flushes. In spring, the wealthy might enjoy the blooms of bulbs such as tulips and narcissi, but the cost of these imported bulbs put large plantings beyond the means of even most middle-class families. Later on there were roses, mostly old-fashioned types that flowered just once a year, in late spring or early summer. Wild azaleas and magnolias were brought in from the woods. Simple and hardy perennials such as the tawny daylily and yellow flag iris added their flowers during their brief seasons. For the most part, however, the emphasis was not on bloom but on fruitfulness, with orchards and fruit bushes commonly occupying the center of the landscape. Even at the homes of the wealthy, ornamental gardening was largely limited to open-air barbering, with the gardeners spending their days clipping evergreen shrubs into cones and balls, columns, walls, and statuary.

The rise of the annual

Styles changed with the arrival of the industrial revolution. The growth of a wealthy middle class created a new market for gardening, and the building of railroads and canals, along with the rise in popularity of the steamboat, made it possible for nurseries to serve customers outside their immediate area. The first mass-market mail-order nurseries appeared, and soon the competition for customers became fierce. To be the first to offer some rare and exotic plant could win great prestige for the nurseryman and might mean great sums in sales. This in turn meant there was money to send explorers out on expeditions to the West and to the Tropics, and the ancestors of our modern annuals came pouring in.

Plant hunters

So, in 1823, a primitive petunia with dull white, night-fragrant flowers, Petunia axillaris, was collected from the banks of the La Plata river in South America. In 1827, portulaca, or rose moss, (Portulaca grandiflora) arrived from Brazil. In

Formal designs are new again as today's gardeners are updating the Victorian carpet bed. (Photo by Michael A. Ruggiero.)

Elaborate embroideries of annuals woven into the intricate patterns of carpet beds need meticulous maintenance to retain their shapes. (Photo by Michael A. Ruggiero.)

1835, a Scottish plant explorer sent seeds of Drummond phlox from Texas to a botanical garden in Glasgow, and from there this flower soon found its way into seed catalogs in the eastern United States.

Among these new arrivals were many tropical and subtropical plants, such as verbenas from Argentina and Peru. And the glass and cast iron that was rolling out of the new factories meant that nurserymen could now afford to build greenhouse ranges in which the frost-sensitive plants were propagated and raised in bulk.

From wildflowers to hybrids

As important as the arrival of the new species was what gardeners and nurserymen did with them. The La Plata petunia was crossed with a related species to produce the first hybrid types by 1837. Within a generation, a French gardener had transformed the coarse, simple wild Mexican zinnia, Zinnia elegans, producing a strain of double (many-petalled) cultivars with flowers resembling dahlias.

Meanwhile, all across northern Europe, amateur gardeners were crossing and recrossing plants of the wild native Johnny-jump-up (Viola tricolor) with another native violet (V. lutea) and eventually one from the Near East (V. altaica), to produce a host of bigger, bolder pansies. The ancestors of the zonal geraniums (Pelargonium x hortorum) had traveled to Europe from South Africa early in the seventeenth century, but it wasn't until the explosion of greenhouse-building in the Victorian Age that the large, vivid blossoms familiar to the modern gardener appeared.

Ornate bedding styles— something old is new again

This flood of brilliant—and longer-lasting—new blooms inspired an entirely new style of gardening. Amateurs and professionals alike began looking at the landscape as a canvas. Using the annuals' flowers and their often colorful foliages as pigments, gardeners began painting them over beds and borders in carefully worked patterns.

This process was called "bedding out," and it began with the raising of huge numbers of seedlings in greenhouses—the wealthy grew their own, and gardeners of more modest circumstances bought from the local nursery. Rarely was the flower seed sown right into the bed or border, for gardeners insisted on color from spring through fall, with one or more complete changes of the display along the way. Such a tight schedule could be maintained only if the plants were grown to the flowering point in the greenhouse, so that the bloom began almost as soon as they were transplanted into the garden.

Double-flowered zinnias such as these caused a sensation when they first appeared in Victorian gardens. (Photo by Judi Rutz; © The Taunton Press, Inc.)

A MODERN CARPET BED

Each generation defines itself by rejecting the tastes of its parents, and then time passes and we are free to find the virtue in what has been lost. So Gertrude Jekyll, the great garden maker of turn-of-the-century England, abhorred the Victorian carpet bed. That means we are due to rediscover its bold, graphic possibilities.

We can't reconstruct the originals, mind you. The Victorians, who took for granted their access to cheap, highly skilled labor, gloried in expansive

Impatiens in two colors and silvery dusty miller combine in this modern carpet bed. (Photo by Michael A. Ruggiero.)

plantings. You, whose garden staff are all the same person, must focus your imagination on a smaller scale. As you design, think prayer rug rather than wall to wall.

Because a carpet bed relies on precision for its effect, this is one style of garden that absolutely must begin on paper. Besides, a plan drawn to scale allows you to calculate exactly the number of plants needed to realize your inspiration (see p. 137), and so predict the maintenance your design will require.

Victorian gardeners, who loved precise geometrical symmetry, designed their carpet beds with a compass and protractor. But an asymmetrical bed with a flowing interplay of plant masses is far more likely to suit a contemporary landscape. Still, the lines should be clean and crisp, as a large part of a carpet bed's effectiveness lies in the abstract precision of the pattern.

Draw the first drafts of your plan freehand. Use thick-tipped colored markers and design with a sweep. You'll probably find a French curve, an inexpensive drafting instrument available at any art supply store, helpful in smoothing and coordinating the outlines in your next draft, the finished plan you'll use for the actual planting. Don't begin with drafting tools, though. Your carpet bed should have the freehand energy of graffiti.

The Victorians commonly laid out their carpet beds around a tall focal point, commonly a tropical foliage plant such as the fountain dracaena, Cordyline australis. By giving a third dimension, height, to the display, such a focal point helps to keep the bed from looking flat and static. A standard, an annual plant that has been trained into a "tree" form, also works well for this purpose. Traditional favorites for training into standards are fuchsias and heliotrope; inserting one of these living heirlooms into your carpet bed will give it an elegant antique flavor.

When it came to working out a bed's color pattern, the Victorians favored strong contrasts. In today's bright-colored world, we are more likely to take pleasure in subtler compositions.

Try using your carpet bed to explore the delicate contrasts provided by tones of a single color. For example, create a most unusual display of green flowers and foliages. Interweave beds of the chartreuse-flowered Zinnia 'Envy' with beds of Nicotiana 'Lime Green' or 'Havana Lime Green', accent them with the taller stalks of an ornamental corn such the white and green striped Zea mays 'Albovariegata', and encircle the whole with a flow of the chartreuse ornamental sweet potato Ipomoea 'Margarita'.

Often such displays were quite elaborate, as in the style known as carpet bedding. This was a sort of horticultural paint-by-the-numbers, in which the annuals were planted out according to a detailed plan drafted well ahead of time. Bright-hued flowers were usually preferred for such schemes: scarlet geraniums or sages; white, purple, or red verbenas; pink, white, or purple petunias; and white sweet alyssum or electric blue lobelias for edging.

These plantings had the effect of a floral Persian rug (which was why the technique was called carpet bedding), and they might extend over hundreds or even thousands of square feet and involve the meticulously spaced planting of tens of thousands of seedlings. Often the beds were cut into the shapes of birds or butterflies, or into patterns such as a fleur-de-lis, with the various parts painted in with annuals of the appropriate colors.

Ribbon beds

Another popular Victorian device was the "ribbon bed," in which strips of annual flowers were alternated with strips of foliage plants. Usually, the emphasis was on startling color contrasts: orange and purple, red and white, or even a patri-

Blue lobelia alternates with white alyssum in edging this ribbon of scarlet sage. (Photo by Michael S. Thompson.)

otic striping of red, white, and blue. Such displays might also be curled into circular patterns, generally with a white foliage plant at the center.

Victorian gardeners preferred dwarf cultivars of the various annuals for use in both ribbon and carpet beds, because a low, even sheet of flowers displayed the designer's pattern most clearly.

> ✳ *Carpet beds are bold and graphic but require continual maintenance.*

If a design demanded a particular annual—an essential blue, for example, might be available only in a lobelia—and there was no dwarf cultivar of that annual, then gardeners made do by continuously trimming and pinching back the plants to keep them to size. These floral displays demanded daily attention, anyway; the plants had to be deadheaded constantly to keep them in the full bloom that made the beds so colorful.

Competitive carpet bedding

As each gardener tried to outdo his or her neighbor, the beds kept expanding, until some reached a monstrous size. From simple geometric patterns, the carpet beds developed into elaborate scrollworks, monograms, coats of arms, and butterflies. City parks departments created giant working clocks, whose faces were entirely composed of flowers, and Chicago's Columbian Exposition of 1893 featured cartoon-like representations of elephants, Father Time, and floral crowns. To realize these designs took tens of thousands of plants.

Undoubtedly, though, the greatest carpet bedding display of all time was an American flag planted by a California seed company in 1942, long after the fashion for this sort of planting had passed. Covering nine acres, it was composed of some 600,000 larkspurs and calendulas.

When Annuals Fell Out of Fashion

Such displays might have been impressive, but they weren't necessarily beautiful. Besides, to buy or grow enough plants for such a horticultural behemoth was crippling, and the labor involved in keeping the planting in shape was oppressive. By the last quarter of the nineteenth century, the tastemakers in the garden world were demanding something more practical, and more subtle. The general response was a shift to perennial flowers that, theoretically at least, did not require yearly replanting.

The best designers, such as England's Gertrude Jekyll, found plenty of niches for annuals in their new herbaceous borders and "wild" gardens. But on the whole, the popular attitude toward annuals became one of suspicion (they were too much work) and disdain (annuals were obvious and garish, a sure mark of vulgarity).

(opposite) A sea of verbena (*Verbena* ssp.) in pink, red, and purple. (Photo by Michael A. Ruggiero.)

Summer annuals can provide a season-long wash of color against which to display the passing colors of perennials. (Photo by Steve Silk; © The Taunton Press, Inc.)

A New Outlook

Fortunately, attitudes about annuals are changing. Over the last decade, garden tastemakers have rediscovered what smart gardeners have always known: Annuals make sense and annuals are fun. Today, the best designers are not only using annuals in their gardens, they are using them in entirely new ways. Annuals are moving back to center stage, and in the process they are transforming American gardens.

Lynden Miller, for example, finds annuals indispensable. She's a designer who specializes in public gardens and has transformed many New York City spaces, from the Conservatory Gardens in Central Park to the display gardens of the New York Botanical Garden in the Bronx. Lynden relies on annuals for the long season of color they give, and she likes to mix annuals with perennials and shrubs, for she finds that annuals enhance other kinds of plants.

In a flower border, for example, she likes to use them as a sort of stable setting against which to display the coming and going of the perennial blooms. She's always experimenting with new annuals. That's important, she believes, for she ascribes the renewed popularity of annuals to an increase in diversity. A generation ago, she says, there seemed to be few annuals available other than marigolds and red salvia. Now she finds 40 pages of annuals in the better catalogs. How can an adventurous designer (or gardener) resist?

These attitudes continued to stigmatize annual flowers, and those who grew them, for generations. Gardeners with taste cultivated perennials—only the unsophisticated concentrated on annuals. Unless, that is, in a triumph of inverted snobbery, you grew rare, unhybridized types unobtainable from the average nursery, those "annuals for connoisseurs."

TERMS TO KNOW

Terminology can be confusing when it comes to annuals. So, when thumbing through catalogs or looking at the labels in the local garden center, you are likely to see each annual described by one of a number of archaic terms. There will be annuals that are classified as hardy and others as half hardy and tender. These classifications date back to the Victorian Age, and they are inherited from the English. As such, they reflect a preoccupation with cold, since that was (and is) the main challenge to annual flowers on that northern island (which actually lies on the same latitude as Labrador).

We offer the following definitions:

HARDY

The seeds of this type of annual, including asters, larkspurs, poppies, sweet alyssum, and sweet peas, may be sown directly into outdoor garden beds even in a northern spring. Seeds of hardy annuals will germinate successfully in the cool, damp conditions they will experience there, and the seedlings will tolerate light frosts. In fact, in mild-winter regions, these plants are best grown as winter annuals.

HALF-HARDY

Half-hardy annuals are not reliably proof against even a light frost, but they do flourish in cool weather. As a rule, such annuals need a long season

of growth and so are still sown in early spring—but indoors. The resulting seedlings are transplanted out into the garden as soon as the danger of frost is past. Examples of this group include gerbera (Gerbera jamesonii) and spider flower (Cleome hasslerana). Many of the most popular half-hardy annuals, such as petunias and snapdragons, are actually frost-sensitive perennials.

TENDER

Annuals labeled tender are sensitive to cold, will not tolerate even a light frost, and do not thrive in chilly spring or fall weather. Some of these, such as zinnias, are true annuals, while others, such as coleus (Coleus x hybridus),

wax begonias (Begonia semperflorenscultorum), and zonal geraniums (Pelargonium x hortorum), are actually tropical and subtropical perennials. As a rule, these annuals bloom generously through high summer in the North, and are the best bet for warm-weather plantings in the South.

(above left) Sweet peas are hardy annuals. (Photo © Michael Gertley.)

(above) Spidery-flowered cleome is half-hardy. (Photo by Michael A. Ruggiero.)

(left) Morning glories are tender and like warm weather. (Photo by Michael A. Ruggiero.)

INTO *the* GARDEN

FOR REAL GARDENERS, design is personal. We wouldn't let someone else choose the house we live in, and we aren't about to let a stranger design our garden. Real dirt-under-the-fingernails gardeners don't want to plant according to someone else's blueprint or work by someone else's rules. And for good reason. Our goal, after all, is to satisfy ourselves, and no one knows how to do that as well as we do.

Just the same, that doesn't mean we can't benefit from the experience of others. If you were setting out to build a home of your own, you would certainly talk to a carpenter, and you'd make sure you knew how to use the tools of that trade. There are tools—basic techniques—for designing a garden, too. Informing yourself about them before you begin will make it much easier to get the landscape effects you want.

(opposite) The hot-colored foliage of *Amaranthus tricolor* 'Aurora Yellow' is as dazzling as any flower. (Photo by Michael A. Ruggiero.)

(left) The maroon foliage of *Hibiscus acetosella* (rear) provides a contrasting backdrop for the yellow and orange flowers of zinnias and cosmos and for the up-thrusting leaves of *Yucca* 'Gold Sword' (front). (Photo by Mobee Weinstein.)

✿ Growing annuals in containers allows the flowers to become part of the architecture of the landscape.

Because design is mostly a matter of satisfying the eye, we are going to do more than just tell you how to get the most from your annuals. In the following pages, we will show you in photographs how other gardeners have handled the process of designing with annuals. In this way, you can benefit from their successes and their mistakes as you learn to handle the design tools in a way that suits you.

Opportunities for Display

Before you begin thinking about designing your annual plantings, you need to know where you want to display them. This is the most basic design decision, for where you grow your annuals will affect how you'll display them. Each situation offers different opportunities, and you will want to make the most of them.

This sort of preparation is valuable even for experienced gardeners because annuals offer unique opportunities for color and creativity. To benefit from these opportunities, however, you have to recognize them and know how to exploit them.

Annuals in containers

Containers offer the easiest and most versatile—and often the most effective—way to display annual flowers. Because their development from seed to blossom is so quick, annuals are the ultimate container plants. Perennials need at least a

THE BEAUTY OF BASKETS

Hanging baskets offer real horticultural advantages. For one, they provide for your plants a breezier, and often less humid, microclimate. In addition, they offer flexibility. You can hang baskets of impatiens or begonias from the limbs of a big crabapple to give it a second season of bloom, and then, on the night of a party, you can move all the baskets to hang over your deck.

Suspend a row of flower-filled baskets from the front of a porch roof to create a living screen. By drawing and holding the eye of passersby, the baskets ensure a certain amount of privacy to those relaxing on the porch behind. At the same time, the porch-sitters enjoy an illusion of isolation—their eyes also stop at the baskets, and they don't see the busy street beyond.

A whole garden in itself, this mixed basket can be moved as the need changes. (Photo by Michael A. Ruggiero.)

Tiers of planters bursting with annuals point the way to the back door. (Photo by Susan Kahn; © The Taunton Press, Inc.)

year of growth in a nursery bed before they are ready to transplant into a window box or basket.

Besides, because of their relatively short season of bloom, most perennials give a poor return for the labor of potting them up. Even spring bulbs, a very popular and welcome early-season display, must be planted into their container early enough to allow many weeks of chilling before they emerge above the soil. For that reason, most home gardeners, when they want a container display of these flowers, prefer to buy

Annuals become architecture: In this row of baskets, petunias are matched with dracaenas. (Photo by Michael A. Ruggiero.)

To create a focal point or to highlight a favorite plant, grow it in a decorative container placed in a prominent spot. (Photo by Delilah Smittle; © The Taunton Press, Inc.)

their bulbs already potted up and ready to bloom—an expensive solution.

Annuals, by contrast, are available as inexpensive seedlings throughout the growing season and can be bought on a whim to pop into a pot, tub, or window box. Because a container of annuals requires such a slight investment of money and time, this style of growing, like no other, encourages experimentation.

Another advantage of growing annuals in containers is that it allows the flowers to become a part of the architecture of the landscape. A rectangular tub of pansies or geraniums can become a divider that marks off an eating area within the

WINDOW BOXES

Window boxes can help visually connect a house with the landscape. Of course, window boxes also transform the view from within, and it's fun to create in them gardens that echo the theme of the room from which you look at them.

Outside a sunny kitchen window, for example, you might mount a miniature salad patch of different-hued leaf lettuces. When summer heat prompts the lettuces to bolt, you could refill with herbs.

Most of the common culinary herbs, such as rosemary, thyme, and sage, are of Mediterranean origin, and they won't mind the droughty conditions of a summertime window box garden. In fact, where summers are hot and humid, the herbs may grow much better up in the air, where they catch every breeze, than they will on the ground, where the air is likely to be stagnant. And when you need a pinch of seasoning, you can get it fresh without ever leaving the kitchen.

White-flowered lobelia makes a counterpoint to pink nicotiana; annuals are the ultimate window box plants. (Photo by Michael A. Ruggiero.)

confines of a patio. Or it can serve as a foot rail to define the edge of a porch, while a row of hanging baskets suspended from the roof serves as a screen, creating a sense of enclosure and privacy. Even a small tub of blooming annuals is sure to draw the eye, so by incorporating a planter into a bench you advertise a seating spot or draw passersby into a shop or a pub. Flowers have a softening effect, and a window box or hanging basket can do much to lighten a facade that might otherwise seem oppressively formal. Containers also allow you to garden in areas that otherwise would not support plants at all. A cluster of pots turns an empty corner of pavement into an impromptu flower bed.

Keep in mind, too, that containers can make your plants inaccessible to many pests—rabbits can't nibble the petunias you suspend 6 ft. up in a hanging basket.

Even where there is plenty of soil to plant in, you may find that you still prefer containers. By planting in pots, you can drop spots of color into the surrounding greenery like exclamation points. And when you become bored by the effect, you can rearrange it in minutes.

A pot of impatiens dropped into a sheet of creeping junipers relieves the solemnity of the evergreens. (Photo by Michael A. Ruggiero.)

(right) Ivy on a trellis adds a third dimension to a half-barrel bouquet of blue lobelia and pink tuberous begonias. (Photo © Michael Gertley.)

(far right) Annual classics—zonal geraniums, petunias, and swan river daisies—bring a traditional look to a formal urn. (Photo by Michael A. Ruggiero.)

Emphasizing your annuals

A final advantage of container plantings is that they give the most impact to the plants. By putting flowers on a pedestal and displaying them like bouquets, containers give them an effect disproportionate to their size. For example, envision half a whiskey barrel on fire with half a dozen scarlet geraniums, with swags of scarlet runner beans spilling over the side. Set that beside the front door, and it will do more to make the entryway inviting than any quantity of foundation plantings. What's more, because of the containers' mobility, they offer a kind of garden that can change to suit your mood or need. You can easily assemble all your pots and tubs on the back terrace for the evening of a party, or move them into the house to dodge a late or early frost.

Massed pots of petunias in a variety of heights and sizes turn a deck into a lush flower garden. Climbing roses frame the door and railing, but annual morning glories would also do nicely. (Photo by Robert Vinnedge; courtesy David Rigby.)

Faux stone containers made of durable Fiberglas add an elegant note to the garden. (Photo by Michael A. Ruggiero.)

Annuals take to all sorts of whimsical containers, such as an old work boot, a garden cart, or a wheelbarrow. (Photos far left and below by Michael A. Ruggiero; photo left by Charles Mann.)

Containers as part of the display

The really unique aspect of planting annuals in containers, however, is that the container can become as much a part of the display as flowers. Old iron kettles, wooden tubs, and terra cotta pots are classic containers for annual flowers, but virtually anything that will contain soil can be pressed into service. We've seen a dozen football helmets upended, filled with potting mix, and hung in a row to make an annual garden in Texas, an old shoe sprouting annuals on a Cape Cod porch, an old garden cart turned into a mobile planter in a New York yard. Turn a tire inside out and you'll make a planter that lends the genuinely rural look to your weekend "farm."

CONTAINER DESIGN TIPS

To put together a lush, professional-looking container planting, design the container as you'd design an in-the-ground planting:

* Choose plants in a gradation of heights—place a tall plant in the center, surrounded by mid-height plants, with smaller plants closer to the container's edge. Finish with trailing or cascading plants to spill over the edges.
* Aim for a variety of forms and textures in flowers and foliage.
* Because the space is small, work with a simple color scheme, whether harmonious or contrasting.
* Don't overlook the importance of foliage.
* Choose plants with similar needs for light and moisture.

Containers provide opportunities for contrasts and harmonies, as in this match of *Zinnia angustifolia* and *Zinnia* 'Red Sun', *Cleome* 'Rose Queen', and ivy-leaved geraniums and blue salvia. (Photo © The Taunton Press, Inc.)

A pot serves as the perfect showcase for one extraordinary plant, such as this bleeding heart vine (*Clerodendrum thomsoniae*). (Photo by Michael A. Ruggiero.)

We've even seen a bed of annuals that was literally just that: an old four-poster converted into a broad, legged tub and then tucked in with a quilt of flowers.

Or you can go for a decorative, classy look and plant your annuals in a Victorian-style urn, a hand-painted oriental cache pot, or a concrete or faux stone planter.

Whether you opt for humor or elegance, annuals and containers are perfect partners.

Container maintenance

The nature of growing plants in a pot makes this type of display, for the most part, exceptionally easy to create and maintain. If you don't want to take the time to mix your own potting soil, you can buy it bagged and ready to plant. If the potting soil you use is free of weed seeds, then your container plantings should need virtually no weeding. Because the container plantings are, by their nature, concentrated, the muscle involved in putting them together is usually slight.

> *✻ Annuals in containers need frequent watering and regular fertilizing as well.*

One aspect of maintenance, though, is increased by container cultivation, and that is watering. The area of soil available to the plants' roots is relatively small, and as the roots draw moisture from it, additional water can't percolate in from the soil around and below, as would happen in an ordinary, in-the-ground planting. As a result, container plantings require conscientious watering; in hot weather, your pots may need daily irrigation.

Annual Beds and Borders

In-the-ground plantings composed entirely of annuals have been, traditionally, the most popular way to display this class of flowers, and they certainly offer many practical advantages. Preparation, planting, and maintenance are far more efficient on a per-plant basis in these types of displays.

In a bed or border that is to be planted entirely with annuals, each growing season starts with a clean slate. Because you aren't trying to carry over any plants from the last season, you can turn the soil in the empty bed with a mechanical tiller. Such a machine will cultivate even a large expanse in a matter of minutes, and it will at the

This bed of petunia 'Carpet Red' and *Salvia farinacea* 'Victoria' makes a bold splash. (Photo by Judi Rutz; © The Taunton Press, Inc.)

Tall cosmos punctuate
this border with vertical
accents. Deep purple
heliotrope and lighter
ageratum grow in front.
(Photo by Michael A.
Ruggiero.)

same time dig in whatever fertilizer, compost, sphagnum peat, or other amendments your soil may need. A general cultivation such as this also gives you the opportunity to eliminate any perennial weeds—just watch the soil as you till it and fish out any roots as they surface.

If you intend to include a large burst of annual color in your garden, you'll find that it is also far more efficient to plant all the plants at once and all together. With a good trowel, you can set out a whole flat's worth of seedlings into an empty, well-prepared bed in less time than it takes to work a single six-pack of the same plants into the openings within an existing planting of perennials and shrubs.

Set out lots of annual plants at the same time to create a mass of color.

Ease of maintenance

Maintaining an unmixed bed or border of annual flowers can also be more efficient than caring for a display composed of several different kinds of plants. If you have chosen compatible species of annuals, then watering is simple. Because all the plants get the same amount of water, you can irrigate with a sprinkler or a drip irrigation system controlled by a timer.

By contrast, when annuals are intermingled with other types of plants, you are likely to find yourself doing a lot of spot watering with a hose or watering can. Especially when the annual seedlings are young, their root systems are almost certain to be less extensive than those of the established perennials and shrubs around

Masses of yellow marigolds and blue mealycup sage create an eye-popping sea of primary color. (Photo by Michael A. Ruggiero.)

(right) Fragrant purple
heliotrope and pale
Madagascar periwinkle
look cool and soft.
(Photo by Michael A.
Ruggiero.)

(above) The silvery
foliage of dusty miller
can visually blend con-
trasting colors or tone
down bright hues like
that of this celosia.
(Photo by Michael A.
Ruggiero.)

(right) Meticulously
pruned evergreen
shrubs make an elegant
formal screen but they
need flowers to soften
their severe look. (Photo
by Michael A. Ruggiero.)

them. If the annuals have less extensive roots,
then they will be less effective at searching out
and collecting moisture from the soil. That
means you'll have to give them more irrigation
than the surrounding plants, and that type of
handwork can absorb a disproportionate share of
your time.

Visual impact

The sheer quantity of blossoms they offer up to
the eye gives annual beds and borders a strong,
assertive presence. And if you follow a traditional
pattern and create the whole planting out of just
a couple of cultivars, then you greatly reinforce
the visual impact: A block of 100 'Orange Lady'
marigolds will be perceived not as 100 individual
plants but as a single, overwhelming unit.

Such a brilliant, even brash, effect may be
just what you want in a situation such as a front
yard planting that will be viewed from a distance—from the vantage of the sidewalk or the
street—and that is designed to catch the eye of
passersby.

In a quieter, more intimate setting, though, a
large, unmixed planting of brightly colored annuals is likely to look obvious or even garish. Here,
you would probably do better to use pastel-col-
ored flowers of related hues. For a quieter effect,
you could mix different shades of pink and rose
with an occasional splash of violet, or blend
together blues and purples.

In this small space, large blocks of identical flowers would be overwhelming. Here, soft colors in a mixed planting are more appealing.
(Photo by Stacy Geiken.)

You can also soften the impact of a planting by avoiding large blocks of single types of flowers. Instead, intermingle the different species and cultivars, planting in clusters of more than three to five individuals of each type.

Softening bright colors

Mixing white flowers in with the brighter colors dilutes the impression that they make on the eye. Whites also have the effect of brightening a shady spot. Of course, some settings, such as a brightly lit seaside garden, demand bright colors. You can temper the effect, though, by interweav-ing foliage plants of eye-soothing greens and grays. A classic seaside planting, for instance, is scarlet-flowered geraniums (Pelargonium x hortorum) mixed with silver-leaved dusty miller (Senecio cineraria). This combination is certainly bright, and it can hold its own even in the blinding seaside light, yet its effect is not loud but elegant.

Starting small

In any case, when you design a garden purely of annuals, what gardeners have traditionally called a bedding display, you should take care not to let

Often, a small cluster of bright flowers, such as these African mari-golds (*Tagetes erecta*), adds zest. Photo by Judi Rutz; © The Taunton Press, Inc.)

(far left) Vibrant contrast is the theme of this knot of *Yucca* 'Gold Sword', blue-flowered *Browallia americana*, and scarlet-flowered *Bouvardia ternifolia*, an exciting new tropical. (Photo by Judi Rutz; © The Taunton Press, Inc.)

(left) A monochromatic garden of zinnias, lilies, tidytips (*Layia*), and tansy. (Photo by Peter Krumhardt; © The Taunton Press, Inc.)

enthusiasm run away with your judgment. A huge expanse of flowers may be attractive in theory, but maintaining it is likely to prove onerous. Routine chores such as deadheading (picking the fading blossoms off the plants), which are easy to keep up with when the planting is small, suddenly become a burden. And if you neglect the upkeep, the bed or border will look simply shabby rather than impressive.

You are far more likely to please your audience, and yourself, with a compact planting that is well designed and well maintained. Besides, it's more fun, and that is what annuals should be.

Mixed Beds and Borders

These days, more and more gardeners are integrating their garden, growing annuals, bulbs, perennials, shrubs, and even small trees together

(left) An ornamental grass adds texture to this combination of *Salvia* 'Victoria' and 'Blue Bedder' and purple-leaved *Setcreasea* 'Purple Heart'. (Photo by Susan Kahn; © The Taunton Press, Inc.)

BACKBONE PLANTS FOR MIXED BORDERS

Pennisetum 'Moudry' provides a soft counterpoint for the blue spikes of *Salvia leucantha* in their late-summer garden. (Photo by Michael A. Ruggiero.)

GOOD SHRUBS FOR MIXED BORDERS
- Corkscrewed European filbert (Corylus avellana 'Contorta')
- Red-barked Tartarian dogwood (Cornus alba)
- Wingthorn rose (Rosa sericea var. pteracantha)

ORNAMENTAL GRASSES TO CONSIDER
- Japanese silver grass (Miscanthus sinensis cvs.)
- Fountain grasses (Pennisetum spp.)
- Dwarf black bamboo (Phyllostachys nigra 'Hale')

ongoing color and bridge the gaps between the blooming periods of the perennials and shrubs.

Caring for a mixed garden is a bit more complex than maintaining an unmixed planting of annuals. That's because the mixed bed or border isn't planted all at once and the individual plants that it contains will require different sorts of care. Obviously, you can't treat an annual and a shrub alike. If you keep maintenance in mind when you are designing the mixed planting, however, you can keep the work to a minimum. The result can still be a remarkably care-free display.

in beds and borders. A mixed display typically includes perennial plants and shrubs, small trees, and annuals. Generally, it is the perennials and shrubs that are the backbone of the design, since they are its permanent features. Annuals are added and replaced on a regular basis to provide

Minimizing maintenance

The secret is to create the backbone of the planting out of shrubs and ironclad perennials such as daffodils, irises, and peonies, which return reliably year after year and need little care. Avoid the spectacular but more demanding sorts of perennials such as summer phloxes—you'll get all the color you could want from the annuals.

When selecting shrubs, look for ones with an interesting branching structure. Larger, clump-forming ornamental grasses, although not shrubs, have a similar bulk and presence, and

Besides supplying season-long color, annuals can also bring interesting forms to mixed beds and borders. In fact, you can choose annuals whose forms complement those of the perennials in your garden. Spiky flowers can be especially useful. One annual that mixes beautifully with perennials in mixed gardens is mealycup sage (Salvia farinacea). Its blue-violet flower spikes are long-lasting and produced in abundance.

Mealycup sage, dusty miller, and pansies integrate easily into a mixed planting. (Photo © Michael Gertley.)

their dry stems and flower stems persist through the winter to add a note of austere grace. The less aggressive bamboos make a very striking backdrop for a mixed planting, although southern gardeners should beware, as the bamboos are likely to spread out of control in their climate.

(left) Antique pansies. (Photo by L. A. Jackson, courtesy Goldsmith Seeds.)

Annuals as Featured Players

In the Deep South and the low-altitude Southwest, of course, the role of annuals in a mixed border is somewhat different, anyway. There, if cool-season annuals such as pansies are injected into the border in mid fall, they will keep the garden in color all winter long.

In any region and any climate, however, a mixed planting offers not only color but also a more sophisticated kind of beauty. In addition, it provides the perfect setting for showing off choice but individualistic annuals, such as the cockscombs (Celosia argentea var. cristata) and the many wonderful cultivars of the common sunflower (Helianthus annuus). These are intriguing as single specimens or in clusters of a few plants, but they are likely to seem overwhelming or even grotesque in a massed bedding display.

Making a mixed planting work also requires forethought: When arranging the more permanent plants, you must make sure to leave opportunities for the annual flowers. Don't stuff the space full of perennials and shrubs and then try to shoehorn in the annuals later. Crowding the plants in this fashion will cause injury to the roots of the perennials and shrubs and stunt the growth of the annuals.

One additional advantage of a mixed planting is that, thanks to the annuals, it can look impressive its very first season. While the perennials and shrubs are young and small (and unimpressive), fill the gaps between them with extra annuals. As the permanent plantings mature and expand, gradually reduce the number of annuals you plant among them.

A Living, Flowering Mulch

Annuals don't always have to be the star attraction in your garden displays: They can also serve in a supporting role. When used as an underplanting around and underneath woody plants, annuals are technically just a background. They are the kind of backdrop, however, that makes the principal players, the plants above, look better than they ever have before.

(above) A container of cypress vine and chartreuse *Ipomoea* 'Margarita' plays off the green-and-white foliage of shrubby variegated dogwood. (Photo by Michael A. Ruggiero.)

(right) Bold shapes and bright colors update the traditional border. (Photo by Steve Silk; © The Taunton Press, Inc.)

ANNUALS TO PLANT UNDER SHRUBS

Portulacas are an ideal choice for planting under shrubs—they are not only shallow-rooted but also drought tolerant. Other suitable plants include Dahlberg daisies (Dyssodia tenuiloba), pansies (Viola x wittrockiana), and sweet alyssum (Lobularia maritima). Some of these are sun lovers, others prefer shade, and the various plants prefer different kinds of soils.

Underplanting among shrubs

You'll benefit in several ways from weaving a groundcover of annuals around the bases of shrubs in a foundation planting or along a fence line, or even under and among the bushes in a bed of roses. Not only will the annuals provide another season and another level of bloom, they will also function as a sort of living mulch to help repress the growth of weeds.

Unlike true mulches, however, an underplanting of annuals will not help keep the soil moist. On the contrary, the annuals will actually increase the need for watering in that area.

An annual underplanting enhances virtually any upright shrub, evergreen or deciduous. You won't want to treat prostrate shrubs in this fashion, for the obvious reason that the annuals would soon swamp their prostrate branches. Nor can you safely underplant annuals among very shallow-rooted shrubs, such as azaleas and rhododendrons, that send their feeder roots

Styrax japonica takes well to interplanting. (Photo by Lee Anne White; © The Taunton Press, Inc.)

right up to the soil surface. A little exploration with a trowel should reveal if the shrubs you contemplate underplanting have shallow roots.

The most important characteristic to look for in selecting annuals for this sort of display is that they are shallow-rooted. Digging the soil to a depth of more than an inch or two would injure the topmost roots of even deep-rooted shrubs, so the annuals you use for an underplanting must be able to flourish in very shallow soils. Because the shrubs' roots suck water from the soil, the area around their bases is especially quick to dry out, so drought-tolerant annuals are often good choices.

FLOWERING TREES TO UNDERPLANT

- Flowering dogwoods (Cornus florida and C. kousa)
- Ornamental crabapples (Malus spp.)
- Flowering cherries (Prunus spp.)
- Eastern redbud (Cercis canadensis)
- Fringe tree (Chionanthus virginicus)
- Yellowwood (Cladrastis lutea)
- Franklinia (Franklinia alatamaha)
- Carolina silverbell (Halesia carolina)
- Golden rain tree (Koelreuteria paniculata)
- Stewartia (Stewartia koreana)
- Japanese snowbell (Styrax japonica)

Impatiens are ubiquitous but still free-blooming, reliable plants to grow under trees and foundation shrubs. (Photo by Michael A. Ruggiero.)

Watering considerations

The only special difficulty involved in maintaining an annual underplanting lies in the watering. Applying the water from above with a conventional sprinkler will wet the leaves of the shrubbery, and, especially in the case of roses, this is liable to promote foliar diseases among the shrubs. What's more, the interference of the shrub canopy is likely to deflect falling droplets so that the water is not distributed evenly over the annuals below. Generally, it's better to water the underplanting and the shrubs, too, with soaker hoses or a drip irrigation system.

Underplantings beneath trees

Surrounding the bases of tree trunks with a circle of pachysandra, ivy, or other groundcovers is a popular way of protecting the tree bark from injury by mowers and string trimmers while also reducing the amount of hand trimming. But why settle for a mere sheet of green? Why not plant annuals and get all the benefits of a groundcover, plus flowers as well?

TREES TO AVOID UNDERPLANTING

- Norway, red, and silver maples (Acer platanoides, A. rubrum, and A. saccharinum)
- Pecan (Carya illinoensis)
- Beeches (Fagus spp.)
- Thornless honey locust (Gleditsia triacanthos var. inermis)
- Walnuts (Juglans spp.)
- Sweet gum (Liquidambar styraciflua)
- Sycamores (Platanus spp.)
- Poplars (Populus spp.)
- Oaks (Quercus spp.)
- Black locust (Robinia pseudoacacia)
- Weeping willow (Salix alba)
- Elms (Ulmus spp.)

Why not, indeed. Many annual flowers thrive in partial shade. In the South and Southwest, a tree canopy can be vital protection against sunburn for flowers as well as for gardeners. Besides, a tree provides a most natural anchor for an island of annuals. A bed of annuals looks adrift if dropped into the center of the lawn; flaring out around the base of the trunk, the planting makes sense. So plant, but before you do, be aware of some potential complications.

Smart planting

Not every tree provides good shelter for an annual planting. Some, such as southern magnolia (Magnolia grandiflora), cast so dense a shade and so thickly carpet the soil with their fallen leaves that no herbaceous plant can survive beneath them.

✳ When trees bloom, the counterpoint between them and the underplanted annuals can be dazzling.

Shallow-rooted trees, species that send their roots right up to the surface of the soil, leave no room for annuals to spread their roots. If you try to turn up the soil under such a tree, you'll injure its roots, and if you layer on fresh topsoil, the roots will reinfiltrate anyway. Unfortunately, many of the popular shade trees fit into this category.

For a quick vertical line, nothing beats annual vines. Climbing snapdragon (*Asarina*) is a beauty. (Photo by Michael A. Ruggiero.)

Luckily, the list of trees that do permit under-planting is even longer. Most of the small to moderate-sized flowering trees respond well to such an arrangement.

When these trees bloom, the counterpoint between them and the underplanted annuals can be dazzling, and their canopy is neither so broad nor so dense as to starve the annuals of light.

There are also a number of fine, though less common, shade trees that partner well with underplantings. The Kentucky coffee tree (Gymnocladus dioica) is one, and the hackberry (Celtis occidentalis) is another. The birches have a light, open canopy that filters rather than blocks the sunlight, an ideal condition for shade-tolerant annuals such as impatiens. The river birch (Betula nigra) tolerates heat and drought better than its better known relatives such as the paper birch, and its cultivar 'Heritage' is resistant to the diseases that plague the other trees in this genus.

A word about water

One more caveat to keep in mind is this: The regular irrigation most annuals require does not suit all types of trees. Some trees native to arid regions don't flourish in soils that are routinely moist. The native oaks of California are a notable example. Detective work by arboricultural researchers has revealed that sprinkler irrigation of surrounding lawns is a cause of the fatal root rot that has attacked many of these trees in recent years.

If you garden in the arid West or Southwest, and your yard boasts established specimens of

A trellis or arbor covered with vines draws the eye and adds another dimension to the garden. Tall zinnias and sunflowers help pull attention skyward. (Photo © Michael Gertley.)

Purple-flowered hyacinth beans on an arch can frame a view, define an entryway or path, or bring height to a flat expanse of garden. (Photo by Michael A. Ruggiero.)

Annual vines offer a marvelous diversity of forms and colors, including canary creeper (*Tropaeolum peregrinum*), right, flag-of-Spain (*Ipomoea lobata*), far right, and trailing nasturtium varieties, below. (Photo right © Michael Gertley; photo far right by Michael A. Ruggiero; photo below © Michael Gertley.)

native trees, check with the local cooperative extension office about the needs of these valuable plants before you install a planting under their canopy. Chances are good that an underplanting won't harm the trees, and that the extra irrigation will even benefit them. But in regions where shade is at a premium, you don't want to kill a tree through ignorance.

Growing Up

One type of annual flower that gardeners tend to forget is the kind that grows on vines. Because of their ability to mold themselves to different

— VERTICAL GROWING —

Every space has three dimensions, yet most gardeners fail to take their planting aloft into the third one. As a result, their gardens look flat, in both senses of the word.

Give your garden some height by planting tall annuals, such as castor beans or sunflowers. You'll achieve far more dramatic effects, though, by leaving the earth behind and training annual vines up a trellis or arbor, or by hoisting plants right up into the air in hanging baskets or window boxes.

Each type of vertical planting has its own applications. Window boxes, by making plantings literally part of the house, help to root the structure into the landscape. Hanging baskets create leafy screens.

A trellis is a great way to expand the planting potential of a small garden, especially a shady one. For by climbing, an annual vine can rise out of the shadows to seek out stronger light.

With a bit of ingenuity, you can turn trellises into living architecture. To do this, you must give the trellis itself three dimensions by turning it from an attached flat sheet into a freestanding structure. You can fold it into an obelisk, roll it into a column, or attach it to posts and erect it as a wall. This can be complicated if you build your freestanding trellis out of wooden latticework. However, there are other, unconventional materials that take much less time and labor to work.

The sturdy wire mesh used for reinforcing concrete slabs, for instance, can be cut and formed into a series of columns that, if securely anchored at the base, will stand alone without further support. Erect a double row of columns and top them with an arched roof or more mesh, and you've got an arbor or an arcade.

If you prefer organic materials, you can lash together tall bamboo stakes to make tripods, teepees, and screens. You can stretch lengths of black plastic bird netting from post to post—at a distance of a few feet it's invisible—so that your climbers will seem to float.

Annual vines are fast-growing— if you match the plant to the site well, any trellis you make will soon disappear.

Lance-leaved and floriferous, morning glories are great for screening and camouflage. (Photo by Michael A. Ruggiero.)

shapes and surfaces, the annual vines are exceptionally versatile and useful garden plants. They also grow satisfyingly fast: They'll produce a sheet, cascade, or pool of foliage and flowers in a matter of weeks.

There are all sorts of supports for vining annuals, ranging from custom-built teakwood panels to simple structures lashed together from twigs collected in a nearby woodlot. No matter what the style of the trellis, however, they all have a similar, transformative effect on the garden: They introduce a third dimension (height) where previously there had been only two.

Creating height with plants can be especially useful in gardens lacking in natural topography. No matter how colorful, a garden that pre-

MAKE YOUR OWN TWIG TRELLIS

(above left) Fasten the branches together with lengths of wire or raffia to build the trellis.

(above right) Plant morning glories or other vines to cover the structure. (Photo by Chris Curless; © The Taunton Press, Inc.)

A rustic twig trellis is quick and easy to make but too attractive to hide. Gather twigs in winter, cutting sturdy shoots from wild bushes and trees while they are dormant and leafless. Any sort of twig will do, but those with handsome bark are best. White-barked birch twigs are striking and flexible, too, bending easily to fit almost any curve you want. Twigs of the scarlet-barked red osier (Cornus sericea) are outstanding, and for contrast there is the osier's yellow-barked cultivar, 'Flaviramea'. The stripe-barked maple (Acer pensylvanicum) is another source of interesting twigs.

To assemble the trellis, cut the shoots to length with a pair of pruning shears and then lay them out in whatever pattern suits you, one side at a time. Where shoots cross or overlap, bind them together with lengths of copper wire. A pair of pliers will help you twist the wire tight and bend over the ends so they won't snag garden visitors.

If you want to round out the profile of your twig structure, wrap it in lengths of dormant (leafless) wild grapevine. Or roll a grapevine into a large ball, and mount it on top of a twig tripod to create a classical obelisk. Soaking the vines for a couple of days before trying to bend them will make them more cooperative.

Design for practicality as well as for beauty. This mix of fountain grass, sunflowers, amaranthus, and bachelor's buttons thrives in a sunny spot with well-drained soil. (Photo © Michael Gertley.)

sents only a flat expanse is boring. Setting the garden on a slope or centering it around a rocky outcrop can solve that problem, but if your yard offers nothing but an uninflected expanse of lawn, then you have to make what topography you can. A plastic or wooden arch or arbor is easy to erect, and purchased kits are not expensive. Once clothed in flowers, it draws the eye irresistibly.

Trellises mounted on a wall are also a most effective way to showcase annual flowers, since they bring the blossoms right up to eye level. In addition, by carrying the greenery and flowers off the ground and up the side of a building or shed, they help integrate the architecture into the garden.

Moreover, if when enclosing your yard you opted for security and economy over beauty, you may find yourself very grateful for the almost magical effect of annual vines. A cloud of blue or pink morning glory (Ipomœa spp.) blossoms, or a carillon of cup-and-saucer vine's (Cobaea scan-

Annuals—white impatiens, nicotiana, red-leaved coleus, and an ornamental sweet potato—add late-summer color to a mixed border of perennials and shrubs. (Photo by Judi Rutz; © The Taunton Press, Inc.)

dens) purplish blue bells transform a chainlink or palisade fence from an ugly necessity to an attraction, in just a matter of weeks.

For gardeners with limited space at their disposal, however, the greatest value of annual vines is the way they can double or triple the scope for flowers. Grow your flowers up rather than across, and you can fit many more of them into a small courtyard or townhouse back yard.

In general, annual vines require much the same maintenance as any other annual. Most of these climbers are sun lovers (annual vines need lots of solar energy if they are to stretch their stems to an adult stature in a single season), so plant them where they can find their way up into full sun-

light. In such a situation, though, the vines are liable to need generous and frequent irrigation.

Consider the Practicalities

Design is an art, but it's also a craft. That is, when you design your garden, you aim to please the eye and nose, and maybe even your fingertips—can you walk through a garden without touching the furry leaf of a dusty miller or the satiny surface of a poppy petal? But to really please, the garden must work. Each plant must be comfortable with its neighbors, and all should be comfortable with the situation in which they find themselves. Nor will you enjoy a garden that demands constant care, no matter how beautiful it may be.

Like visual and tactile pleasures, practical virtues don't happen by accident. You have to keep them in mind while you are selecting plants and planning how to arrange them. It is easy to forget the practicalities as you immerse yourself in the colors, textures, and perfumes of the annual garden. However, the simple checklist that follows should keep you on track as craftsman as well as artist.

Working with your climate

What does the local climate have to do with garden design? Everything. To begin with, it determines which annuals will succeed in your garden during each season. What a Pennsylvania gardener plants as spring annuals are winter annuals in southern California, and many annuals that thrive in the cool, moist summers of the Pacific Northwest must be reserved for spring or fall planting in the Southeast.

A thorough understanding of climate is particularly important to Southern gardeners. Hardiness is the term that horticulturists use to define a plant's tolerance for climatic extremes, but unfortunately, the traditional methods for rating plant hardiness concentrate on tolerance for winter cold and ignore the challenge posed by summer heat. So, a "hardy" annual is proof against the occasional frost, but it may or may not be able to withstand the heat and humidity of a New Orleans summer.

To help Southerners with selecting plants hardy in their climate, we have included in the appendix a list of annuals tolerant of heat and humidity. Gardeners from droughty regions will find there a list of annuals adapted to hot, dry climates.

Accessibility

The worst thing you can do to your garden soil is to step on it. The pressure from your foot compresses the soil, driving out the air that roots

(above) Design freestanding beds and borders so you can reach into the center. (Photo by Chris Curless; © The Taunton Press, Inc.)

(left) Stepping stones between or behind garden beds also allows easy access to plants. (Photo by Judi Rutz; © The Taunton Press, Inc.)

A drift of *Verbena tenui-secta* brings a cloud of soft color to the front of this garden. (Photo by Chris Curless; © The Taunton Press, Inc.)

need, and making the soil impenetrable to water. Step on your garden beds too often and you will destroy the structure of your soil. You can repair such hard-packed soil by forking it up and turning in compost or some other organic material, but that's a lot of work. In the meantime, your annuals will not thrive in the compressed soil.

What does this have to do with garden design? The best way to protect your soil from compression is to design beds so that you can reach all the way into their centers while standing outside them. So before you start to lay out any new garden bed, measure your reach: the distance that you can reach out with your hand and arm to plant or weed without straining or overbalancing.

Take the length of your reach as the basic unit for designing the depth of any garden bed. A bed that is accessible from only one side, such as a flower bed that runs along the base of a fence or wall, should be only one reach across from front to back. A bed that is accessible from both the front and the back may be two reaches across.

Sometimes your garden scheme may call for a planting area that is broader and deeper than this. That's no problem: Just plan to run one or more lines of stepping stones across the bed. Space the stones no more than two reaches apart, and no farther from the edge of the bed than two reaches. In this way, you'll always be able to reach into every part of the bed's interior while standing on one of your stones, so that you'll still have no need to step onto the soil.

Planting singly vs. in drifts

Conventional designer's wisdom is that when planting a flower garden, solitary specimens look paltry. According to this view, for a strong visual statement, you should always plant in what the turn-of-the-century English gardener Gertrude Jekyll referred to as "drifts." These are irregular masses of three, five, or more specimens of a given type of plant.

✳ Massed plants have a more dramatic effect than solitary plants.

It's true that massed plants have a more dramatic effect, but there are also some good reasons for violating this rule. Practically speaking, drifts are far more likely to suffer from insect pests. These are usually quite specific in their diet, and usually a given pest will attack only plants of a particular genus or family. Tomato hornworms, for example, feed only on plants of the tomato family, so they will attack petunias, which are a tomato relative, but not marigolds or snapdragons, which are not related to the tomato. Clustering many petunias together creates a larger target for hungry hornworms, or, actually,

for the moths that are the adult form of this pest and that range the landscape looking for an appropriate plant on which to lay tomato hornworm eggs. Planting in drifts, then, makes your flowers easier for their enemies to find.

In contrast, intermingling many individual specimens of different flowers, or smaller clus-

Intermingling different flowers in a casual cottage style creates a naturally pest-resistant planting. (Photo by Judi Rutz; © The Taunton Press, Inc.)

type of soil, and a similar level of moisture makes it easier to care for your garden and helps ensure that your annuals will thrive. Compatibility extends also to the relationship between the plant and its site. Don't try to force a sun-loving verbena to exist in a shady spot, or set a moisture-loving New Guinea impatiens out in the dry heat along the road.

These may seem like obvious points, but too often gardeners ignore them in their quest for the right color of flower or the right type of foliage to complete the picture they have in mind. Remember, as you are planning your garden, that putting incompatible plants together will make it impossible for you to care for all of them together as a single unit, as you would with a better-matched selection. You'll be fertilizing the plant that needs rich soil, but not its neighbor that prefers a poor soil. Instead of irrigating all at once with a single sprinkler, you'll be making the

(above) Tuberous begonias light up the shade with their bright, warm colors. (Photo by Michael A. Ruggiero.)

(right) This sun-loving strawflower is a lovely shade of pink. (Photo © Michael Gertley.)

ters of each, makes the various types of plants less easy for the pests to locate. Perhaps that's the reason that old fashioned cottage gardeners generally planted in this fashion. Or maybe they preferred the informal, tousled look of a thoroughly mixed-up planting. Maybe you will, too.

Designing for compatibility

Compatibility is largely a matter of common sense. Planting together flowers that prefer the same intensity of sunlight or shade, the same

rounds, hose in hand, giving this one twice as much water as that one. Even so, the dryland flower will still resent the water oozing in from its wetland neighbor, which in turn will pine for the moisture that escapes its reach. It's worse than a pack of kids in the back seat of the car. Ignore compatibility, and your plants are sure to sulk—they'll grow poorly and fail to bloom.

Learning from Your Garden

As gardeners, most of us are intimidated by the design process. We think that because we can't compose like Gertrude Jekyll, we can't design at all. It's as if we refused to make ourselves dinner because we can't cook like a Cordon Bleu chef. In fact, garden design is a lot like cooking in this respect. You can practice it as high art, or you can practice it as a practical, uncomplicated craft, something you do to please yourself and get the job done.

The basic skills of garden design are easy to pick up; you learn them by doing. And if you want a crash course in garden design, there's nothing better than planting annuals. Your successes will be dramatic, and your mistakes will vanish with the first frost. Every spring will bring a fresh start, too. You'll have another opportunity to experiment and learn, a chance to express yourself and amaze the neighbors, perhaps, and above all to enjoy.

Sunflowers can be had in a variety of sizes and colors. (Photo © Rick Mark.)

PLANTING WITH STYLE

S TYLE IS REALLY NOTHING MORE than self-expression, and whatever you are comfortable with is the right garden style for you. You don't need to study that. But you should spend a bit of time learning the vocabulary of style. These are the visual devices you can use to express yourself easily and forcefully. Becoming fluent in these will make your style even more your own.

Formal or Informal

The choice of a mood for your garden is the most basic style decision, as it determines where you put everything, from paths to beds to pots. Formal garden plans depend on symmetry and precise, geometrical patterns; informal garden plans should exhibit balance and comfortable proportions, but without the obvious, predictable structure of a formal design.

(opposite) The bold foliage of New Zealand flax (*Phorminum tenax*) adds drama to beds and borders. (Photo by David Cavagnaro.)

(left) Neatly maintained marigolds, salvias, and other annuals can be massed in precise formal designs. (Photo by Michael A. Ruggiero.)

Neatly edged turf and a margin of sweet alyssum gives structure to an otherwise casual planting. (Photo by Michael S. Thompson.)

around a casual country cottage, though, might just seem pretentious and oppressive. Here, a looser, more flowing design would feel more appropriate.

Breaking the rules

However, you may decide that in your garden, rules are made to be broken. In fact, the most dramatic style of planting is the one that goes against the grain of its setting. A tousled, lush border looks even lusher and more delightfully unpredictable in a symmetrical formal space. Likewise, a touch of formality—perhaps a pair of matched, flower-filled urns set on either side of an informal front entrance—can strike a pleasing note of casual elegance.

You may also wish to plant against the style of the setting to soften or temper its effect. A tangled strip of mixed flowers set at the foot of a fence can be a relief from the harshness of an urban alley. Edging the shrubbery with a neat stripe of impatiens or begonias can impose just enough order to keep an informal bed from degenerating into a messy wilderness.

You can also inject excitement into your garden by mixing your planting styles. The formality of a standard fuchsia, an annual artificially trained into the form of a dwarfed tree, is particularly arresting when set amid an informal carpet of mixed flowers.

Vita Sackville-West used this sort of contrast especially effectively in her famous garden at

Which of these moods is right for your garden depends, ultimately, on what you find easiest to live with. In addition, you may want to take some direction from the style of your house. An elegant, Georgian-style brick house may cry out for a formal, decorous landscape to surround it. Similarly, the clean geometry of a contemporary house and pool may look more at home in a geometrical, formal setting. The same planting

(left) An informal garden of snapdragons, violas, and perennials looks at home in front of a country bungalow. (Photo by Delilah Smittle; © The Taunton Press, Inc.)

(above) A fuchsia trained as a standard adds an exciting formal note to an informal planting. (Photo by Michael A. Ruggiero.)

Lush, informal plantings within a formal structure create an appealing contrast of styles. (Photo by Dency Kane; owner/designer Elisabeth Sheldon.)

Sissinghurst Castle in Kent. With the help of her husband, Harold Nicolson, she laid out her gardens in a meticulously formal pattern of paths and hedged or walled-in "rooms." Then, within this carefully regulated framework, she planted lushly and informally. The effect of the contrast was exciting and elegant, yet also warm and inviting.

As you choose between formality and informality, though, keep in mind this fact: Formal designs are far less tolerant of casual mainte-

nance. Suppose, for instance, that you plant four knots of blanket flower (Gaillardia pulchella) to mark the four corners of intersecting paths. If you let one knot go to seed, the whole detail will look sloppy. Furthermore, you can't let plants stray out of their allotted spaces in a strictly formal design or the precise lines will be blurred. And the death of one plant in a formal carpet bed will leave the whole planting looking incomplete. Lapses of this sort are far easier to overlook in an informal planting.

AN ANNUAL CUTTING GARDEN

Because they bloom so generously, annuals are ideal for a cutting garden. A cutting garden of annuals can be quite compact—perhaps no more than 5 ft. by 10 ft.—because every plant in it will remain in bloom throughout most of its growing season.

A cutting garden will do best in a spot that is flat, well drained, and, most important, sunny. Most annuals perform best in full sun. You make heavy demands on cutting flowers, regularly removing whole stems with their leaves and flowers. To withstand this kind of continual drastic pruning takes a vigorous plant. And that plant depends on sunlight as its energy source.

The best site is also one that is out of the way but not too remote. This planting is designed for productivity and is likely to look obtrusive if set down in the middle of your decorative beds. Besides, you'll want to mix flowers of diverse, even clashing, colors and forms in your cutting garden, so that you can assemble many different styles of floral arrangements and bouquets. You'll be planting the cutting garden in a practical rather than a pragmatic way, as well. The tallest flowers, for example, should be lined up on the north end of the garden so that they don't shade the other plants.

One easy solution to this dilemma of convenient-but-not-too-obvious is to incorporate the cutting garden into an existing vegetable garden. If you want to give the cutting garden its own space, you can set it apart and reduce its visibility by surrounding it with fencing and draping that with annual vines. A curtain of sweet peas will hide the fencing and furnish armfuls of cut flowers itself.

When selecting annuals to plant in the cutting garden, aim for a variety of flower forms. To make balanced-looking flower arrangements, you'll need some tall, spiked flowers such as snapdragons, some rounded blossoms such as marigolds or dahlias, and some airy, textural flowers such as annual baby's breath (Gypsophila elegans).

Take care as well, to include both bold flowers such as sunflowers and some delicate ones such as rocket larkspur (Consolida ambigua). Draw attention to your arrangements by growing one or two striking novelties you'll never find at the florist, such as the chartreuse green zinnia 'Envy'.

Because long, strong stems make flower arranging easier, choose "standard" or "tall" cultivars and avoid those labeled as "bedding" flowers, since this is a term typically applied to short-stemmed dwarf varieties. Try also to select plants that are horticulturally compatible. If you interplant cool-weather-loving snapdragons with heat-craving celosias, one of the

two will be dissatisfied and bloom poorly.

To harvest more flowers and do less staking of tall stems than in a traditional single-row layout, plant in wide rows. These are essentially narrow beds 18 in. to 36 in. wide, which, like the single rows, you run from north to south. Within each row, stagger the seedlings at the spacing recommended in the entries in The Essential Annuals, beginning on p. 152. Growing as part of a mass in this fashion, the flowers will hold each other up, and all the support you'll have to provide will be rows of brush stakes (see p. 149) down the outsides of each wide row.

For a list of annuals for cutting, see p. 224.

Planting a cutting garden allows you to enjoy your annuals indoors as well as out. (Photo by Steve Silk; © The Taunton Press, Inc.)

Dahlias offer a tremendous diversity of flower forms and sizes, and a range of colors, from pale pastels to bold brights. (Photo © Allan Mandell.)

Using Color

Some people like their food highly spiced, others don't, and neither way of cooking is right or wrong. So it goes with color in the garden. There are annuals in bold, dramatic colors, soft pastels, and gleaming whites. Try different combinations of flowers and foliages to create different effects until you discover the mixtures of hues you like best. The wonderful thing about annuals is that experimentation is so easy and costs so little in time and work.

However, besides personal preference, there is also a certain amount of science to the use of color. Certain colors or combinations of colors, for example, produce in us definite, predictable reactions. It's no accident that we commonly speak of emotions in terms of colors, that we "see red" or "feel blue." Color has an immediate impact on our feelings. Because annuals are the most colorful of garden plants, they provide an unmatched opportunity for directing and changing the reactions of garden visitors.

The most common distinction that gardeners make with regard to colors is between "hot" ones and "cool" ones. Hot colors are reds, oranges, yellows, and the more vivid pinks; cool colors are blues, purples ranging to lavender pink, greens, and whites. As the name suggests, hot colors tend to have a stimulating effect, and they tend to leap out at the eye, dominating a landscape. Cool colors are calming, and they seem to recede into the distance, which makes them useful for giving a feeling of greater expanse to a small space.

The type of colors you plant—hot or cool—will also depend on where you garden. Where the light is intense, as in the Southwest, the hot colors do better at holding their own. In the harsh desert sunlight, the cool colors tend to wash out, to look anemic. The cool colors show up better in cloudy weather, as is often found in the Northwest and the Northeast. In the filtered light that predominates in those regions, cool colors can give a very lush but delicate effect, especially when mixed with delicate pastel pinks. In the same setting, hot colors may look obvious and loud.

(above) A pale pink rose campion (*Lychnis coronaria* 'Angel's Blush'), a biennial that can be grown as an annual, softens a combination of perennial salvia and *Sedum alboroseum* 'Medio-variegatus'. (Photo by Peter Krumhardt; © The Taunton Press, Inc.)

(left) A hot combination of coleus and celosia. (Photo by Michael A. Ruggiero.)

BEAUTIFUL BLACKS

Vita Sackville-West won fame in the 1950s with the all-white garden she designed for her home, Sissinghurst Castle, in Kent. Tourists still flock there. But her achievement will pale—literally—beside the black garden you are going to plant in your backyard.

'T&M Black Pansy' is just what the name suggests—a dark note for a spring or fall garden. (Photo courtesy Thompson & Morgan.)

You must be resourceful, for black is an exceedingly rare color in the plant kingdom. In fact, there are no truly black plants, just virtual blacks that are actually darkest shades of purples, reds, blues, and greens. Tulip 'Queen of the Night', for example, bears blossoms that bulb

catalogs may describe as black but which are, really, a deep maroon; the flowers of snapdragon (Antirrhinum majus) 'Black Prince' are actually a dark crimson; and those of cornflower (Centaurea cyanus) 'Black Ball' are deep purple.

Such plants are close enough to black to create that impression, but the true colors will emerge as undertones, and you must be aware of these as you design. Otherwise, you may create subtle, but nevertheless disturbing, disharmonies. A greenish black, for instance, will not rest easy next to a purplish black.

Designing a black garden also involves a reversal of the customary situation, in which flowers are the star and foliage the backdrop. Because black flowers are rare and anyway don't leap out at the eye, foliage will play the starring role here. Should you plant the tropical plant Alocasia 'Black Beauty', for instance, or the black-leaved taro, Colocasia esculenta 'Illustris', you'll find their huge, inky leaves making more of an impression than the jewel-like but petite blossoms of pansy 'Black Devil' or hollyhock (Alcea rosea) 'Nigra'.

WHITES AND LIGHTING

In your enthusiasm for black flowers and black foliage, though, you shouldn't forget the importance of contrast. At least a hint of this is essential spice for

any planting, and nowhere more so than in the black garden, which without it would look simply grim. White, of course, poses the starkest contrast to black and is also the most cooperative. Other colors, such as reds, yellows, oranges, and blues, are likely to coopt your planting, turning the blacks into a mere background. The relatively characterless white, on the other hand, accentuates blacks, making them look even blacker. Yet at the same time, calculated spots of white serve as a visual punctuation, defining masses and drawing the eye to areas you wish to emphasize.

To inject the vital note of white, you can use white flowers. White-flowered impatiens are particularly effective, though for a more delicate texture, you could plant puffs of white-flowered annual baby's breath (Gypsophila elegans) or a drift of some white-flowered sweet alyssum (Lobularia maritima), perhaps the honey-scented 'Sweet White'. Alternatively, you may select flowers in which the contrast is inherent. Nemophila 'Pennie Black' bears blossoms of black petals tipped with white; so does China pink (Dianthus chinensis 'Heddewigii') 'Black and White Minstrels'.

In no other kind of garden is the quality of the light so important. You'll find that black foliage and flowers do not look their best in the harsh, overhead light of midday. The cool, gentle lights of

early morning and of evening are more flattering to these plants, and backlighting really makes their dark, rich tones glow. So set your black garden to the east or west of a path, lawn, or terrace and in a spot where it isn't backed by a dense screen or canopy. As the sun rises or sets, there will come a moment when the rays angle in just right. As they strike your black plants from behind, what had been leaves and foliage will turn into a jigsaw of living stained glass.

BLACK-FLOWERED ANNUALS
* Bat plant (Tacca chantrieri) tropical perennial
* Cornflower (Centaurea cyanus) 'Black Ball'
* Hollyhock (Alcea rosea) 'Nigra'
* Pansy (Viola x wittrockiana) 'Black Devil', 'Black Prince', 'Springtime Black', and 'T&M's Black Pansy'
* Snapdragon (Antirrhinum majus) 'Black Prince'

BLACK-AND-WHITE FLOWERS
* China pink (Dianthus chinensis 'Heddewigii') 'Black and White Minstrels'
* Nemophila 'Pennie Black'

BLACK- OR VERY DARK-LEAVED ANNUALS
* Basil (Ocimum basilicum) 'Dark Opal'
* Canna (Canna x generalis) 'Egandale'
* Coleus (Coleus x hybrida) 'Black Cloud' and 'Othello'
* Elephant's ear (Alocasia) 'Metallica' and 'Black Beauty'
* Fennel (Foeniculum vulgare) 'Purpureum'
* Perilla (Perilla frutescens) 'Crispa'
* Sweet potato (Ipomoea batatas) 'Blackie'
* Taro (Colocasia esculenta) 'Illustris'
* Taro (Colocasia esculenta) 'Fontanesia'

ANNUALS WITH BLACK LEAVES MARKED BY LIGHTER PATTERNINGS
* Elephant's ear (Alocasia) 'Black Beauty'
* Elephant's ear (Alocasia watsonia)
* Taro (Colocasia esculenta) 'Black Princess'

(left) *Nemophila* 'Pennie Black' provides contrast in flowers of midnight edged with silver. (Photo courtesy Thompson & Morgan.)

(above) A "black" planting with reddish-purple undertones: canna 'Red King Humbert', coleuses 'Purple Emperor', 'Inky Fingers', and 'Black Magic' edged by *Ipomoea batatas* 'Blackie'. (Photo by Suzanne O'Connell.)

(above left) The blue flowers of scaevola contrast beautifully with a lime green coleus. (Photo by Michael A. Ruggiero.)

(above right) Warm reds, pinks, and yellows harmonize well, but for a cool note, add touches of white and green. (Photo by Michael A. Ruggiero.)

Harmony and contrast

A handy device for selecting colors is a color wheel. This shows relationships and interplay between the colors. Colors found next to or near each other on the color wheel associate easily and comfortably. Intermingle flowers of yellow, orange, and red, for example, and you create a naturally harmonious display.

Colors found directly across the color wheel from each other are "complementary"—having the strongest possible contrast. Juxtapose a purple flower with a yellow one, or an orange one with a blue one, and you will create a powerful and dramatic, even a jarring, effect. Use such effects sparingly, however; too many complementary contrasts makes the garden a visual battlefield. Often, just a touch of complementary contrast is enough. Just a spot of yellow, perhaps from a golden-leaved foliage such as a coleus, among a bed of purple flowers will make the blossoms seem to vibrate with energy.

Color and light

When selecting flower colors for your garden, you should also consider the season at which the plants bloom, as the light in which you will view the flowers, and hence the quality of the colors,

(top) The variegated flowering maple (*Abutulon*) glows against a sea of purple ageratum. (Photo by Michael A. Ruggiero.)

(above) A harmonious composition of pinks and purples combines rosy zinnias, cleome, and tall vervain (*Verbena bonariensis*). (Photo by Michael A. Ruggiero.)

(left) Blue bachelor's buttons and yellow rudbeckia are a lovely duo. (Photo by Michael A. Ruggiero.)

CLASSICAL HARMONIES

For most American gardeners, the style of planting developed by the English designer Gertrude Jekyll at the end of the nineteenth century remains a model. Jekyll brought an artist's sensibility to garden design. Though not afraid of strong colors, her forte was the delicate harmonies and contrasts that could be achieved by juxtaposing related hues.

In her book, Colour Schemes for the Flower Garden, she wrote of planting together in her own garden the soft pink, old-fashioned rose 'Mignonette' with masses of slate-blue-flowered catmint and silver-leaved artemisias. In the length of a border, she might move from a pale salmon-pink-flowered geranium to a cultivar with blossoms a shade deeper in hue, then a

salmon-scarlet, and finally a "pure good scarlet."

She promotes a plan for another border in which the background is a fabric of gray-foliaged plants, such as lavender, yucca, achillea, and stachys (all perennials), into which she could inject the pastel blues and pinks of annuals (or biennials grown as annuals) such as ageratum, hollyhocks, dahlias, and sweet peas. Clouds of white-flowered gypsophila further enhanced the delicacy of the effect.

HARMONIOUS CONTRAST
Jekyll was a master of working with different hues within a range of related colors. She had a sensitive eye for the affinities of the different reds and pinks, of yellows, gold, and greens, or

of apricots and scarlets. She interspersed masses—"drifts," she called them—of these harmoniously contrasting colors, working them into a running counterpoint of gray and green foliages. Whenever boredom threatened, she'd slip in a spot of some muted, but definite, complementary contrast. In her description of a border of mixed blues and silvers, for example, she wrote of it "hungering" for a spot of "palest lemon-yellow."

The passage of time has given a patina of nostalgia and romance to this style of design, and its understated sophistication can make it a welcome refuge from an aggressive modern world. It works particularly well where the light is gentle, as it was in Jekyll's native landscape.

Brightly lit southern gardens may demand stronger colors, especially in summertime. Even there, Jekyll's reliance on different color tones within a single range can still apply. You'll just need to turn up the volume, planting more oranges, brilliant yellows, and reds with your grays and greens, rather than the violets, soft blues, and pale rose.

A cool border in the classic Jekyll style includes blue campanula, white nicotiana, and soft pink cleome. (Photo by Laurie Clement-Lawrason; courtesy Glebe House Museum.)

changes with the time of year. Sunlight changes with the seasons: Spring and fall light tends to be clear and crisp and is particularly kind to bright colors such as the clear, bold yellows and reds found in so many of the hybrid tulips.

Midday in the summer, with its blazing sunlight, is the time for loud, tropical colors, but maybe you find that you spend those hours indoors. Maybe you save your summertime visits to the garden for evening and morning, when it's cooler outside. That season's rising and setting

Bright, hot colors hold up well in the blazing midday sun, when softer pastels look washed out.

sun shines with a warm light that casts bluish shadows, flattering and reinforcing the effects of the cooler colors.

Caress the eye with harmonies or wake it up with bold contrasts—in large part, the choice will depend on the situation and the effect you want to create. Maybe you relish the subtle effect of a border of blues, greens, and silvers. Equally, you may be a risk-taker who needs the excitement of blue warring with orange. Either way, annuals offer all the alternatives you could desire.

(above) Pale pink verbena harmonizes beautifully with deep purple petunias. (Photo by Michael A. Ruggiero.)

(left) This pansy combines delicate shadings of yellow and mauve for subtle contrast. (Photo by Michael A. Ruggiero.)

DANGEROUS LIAISONS

The angular red-bronze foliage of amaranthus is brought to life by a shot of gold. (Photo by Michael A. Ruggiero.)

Subtlety is all very well, but there are times when it's more satisfying to shock. Besides, a simple, sharp contrast of two discordant colors, or even two colors that harmonize but strongly compete, can have a wonderful tang. The tension of such a forced partnership works especially well with the formal abstraction of modern design. As the theme of the planting around or on a terrace, or in small and enclosed yard, the duel of the two colors can crackle with energy, turning the garden into a set for high drama.

One of the most remarkable examples of this style of planting that we have seen was a flowingly contoured spring bed of tall hybrid tulips and massed pansies. The two were inter-planted, so that the sheet of dark purple tulip blossoms hovered over the purple and apricot floor of pansy flowers. The eye kept jumping back and forth, from one level to the other. In summertime, the effect might have been blazingly harsh; in the cool light of spring, it was unspeakably stylish.

YELLOW AND VIOLET

Yellows and violets engage in another such color battle. Okra, though better known as a food crop, is an annual relative of Hibiscus, and it bears lemon yellow blossoms of a similar form. Set its flower spikes against a sheet of purplish-flowered hyacinth bean (Lablab purpureus) and you have a striking ornament for a Southern fence line.

Or you could mix globe amaranth (Gomphrena globosa) 'Buddy', with its intense violet flowerheads, blue-purple rocket larkspurs (Consolida ambigua), yellow snapdragons (Antirrhinum majus), and signet marigolds (Tagetes tenuifolia).

There's also a good deal of yellow in chartreuse green, and planting blue flowers nearby brings it out. Set some blue rocket larkspurs and blue bachelor's button (Centaurea cyanus) against coleus 'Super Chartreuse' or 'Moonbeam', and the foliage will develop an almost incandescent glow.

BRONZE AND RED

Finally, there's one instance of a color that is leaden and dull until a dash of contrast turns it into one of the most exotic hues in the garden: a peculiar purplish red that catalogs persist in describing as "bronze." It's found in the foliage of several annuals, notably the castor bean (Ricinus communis) 'Sanguineus' and the beefsteak plant (Perilla frutescens) 'Atropurpurea' that, as the last name suggests, recalls nothing so much as raw meat or liver when it stands alone. Set a clump of scarlet sage (Salvia splendens) or of canna (Canna x generalis) 'Red King Humbert' amid the mass of homely bronze, and it's transmuted into something as suave as a tuxedo.

So, when selecting annuals for your garden, be sure to really look at the leaves. Check the texture of the foliage. Delicate blossoms may look insignificant on a coarse-leaved plant, while fine-textured, lacy foliage will make showy blossoms look even more spectacular. You can also use contrasting leaf textures to develop drama in your garden, juxtaposing the broad leaves of flowering tobacco with the feathered foliage of the signet marigold (Tagetes tenuifolia) for example, and using this as a sort of counterpoint to the floral display.

Foliage color is also important, even with plants whose leaves offer no hue other than green. What shade of green do the leaves contribute? A deep, lustrous green? That makes a particularly dramatic contrast to a red, making a

Foliage can be as interesting as flowers. Here, front to back, are bold, jagged cardoon, deep bronze coppertone mallow, and a green-and white grass. (Photo by Michael A. Ruggiero.)

The Importance of Foliage

When selecting plants, especially annuals, we tend to focus on the flowers. What color are the blossoms? How big are they? When does the plant bloom? As we indulge this preoccupation, too often we forget that even when the plant is in bloom, the greater mass of it still lies in the foliage. And when a plant isn't in bloom, then its visual effect derives entirely from the leaves. Flowers will always be the stars of the garden, but they can't succeed without the help of the supporting cast, the foliage, and sometimes an understudy will surprise you and steal the show.

Spiky New Zealand flax is the centerpiece of an all-foliage composition that includes purple Setcreasea and pale pick-a-back plant. (Photo by Michael A. Ruggiero.)

The silvery foliage of *Helichrysum petiolare* tones down brilliant flowers like this *Zinnia angustifolia* and makes them more palatable. (Photo by Chris Curless; © The Taunton Press, Inc.)

bright red seem even brighter. Paler greens have a lighter effect, combining well with less intense yellows and blues, while gray-greens can help to temper vivid flowers that might otherwise seem too intense.

Colored and variegated foliage

The leaves of annuals offer many more colors than simple greens. You'll find reds, bronzes, purples, golds, even whites in the foliage of different annuals, many of which, such as coleus, are grown entirely for their foliage effect. Colorful foliages are especially important in shady gardens, where the flowers are fewer and less spectacular. There, the tropical splashes of

(left) Perilla offers bronze foliage. (Photo by Michael A. Ruggiero.)

(below left) Blue-green foliage of myrtle euphorbia mixes well with the purple flowers of annual larkspurs and pale yellow nicotiana. (Photo by Michael A. Ruggiero.)

(below right) Light greens are good companions for warm golds. (Photo © Michael Gertley.)

VARIEGATED PLANTS

We know an ordinarily broadminded gardener who dismisses variegated plants as "the golfing pants of the plant world." Yet we also know of a renowned nursery that sells nothing but and many gardeners who collect variegated plants the way your aunt collects Hummel figurines. Really, all you can

Coleus foliage comes in many color combinations, shapes, and sizes. (Photo by Michael A. Ruggiero.)

safely say about variegated plants is that they always excite strong feelings.

Variegated plants are those whose leaves are not single-colored but striped, splashed, spotted, or edged with two or more contrasting hues. One of their intriguing aspects is that they allow you to interject a color contrast into the garden with the use of a single plant.

There are many annuals in this group, and their most common type of variegation is the combination of green and

white, as in the Japanese imperial morning glory (Ipomoea nil), nasturtium 'Alaska', and snow-on-the-mountain (Euphorbia marginata). But there are also many plants with green and yellow variegations—as on the long, striped leaves of the ornamental corn Zea mays 'Variegata'—green and pink, and green and cream foliages, and once you start planting coleuses, almost any combination of colors is possible.

All of these plants are eye-catching; some are eye-stunning, a sort of visual exclamation point. Generally, their look is somewhat artificial as well. Despite the current prejudice for the so-called natural garden, artificiality isn't necessarily bad. When well chosen and well placed, a variegated plant can give a scene a sort of stylish chic.

Restraint is usually the key to successful use of variegated foliage. In most gardens they should be treated as a spice rather than as the main course. Be careful, too, about mixing two different variegated annuals. Plants with plainer green and white variegations can be intermingled more easily, but even there, the result is likely to look like the morning you wore a checked tie with a checked sports jacket. Everyone knew you dressed in the dark.

Rules were made to be broken, though, at least when it comes to annuals, and one occasion when you should abandon all good taste and apply the

variegated foliage with a broad brush is when you are planting one of the tropical-style gardens that have become so popular in recent years. Yet even here, you'll want to intersperse masses of bold-textured but evenly green-leaved plants such as elephant's ears (Colocasia esculenta) and banana trees. For without such visual rests, your garden degenerates into a noisy mob of stripes, spots, and smears, and the variegation loses its impact.

SOME VARIEGATED ANNUALS

* Alternanthera ficoidea var. amoena (parrot leaf): yellow to green leaves marked with red, orange, purple, yellow
* Amaranthus tricolor (tampala): leaves combine bronze, red, green, gold
* Caladium: combinations of red, green, white, rose, salmon
* Canna 'Pretoria': green and yellow striped
* Coleus x hybridus: combinations of white, yellow, red, bronze, chartreuse, gold, copper, pink, purple, green
* Impatiens spp. (New Guinea impatiens): combinations of red, green, bronze, yellow
* Vinca major 'Variegata' (greater periwinkle): green and cream
* Zea mays 'Quadricolor' (variegated corn): white, yellow, pink, green leaves on each stalk

'New Guinea' impatiens leaves are likely to out-shine any of the blossoms. A few annual foliages are assertive enough to compete with the bright-est flowers and hold their own even in the full sun. Certainly, the hot pink bracts of the Joseph's coat, Amaranthus tricolor 'Illumination', stand out in any company.

Most plants are valued either for their foliage or their flowers, but some plants are outstanding in both departments. The 'Red King Humbert' canna, for example, bears an attractive and very tropical-looking spike of orange-red flowers, and its leaves—long, broad blades of reddish purple borne on 5-ft. stalks—are extraordinary as well. Such a plant provides excitement from the moment it pokes the first shoot out of the ground until the last petal fades and drops and frost cuts it down.

Consider the Scale

When you are designing a planting, the size that matters is the size of each plant relative to the other elements of the garden. You can make a 2-ft.-tall dwarf spruce look like a towering forest giant by swathing around it a mat of diminutive, creeping sweet alyssums. On the other hand, a 'Russian Mammoth' sunflower may lose its gigantic effect and seem almost ordinary if you surround it with tall prairie grasses.

These differences in scale can be a very effec-tive tool. If your garden is a constricted court-yard, you can plant it with miniatures and make

A big annual like this imposing *Brugmansia* can take the place of a shrub or small tree, dwarfing a bench. (Photo by Michael A. Ruggiero.)

91

effects. Wrapping the front of your little clapboard Cape Cod house with a bed of towering, broad-leaved castor beans (Ricinus communis) can transform an ordinary structure into a storybook hobbit house.

You can also use contrasts in scale to inject drama into the garden. A cluster of coarse caladium leaves will draw the eye while emphasizing the delicacy of the baby's breath (Gypsophila elegans) by its side. Of course, by massing together identical, though small, plants, you can also achieve an appearance of increased scale. This was one goal of old-fashioned carpet bedding: By setting the annuals close enough together so that their foliage and flowers merged into a sheet, the Victorian gardeners turned their beds into grand sweeps of color, on a scale far larger than individual plants could ever supply.

(above) Scarlet sage (*Salvia splendens*) with fountain grass. (Photo by Mobee Weinstein.)

(right) This mass of delicate cupflower (*Nierembergia hippomanica*) is in scale in a small garden. (Photo by Michael A. Ruggiero.)

it look expansive. Alternatively, you can bury it under huge, broad-leaved tropical foliage plants—such as elephant's ear (Colocasia esculenta) and bananas (Musa spp.)—and turn it into a nook in the middle of the jungle.

The standard practice is to match the scale of the planting to the scale of the house—a ribbon of lowly ageratums is likely to look meager at the foot of a massive stone facade. Playing tricks with the scale, though, can produce appealing

Profile

Every annual has a characteristic silhouette, or visual profile, and this is yet another tool to use in creating a design.

Profiles are what horticulturists call the plant's habit of growth. That may sound like jargon, but pay attention. Unless you have a very good reason for doing so, you won't try to break a plant of this habit. You can affect the shape of the plant somewhat, by pinching back unwanted growth or staking the stems. Generally, though, such training works well only when you are seeking to reinforce and enhance the natural pattern of growth. In other words, you can make a rounded plant even more cushion-like, but in general you can't turn a creeper into a spike.

⁂ Visual punctuation can give a sense of rhythm to a planting.

The only notable exceptions to this rule are found in a few normally shrubby plants such as fuchsias or geraniums, which through persistent discipline are sometimes trained into tall-trunked lollipops, or "standards." In the right setting, these give a fine effect, but they are about as natural, and as laborious to create, as bonsai.

It's important to know the natural profiles of your plants because it is by varying and matching

PLANT PROFILES

* Upright plants are tall and thin with a soaring stalk or stem of flowers.
* Erect plants are upward reaching, but clump forming and perhaps branched.
* Vase-shaped plants send stalks and leaves soaring upwards and out.
* Rounded plants may be loosely mounded or perhaps densely rounded and cushion-shaped.
* Prostrate plants are low and spreading, flowing across the ground in a mat of leaves and blooming flowers.

(below) Upright orange cannas, vase-shaped cardoon, arching fountain grass, and rounded zinnias. (Photo by Michael A. Ruggiero.)

(left) A mass of variegated garden impatiens. (Photo by Michael A. Ruggiero.)

(above) Spiky mealycup sage partners with funnel-shaped petunias. (Photo by Michael A. Ruggiero.)

(above right) Petunias are paired with narrow-leaved *Zinnia angustifolia*. (Photo by Michael A. Ruggiero.)

(right) Cactus-type dahlia. (Photo by Michael A. Ruggiero.)

these in different combinations that you give form to your garden. Typically, gardeners tend to place taller, more upright plants at the back of their plantings and then work downward to a border of low spreading plants in the front. This placement keeps every plant fully visible to the onlooker.

But you can also use profile to create variety. For instance, you might set a cluster of tall, spiked plants among a throng of lower, rounded ones. Visual punctuation of this sort, if repeated at intervals down the length of a bed or border, can give a sense of rhythm to a planting and endow it with a stronger stucture.

Tall, airy *Verbena bonariensis* acts as a scrim through which to view the shorter plants behind it. (Photo by Susan Kahn; © The Taunton Press, Inc.)

(right) An impatiens trained as a standard is the centerpiece of this bed, with pinks and purples in a gradation of heights. (Photo by Michael A. Ruggiero.)

(below) Annual vines add a third dimension—height—to the garden and can also serve as cover-ups for eyesores and mistakes. (Photo by Lee Anne White; © The Taunton Press, Inc.)

Quick Fixes

Designers may talk of a garden as a composition, but as any real gardener knows, a large part of any design is simply made up on the spot. It helps to establish ahead of time a clear idea of how you want the landscape to look when you are finished with it, but in reality, much of what you do in the garden is to solve problems as they arise.

This is what makes annuals so especially valuable. With their fast, exuberant growth and adaptability, annuals are a great resource for gardeners who need a quick fix for some unforeseen difficulty, or a temporary solution that will keep a problem under control until they have time to arrange a more permanent resolution. Understanding the kinds of stopgaps that annuals can provide may not seem like great gardening, but it's essential to making almost any garden design work.

Cover-ups

Fast-growing annual vines are invaluable for covering up mistakes and eyesores. If allowed to ramble without the constraint of a trellis, annual vines can quickly hide a tree stump, a utility box, or any other low-lying blemish. Ornamental gourds are invaluable for this purpose, as their leaves are large and the foliage dense. Japanese hops (Humulus japonicus), a perennial vine that may be grown as an annual, will also quickly swallow up any stationary object.

(left) Decorate an arbor with the large, heart-shaped leaves and sprays of hyacinth bean (*Lab-lab purpureus*). (Photo © Michael Gertley.)

(below) A fast-growing cardinal climber is excellent for camouflage and screening. (Photo by Lee Anne White; © The Taunton Press, Inc.)

Other good cover-ups, though less rampant than gourds, are the morning glories (Ipomoea spp.), the black-eyed Susan vine (Thunbergia alata), and the many creeping nasturtiums (Tropaeolum majus), such as the old-fashioned 'Empress of India' and 'Glorious Gleam' strains. The black-eyed Susan vine (Thurbersia alata) is particularly useful because it tolerates partial shade. Nasturtiums and morning glories prefer a sunny spot, though in regions such as the Rocky Mountain West and the Southwest, where the sunshine is extra strong, they will thrive in a situation of light shade.

Easy-to-grow morning glories come in single colors or various mixtures like this assortment of pink, blue, and purple shades. (Photo © Michael Gertley.)

Plugs

Because annual flowers grow so quickly, they are uniquely useful as patches for the gaps that periodically appear in garden beds and borders of longer-lived perennials and shrubs. For no matter how skillfully you garden, such holes will appear. Even the hardiest perennial peony or daylily has a finite life span and will die eventually, and many other popular perennials such as columbines (Aquilegia spp.) or summer phlox (Phlox paniculata) are notoriously short-lived in many North American climates. The beauty of these plants may persuade you to grow them anyway, but you do so knowing that there will be casualties. Unfortunately, these deaths usually occur without notice, and often at the wrong season for replanting with a perennial. That's when you call in the annuals.

❧ Annuals are useful as patches for gaps that appear in beds and borders.

Given that the problem is immediate, this is no time to start from seed. Instead, make a mental note of the color and habit of growth of the deceased, and then make a trip to the garden center to look for an annual plant that can substitute. In the North, it's usually the stress of winter weather that produces such gaps, and so you'll find yourself shopping for plugs in springtime when retail nurseries stock the best selection of annuals.

In the South, the season of greatest stress to annuals is often summer, which means that you'll be shopping for plugs in the fall. That's an excellent season for planting annual displays in warm-climate regions, and Southerners should find a good selection then, as well.

Understudies

Many kinds of perennials, such as oriental poppies, old-fashioned bleeding heart, and most of the flowering bulbs, are ephemerals. They emerge from the ground, throw up leaves and flowers, and then retreat back under the soil surface. Such plants are stars when they are on stage, but if the show is to go on, understudies are needed. Again, it is annuals that are best at filling in.

If you are the kind of gardener who is good at planning, you could sow a row of annuals along one edge of the vegetable garden, in preparation for transplanting to the flower garden when understudies are needed. Most of us, however, have to depend on whatever plants we find in packs and containers at the garden center.

In any case, resist the impulse to cut back the aging and shabby foliage of the ephemerals before it has yellowed and withered, as the foliage continues to manufacture and store food in the

perennials' roots as long as it is green. Instead, plant the annual seedlings among the perennials as the foliage flags, fertilize and water, and let the understudies fill in gradually.

Chartreuse-leaved *Ipomoea* 'Margarita' fills a gap left by a spring-blooming perennial. (Photo by Judi Rutz; © The Taunton Press, Inc.)

Grow garden chrysan-
themums as annuals for
masses of carefree
autumn color. (Photo
by Derek Fell.)

Planting through the Seasons

The use of annuals as a seasonal design element often begins as a quick fix, too, but over time you'll find yourself including them in your plans well ahead of time, as they become a regular feature of your gardening calendar.

At least initially, most of us plant annuals reactively. We begin by surrounding the house with the basic shrubbery and groundcover, a sprinkling of spring bulbs, and perhaps an assortment of the more reliable, summer-flowering perennials. Yet afterward, from time to time we notice with disappointment that despite all our efforts, the yard is colorless. Lapses in the original planting have left the yard flowerless through extended periods of the growing season.

In late spring, for instance, after the spring bulbs have finished blooming, there may be a lapse before the roses and perennials swing into action. In late summer, the perennials seem to go on strike, and there's likely to be another lapse during the period from the first fall frost until the leaves drop.

The common response to these lapses is to buy several packs of annuals and jam them into the garden wherever there is room. This is unlikely to really solve the problem, because even annuals require a few weeks to recover from transplanting and start blooming in earnest. The better response is to plan ahead when you lay out the landscape, and set aside space within your garden for annuals that you will replace seasonally.

If you neglected to do that, and your garden is already fully planted, then you should step back, look at your landscape, and decide what you could remove to create some opportunities for annual flowers. If you can't bear the thought of removing any of your perennials, or even rolling

Fill a gap in the garden with a decorative urn of annuals, such as red-flowered cypress vine and *Ipomoea* 'Margarita'. (Photo by Michael A. Ruggiero.)

Petunias can get straggly and leave gaps in the garden when cut back. Solve the problem by planting them with vines or spreaders like artemisia. (Photo by Michael A. Ruggiero.)

back the ground cover, you should consider where you can drop in an attractive and annual-hospitable planter or urn.

Planning the seasonal changes

In her own garden, Lynden Miller, the public garden designer, made sure to leave opportunities for annuals when she planted the glorious mixed borders that are her trademark. The backbone of these beds are perennial flowers intermingled with bulbs, but Lynden reinforces these with

annuals. In each border, she has included spots into which she cycles a succession of carefully chosen annual flowers. Because she plans ahead—and shops ahead of time, too—she can plant what she wants, and not just whatever the nursery happens to have in stock when she stops in. A spot she has dedicated to pink could follow this scenario: It begins the spring hosting a cluster of some pink-flowered tulip such as Tulipa kaufmanniana 'Ancilla'. Then, as their blossoms fade, a cluster of pink-flowered snapdragons

THE NOCTURNAL GARDEN

It's the distillation of summer's sweetness: sitting in the backyard, watching the moon rise, while over you washes the perfume of your night-blooming flowers.

What are night-blooming flowers? They are plants that long ago opted out of the competition to attract daytime's busy pollinators. Instead of butterflies and bees, night-bloomers rely on moths and bats for fertilization. Their buds generally stay shut until dusk, and after spreading their petals through the hours of darkness, the blossoms close again or wilt with the dawn.

As you might expect of such night watchers, these flowers are generally pale faced. Most, actually, are white. In the weaker illumination of the moonlight, more vivid colors turn black and become invisible. But the white blossoms of the night-bloomers fairly glow.

To make sure that the pollinators find them, even on cloudy, moonless nights, most of the night-bloomers are also intensely fragrant. This characteristic makes them very efficient: A few have the impact of many, especially in the darkness when smell becomes a more important sense than sight.

A handful of night-blooming annuals is probably all you will want to plant. When placing them in the garden, keep in mind not only the needs of the plants—their preference for full sun or shade, well-drained soil or moist—but also your own nocturnal habits.

If you like to sit outside on a terrace or deck in the evening, set a few pots of night-bloomers there. Or plant them on either side of the front door, to greet you as you get home from an evening out. Better yet, plant them under your bedroom window, so that the perfumes will find their way in with the night breezes as you lie in bed.

NIGHT-BLOOMING ANNUALS

* Angel's trumpet (Datura inoxia): large white or pink trumpet-shaped fragrant flowers
* Horn of plenty (D. metel): best cultivars are 'Aurea' (yellow-flowered) and 'Flore Pleno' (double flowers, off-white to purple)
* Moonflower (Ipomoea alba): white-blossomed vine to 10 ft. tall, sweet fragrance
* Bottle gourd (Lagenaria siceraria): rampant annual vine to 25 ft. tall, with white flowers followed by huge fruits, musky fragrance
* Evening-scented stock (Matthiola longipetala): soft lilac-colored flowers with potent, sweet perfume
* Flowering tobacco (Nicotiana sylvestris): white flowers, sweet fragrance

The gloriously fragrant moonflower. (Photo by Delilah Smittle; © The Taunton Press, Inc.)

(Antirrhinum majus)—'Little Darling', maybe—are tucked in among the ripening tulip leaves.

The leaves are removed as they yellow and wither, and the snapdragons carry the display until the full heat of summer settles in, at which point those plants are pulled and some heat-hardier flowering tobaccos—Nicotiana × sanderae 'Nikki Red' would qualify—are planted in. Their stronger-colored blossoms show up better in the intense summer sunlight, but as fall arrives with cooler nights, the flowering tobaccos look increasingly ragged. They, in turn, are pulled, and a pink-variegated flowering cabbage is inserted.

Despite the name, the color of cabbage and kale is in the leaves, which even in the North continue to provide a good show until winter settles in. In the South, the flowering cabbage may well carry on right through winter, until the next spring, when the cycle of seasonal annuals begins again.

The greatest pleasure of such seasonal plantings is that they let you enjoy a whole series of distinctly different gardens. Even if your grounds are limited to a window box, you can give your apartment a different view each season. Or give your garden a new mood as your own changes.

Use seasonal annuals to bolster the display in a perennial border, as seen in designer Lynden Miller's garden. (Photo by Michael A. Ruggiero.)

The delicate blooms of star of Persia (*Allium christophii*) seem to glitter in a dark, leafy sea of annual shiso (*Perilla frutescens*) in this design by Lynden Miller at New York's Central Park Conservatory Garden. (Photo by John M. Hall.)

MAKING THE

PART TWO

GARDEN
GROW

GETTING STARTED

EVERY GARDEN BEGINS in the imagination, but from there it moves quickly to the sales yard of the garden center or the pages of the nursery catalogs. Shopping may not seem like an essential horticultural skill, but in fact it is. For no matter how inspired your planning may be, it's useless unless you can lay hands on the plants you need. You may be right, that a window box full of just the right pink petunias will transform the facade of your house. But if you have to settle for white ones because that's all you can find, your gardening is compromised right from the start.

So, getting to know all the sources for plants is a basic part of the annual gardener's education. It's also important to understand the product. Annual plants are sold in a number of different ways, and depending on the needs of your garden and your per-

(opposite) Annuals can be purchased locally or from mail-order catalogs in the form of seed, bulbs, rhizomes, or garden-ready plants. (Photo © Michael Gertley.)

(left) Seeds offer a wide variety of choices. (Photo by Michael A. Ruggiero.)

Buying nursery plants allows you to see the whole plant and often the actual flower color as well. (Photo by Michael A. Ruggiero.)

that are new or on the unusual side, novelties that haven't trickled down to those shops where annual plants are a sideline and not the basis of their business.

There are pros and cons for buying annuals, as opposed to starting them yourself from seed, bulbs, or rhizomes. The primary advantage, of course, is that with plants, you can see just what you are buying. You can see the whole plant, and if it's in flower, as annual seedlings commonly are today by the time they hit the sales shelves, you can see the actual color, rather than trying to imagine it from a catalog description. You should also look closely to determine if the plant is infested with insects or diseases. Shopping for annual plants is not so different from shopping for produce in this respect: You look at them all and pick the best.

The second advantage of buying your annuals as plants is that usually they have been grown in a greenhouse. This gives the plants a head start, both because the seeds can be sown long before you can plant outside, and because a greenhouse provides nearly ideal growing conditions.

sonal style, you may prefer one form to another. In addition, each type of plant has its own advantages and disadvantages, and you should understand these, too.

Purchasing Plants

Most annual plants can be purchased either in local nurseries or from mail-order catalogs in the form of seed, bulbs, or rhizomes, or as plants ready to move out into the garden. In today's world, everyone from supermarkets, home improvement stores, fruit and vegetable stands, and garden clubs sells annual plants. Nurseries and catalogs usually stock a wider diversity of types of plants and almost always offer species

Starting from Seed

Not so long ago, any gardener with imagination was forced to be a do-it-yourselfer when it came to annuals. The selection of transplants found at even the better garden centers and nurseries was usually poor, so that if you wanted to grow anything other than the half-dozen standards, you had to order seed and start your own plants. This is less true today. Just as mesclun, radicchio, and other exotic greens are appearing at local supermarkets now, so too are choice selections of annuals starting to appear at local nurseries and garden centers.

Nevertheless, there are still persuasive reasons for growing your own. It's cheaper; for the price of a few packets of seed, you can start a herd of annuals that would cost you big money at the garden center. And the selection of species and cultivars available as seed is still far greater than the selection found in garden-ready plants. Besides, starting from seed is, in most cases, easy.

Usually, seed-starting is a springtime activity, and in that season you have options: You can sow your seeds indoors in pots, or you can wait until all danger of frost has passed (consult your local cooperative extension office for the average last frost date in your area) and sow the seeds outdoors, directly into the garden. Once again, there are advantages and disadvantages to either method of starting annuals from seed.

Pros and cons of starting from seed

Some popular types of plants are slow to germinate and grow—wax begonias, for example, need between 15 and 20 weeks to produce a flowering-size plant—so for them, direct sowing outdoors is a poor option at best. In addition, the seeds of some annuals, such as wax begonias, are so small

and dustlike that they most likely will be lost if sown right into a garden bed.

You can start seeds indoors, using fluorescent lamps to provide high enough levels of light to produce vigorous seedlings. Shop-light fixtures that mount two 4 ft. tubes are the least expensive alternative. They can support healthy growth if equipped with one cool-white and one warm-white tube and hung about 6 in. directly above the seedlings. As the plants grow, gradually raise the lights to preserve the space between them and the topmost leaves.

Sowing outdoors leaves your seeds at the mercy of the weather, and young seedlings will have to compete with germinating weed seeds for light, space, water, and nutriments. It can be hard to tell the young weeds from your germinating

A specialist nursery offers many varieties of a given plant, like these dahlias. (Photo by Michael A. Ruggiero.)

books such as this one can provide you with the basic guidelines and schedules for growing your plants, but they cannot offer specific instructions tailored to your local climate and regional conditions.

In most cases, this book will list a 2- to 3-week range for the interval of time needed from sowing to planting (for example, 6 to 8 weeks, or 10 to 12). Until your experience and records can pinpoint a date that has worked out best for you, it is wise to sow your seeds using the middle of the range. If the recommended sowing date is 6 to 8 weeks before the last frost date, sow your seeds 7 weeks before that milepost. The middle of the range will give you a place to start.

Before you get to the point of sowing, however, it is advisable to have a plan that will cover all aspects of growing or purchasing the annuals that you want. Consider how many plants it will take to create the design you envision (see p. 137 for a handy formula). Increase this number by at least 25 percent when calculating the number of seeds you need to order, because 100 seeds almost never produce 100 seedlings, and some of the seedlings that do grow will undoubtedly prove to be runts.

Use a calendar to calculate the date you want to sow each type of seed. The time required to raise different plants from seed to transplant varies considerably: Verbena, for instance, may take 10 weeks, while marigolds only 4 to 6 weeks. This means that if you want to plant out your verbe-

annuals. However, some plants, such as giant sunflowers (Helianthus annuus), are best sown directly into the garden. If started indoors in containers, giant sunflowers tend to develop weaker stems that later on will be likely to snap under the stress of wind or rain. Even if they do survive, the weak-stemmed sunflowers bear inferior flowers.

Keep records to keep your sanity

It is always a good idea to keep simple records of all the plants that you grow from seed, for your notes will provide the most accurate account of what went on in your garden. Catalogs and nas at the same time as your marigolds, you must sow the verbena 4 to 6 weeks before sowing the marigolds.

Growing media for starting seeds

Either soil or a soilless growing medium (commonly sold as "seed-starting mix") can be used for starting seeds. Most professional gardeners prefer to use a soilless medium because of the unpredictable quality of real soils.

If you do choose to use a soil-based seed-starting mix, be sure to start with a good loam, and test it with an inexpensive soil-testing kit (available at any garden center) to make sure that the soil is of only average fertility. Then pasteurize the soil by heating it in a 250°F oven for 30 minutes, and blend with other ingredients, following one of our recipes (see p. 114).

Soilless mixes

These usually consist of a combination of finely screened sphagnum peat moss and a variety of soil conditioners that add texture to the mix. Perlite, vermiculite, and coarse sand are the mainstays of most soilless mixes. Such blends are convenient to use. They are also, for the most part, sterile, and they are much more consistent in quality than soil-based mixes, which may vary drastically depending on the type of soil they contain. The texture of the soilless mixes is ideal—both small and large seeds germinate easily in such a medium. And you needn't worry

---

STORING SEEDS

Until you are ready to sow them, keep your seeds where the temperature stays between 45° and 50°F, and where the humidity is low—the vegetable crisper drawer in your refrigerator is an excellent place. Keep unopened seed packets in their shipping container, as most of the reliable seed companies package the seed well, and sometimes even insert a package of silica gel in the shipping envelope to stabilize the humidity.

Always save the silica gel sachets that come with seed packets, or with electronic gear such as cameras and computers. You can dehydrate them by leaving them in a 200° oven for 8 hours. Then put one in a large, screw-top jar to make an ideal storage container, in or out of the refrigerator, for seed packets you have opened but only partially sown. The jar will protect the seeds from hungry mice, and if kept sealed and in a cool spot, the seeds inside should maintain their viability through that growing season.

---

about excessive nutrient levels. In fact, because soilless mixes typically contain little or no nutrients, you should plan to start a program of fertilization as soon as the seedlings have emerged and grown their true leaves.

Sowing seeds

Whether you choose to sow your seeds into a soil-based mix or a soilless one, you should be sure to use a shallow container. Wooden seed flats, plastic or clay pans, cell packs, peat pots, or individual small clay or plastic pots can be used, depending on the number of seeds you are planting, their size, and their requirements for germination. Most annuals can be sown in community containers; that is, a large number of seeds may be sown across the surface of a container. Later on,

---

✿ SOIL MIXES

For starting most annual seeds, use a mixture containing equal parts of the following:

    loam (screened topsoil)

    leaf mold, compost, or peat moss

    coarse sand, perlite, or vermiculite

For starting annuals that require a more organic soil (such as begonias and impatiens), mix the same ingredients in the following proportions:

    1 part loam

    2 parts leaf mold, compost, or peat moss

    1 part coarse sand, perlite, or vermiculite

For starting annuals that do not like wet soils (such as portulaca), mix the same ingredients in the following proportions:

    1 part loam

    1 part leaf mold, compost, or peat moss

    4 parts coarse sand, perlite, or vermiculite

---

the seedlings can be pricked out—carefully dug and separated—and transplanted into individual cell packs or pots.

The roots of some plants, however, are easily damaged and therefore should not be subjected to this extra transplanting. Instead, sow these seeds into individual 3-in. pots or into cell packs, two seeds to each pot or cell. Sweet alyssum and portulaca also need to be sown in individual pots or cell packs, but for a completely different reason. They do not produce husky, substantial transplants unless you sow between 10 and 20 seeds in each container and let the seedlings grow up together.

When the container has been properly filled with seed-starting mix and you are ready to sow your seeds, it is important to first check the individual requirements of the seeds you have selected. You'll find specific sowing and germination requirements of different kinds of plants in The Essential Annuals. Here we will discuss only general requirements and factors that affect the germination and growth of all annuals.

When sowing seeds, the general rule is to cover them with the seed-starting medium to a depth equal to the thickness of the individual seed. Achieving the fine layer of coverage this requires is easier if you sift the medium down onto the seeds through a fine screen. Keep in mind that it is always better to err on the side of covering too thinly than to cover too thickly.

Some seeds need light to germinate and should not be covered at all. Others, such as the seeds of petunias and begonias, are so fine and dustlike that they are easily buried too deeply, and these also should be simply scattered over the surface of the seed-starting medium and then left uncovered. These special needs are noted in The Essential Annuals.

Except for those annuals that need total darkness for germination, it is important to keep the seed containers in the light but out of direct sunlight. Seeds that require total darkness should have their containers placed in a black plastic bag, for even the light from an ordinary household lamp may be enough to prevent them from sprouting.

Because you have soaked the medium before sowing and covered the containers with plastic, the seeds will probably not need to be watered again before they germinate. Most seed packages offer planting instructions, and usually these cite the range of temperatures that is most favorable for the germination of that particular kind of seed. Most annuals have an optimal range of 5 to 10 degrees. Most germinate best at 70° to 75°F, but some species require temperatures as high as 80° to 85°F or as low as 50° to 55°F.

You can set seed containers on a waterproof horticultural heating pad (available through your local garden center) set to the proper tempera-

1. Put a single layer of newspaper over the drainage holes in the bottom of the container to keep the medium from being washed out. Fill the shallow container to the top with the growing medium.

2. Firm the medium down using the bottom of a pot or a piece of wood, so that when wet it will not sink irregularly; leave room for the seeds.

3. Using a watering can with a fine rose, wet the medium using HOT water (cold water will be shed off soilless mixes).

4. Sow the seeds, tapping open the packet with your forefinger and shaking out seeds one by one.

5. Cover the seeds (if appropriate) and label the container.

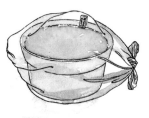

6. Cover with plastic, glass, or Plexiglas to retain humidity, then place a sheet of newspaper over the cover. The paper allows some light to reach the soil, but keeps out the more intense radiation that can dry the soil or "cook" the seeds.

Fine seeds are difficult to distribute evenly. The tendency is to drop them all in one corner, and this makes pricking out the seedlings more difficult later. Mix these dustlike seeds with fine sand and put them in a salt shaker, and they'll be easy to shake out in an evenly dispersed pattern.

ture, or 6 in. to 8 in. below a 60- to 70-watt electric bulb, although the latter doesn't produce as consistent a heat as the pad. If you've chosen to grow your seedlings under fluorescent lights, you'll find that lowering the lights so that the tubes rest 2 in. to 4 in. above the surface of the seed-starting mix provides a good, even warmth. Some seeds require special treatment, as described at right.

The seed packages will also give you a range of days in which you can expect germination to occur. This is meant to be a general guide, and even though seeds of a particular species should germinate in 7 to 10 days, it may take only 3 or 4 days in the conditions you provide. Or it may take 12 days, or even 14. For this reason, you should check the seeds at least daily after sowing them; if it is at all possible, check them in the morning, and then again in the afternoon.

Caring for new seedlings

As soon as you find seedlings emerging from the seed-starting medium or root tips poking out of the seeds, remove the covering and place the container in strong but indirect light, such as is found on a north-facing windowsill. If you are growing the seeds under fluorescent lights, raise the lights at this point to a height of 6 in. above the surface of the seed-starting mix.

If you aren't vigilant enough and do not uncover the containers as germination occurs, the emerging seedlings will stretch and become spindly in just a day or so. Such damaged seedlings will develop into poor plants that may never reach their potential.

Once the seedlings show their cotyledons (the seed leaves), it is best to move them into stronger light, though the intensity of the light should vary according to the type of plant. You'll find the needs of each kind of annual seedling listed in that plant's entry in The Essential Annuals.

SPECIAL TREATMENT FOR SEEDS

Before sowing, check the entry in The Essential Annuals for each kind of annual you plan to grow.
* Hard seeds may need to be soaked overnight in warm to hot water prior to sowing.
* Others may need their seed coat nicked with a knife or file.
* Some seeds need to be chilled for a few days prior to sowing and to be kept at a warm temperature afterwards.
* Others require alternating warm and cool periods after they are sown.

Prick out seedlings when the first true leaves appear. (Photo © Michael Gertley.)

Sun lovers should get full sun, while shade lovers need subdued morning or afternoon sun. The latter may seem to be too strong for a shade lover, but remember that in springtime, the season when you will most likely sow your seeds, the sunlight is less intense than it is later on in the summer. If you happen to be sowing seeds in summertime, then be more cautious about the amount of sunlight in which you set your new seedlings.

Be sure in succeeding days and weeks to provide the seedlings with adequate light and air circulation, or damping-off may occur. Extremely wet conditions, poor drainage, poor air circulation, and high temperatures promote the growth of damping-off fungi. Snapdragons and cockscombs are among the annuals that are prone to damping-off, and it may be wise to drench their growing medium with a fungicide to prevent the disease from taking hold when you start them indoors.

Pricking out

As your seedlings emerge from the seed-starting medium, they will probably be topped with one or two simple, rounded appendages. These are the cotyledons, the first embryonic leaves. Soon, however, if all goes well, the seedlings will sprout their first true leaf or pair of leaves; though small, these will be formed like the leaves of the mature

PRICKING OUT SEEDLINGS

1. Hold seedlings by leaves, not stems.

2. Place seedlings in individual pots with holes already made for them. Firm the soil around the plant, then moisten it by misting well or watering gently. Cover the pot with a piece of newspaper.

plant. The appearance of the first true leaves is the signal that it is time to prick out the seedlings.

Pricking out is the process of transplanting individual seedlings from the community container and planting them either outside directly into the garden or into individual pots or cell packs to grow them longer indoors. If you choose to transplant the seedlings out into the garden immediately, you should do so on a cloudy, calm day, to reduce the shock that the plant will experience from exposure to sun and wind. Because seedlings this young are so sensitive, however, you'll typically get better results by growing them on indoors. Even there, you should take care not

to expose newly transplanted seedlings to direct sunlight right away. Instead, set the seedlings where they will receive strong light, but cover them loosely for a few days with a single sheet of newspaper. Deflecting the stronger rays of sunlight helps prevent transplant shock.

When pricking out your seedlings, never tug them or hold them by the stems, as this rough treatment of an essential part is likely to damage or kill them. Instead, lift the seedlings from the seed-starting mix in the community container with the tip of a plant label or knife, and if they come up in a clump, shake them apart, holding them by either the seed leaves (cotyledons) or the true leaves. This may damage the leaf, but the seedlings will soon sprout more of those.

All pricked-out seedlings should be transplanted into their individual containers with their stems buried up to their cotyledons. By burying them to this level, you encourage the emergence of roots along the base of the stem, which produces a stronger, more stable plant. But don't set a seedling too deeply, or it may rot.

Transplanting seedlings as soon as they have produced their first set of true leaves is critical, as important as anything else you may do toward growing good plants. Prick out too early, and the seedling may not have enough roots to survive transplanting. Leave the pricking out until too late, and the result will be lanky seedlings whose future growth is likely to be stunted.

Acquiring Annuals by Other Means

While true annuals do not survive beyond their first growing season, many of the tender perennials used as annuals will overwinter, if protected from the cold. Dug from the garden before the first fall frost and brought indoors, these salvaged specimens can serve as stock plants the following spring. By removing and propagating pieces from the stock plants, you can start new specimens to set out in the garden and renew, even expand, the display.

Of course, preserving and multiplying plants in this fashion requires more investment of effort than starting plants from seed or buying them from a nursery. However, it reduces your expenses, and in the case of an especially treasured but uncommon plant, you may have little choice. There may be a coleus or begonia, for example, that you received as a "start" from a friend who couldn't remember the plant's name; how do you purchase seeds or seedlings of that? Unless you can identify what it is that you have and then find a nursery that grows it, the only way you can reproduce the plant is to clone it yourself. That is, you must take a piece of the parent and induce the piece to grow roots so that it develops into a new (though genetically identical) individual.

This cloning can be accomplished by division. That is, after digging a mature plant from the ground, you cut the mass of roots and stems into two or more separate clumps and replant each of these separately. A far more efficient method, however, is to root cuttings of the parent plant.

Cuttings

When you set out to create new plants from your overwintered coleus or begonias, the technique to use is propagation by cuttings. This method involves cutting pieces from the stock plant and placing them in an atmosphere and medium that allows the pieces to take root and grow into new plants. Cuttings normally give you plants sooner, and of a larger size, than if you had started from seed, and they are, of course, identical in appearance to the parent plant.

BEST SIZE FOR CUTTINGS

It may be tempting when you are taking cuttings from a stock plant to take extra-large pieces. This would seem likely to produce a bigger plant as it roots. In fact, though, outsized cuttings are often slower to root, and because their surface area is greater, and often their leaves are too, they transpire more and commonly die. On the other hand, you also want to avoid taking cuttings that are too small. Such meager pieces lack sufficient leaf area to produce all the food they need, and as a result they often do not root.

You can take cuttings from various parts of a plant; some types of plants are regularly propagated by root cuttings and leaf cuttings. The most common type of cutting, however, is the terminal—or stem—cutting. Stem cuttings are usually made from the tips of growing shoots, but they can also be made from sections of stem closer to the plant's base. Whatever part of the stem you use for your cuttings, make each one long enough to include three to five nodes (leaf joints). The topmost two or three of these will remain above the rooting medium, while the bottommost one or two will be located along the area of stem that is to be inserted into the medium.

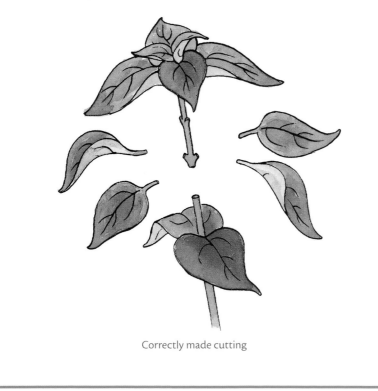

Correctly made cutting

For guidance about which plants can be propagated by cuttings, consult the individual plant descriptions in The Essential Annuals. The advice given there is important because, depending on the type of plant, the part that roots most easily (and thus the part from which you should take the cutting) varies. Furthermore, success depends on taking the cuttings at the right season, and the timing varies from plant to plant.

Getting cuttings to root

Don't waste your time taking cuttings from plants that are diseased, wilted, or otherwise stressed. Choose only the healthiest part of the plant. Removing any flowers, flower buds, or seeds will reduce the stress on the plants and may make the difference between success and failure.

Creating the proper environment for rooting is crucial to success with cuttings. The rooting medium, the quality of the light that the cuttings receive, the humidity within the rooting area, and the temperature, all play important parts in preventing the cuttings from dehydrating. If a cutting dries out before it has grown roots, it usually dies, for without roots, it cannot easily replace the moisture lost from its tissues.

Rooting media can consist of many different materials, or blends of materials. Water, soil, sand, perlite, sphagnum peat, sphagnum moss, and vermiculite are all used, with varying degrees of success.

1. Fill a pot with medium and moisten it.

2. Trim the cutting with a sharp knife, slicing straight across the stem, just below the bottom node. Then slice off the leaves from the section of stem that will be buried in the rooting medium—if left intact, they'll only rot.

3. To apply rooting hormone to the base of the cutting, remove a small amount of the chemical from the package. Don't dip the cutting into the package or the remainder of the hormone might become contaminated and unusable. Dip the base of each cutting into the powder. Shake off any excess.

4. Poke a hole in the medium with a pencil, then slip the base of a cutting into the hole.

5. Firm the medium around it with your finger or the pencil.

6. When you have inserted all the cuttings, carefully water the container; a gentle shower of moisture is what you want, such as you get from a watering can equipped with a fine rose (a tip resembling a shower head, with many tiny holes). Finally, cover the container with a plastic bag or a jar.

TRANSPLANTING CUTTINGS

1. Slip rooted cuttings out of the pot and gently tease apart the roots. Place each cutting in its own pot.

2. Fill the pot with soilless mix.

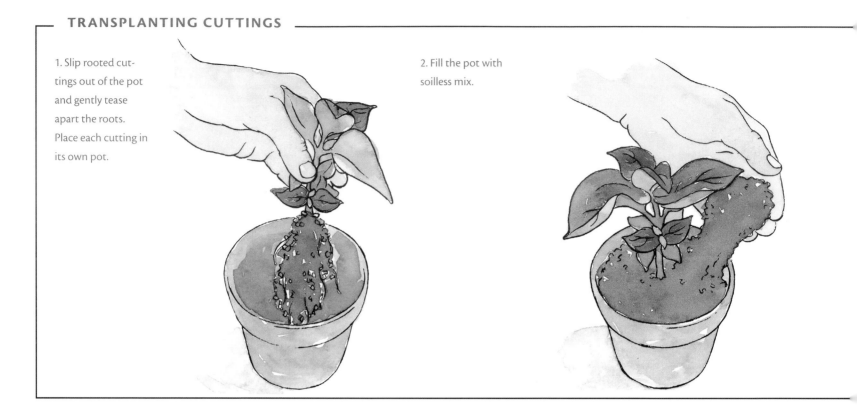

Among experienced gardeners, the most popular rooting media consist of coarse sand, perlite, and vermiculite, particularly in a peat/sand, peat/perlite, or peat/vermiculite combination. Most nurseries sell at least one, if not all, of these media. Don't use beach sand to root cuttings; although you may have as much as you want for free, the salts it contains will kill your cuttings.

Make sure the medium is as sterile as possible. To keep cuttings from rotting, the medium should provide good drainage, yet it should also be absorptive and loose in texture, so that it encourages root growth by providing an environment with a good mix of moisture and air.

Light is necessary for all cuttings to remain healthy while they are in the process of rooting. Generally, the stronger the light, the faster a cutting will root. But excessively strong light will speed transpiration—the loss of water from the leaves—and increase the risk of dehydration and death. So it is wise to filter direct sunlight so that what reaches the cuttings is strong but indirect. Set a window screen or a panel of cheesecloth between the container and the windowpane.

Place your container of cuttings in a plastic bag or under an inverted large jar, to ensure a constant level of humidity and protection from drafts throughout the rooting period.

3. Tap the pot on a hard surface to settle the mix around the roots.

4. Water well.

In general, most annuals root best when kept at a temperature equal to or even slightly higher than the temperature at which they achieve the best growth. In practice, this generally means a temperature between 60° and 80°F. Keeping your cuttings in this ideal temperature range can be tricky, but you can usually manage it with the help of a heating pad or lights.

Wrap the cuttings in wet newspaper or seal them with a damp paper towel in a plastic bag. Leave your cuttings in the protective wrapping until you are ready to stick them into the container of rooting medium.

Rooting hormones can encourage rooting in hard-to-root cuttings. Always follow the steps indicated by the manufacturer of the hormone—all brands are not applied in the same way.

New leaves and stems should start sprouting from the planted cuttings in a few weeks, which is a sign that they are ready to transplant into individual pots. Holding each cutting gently by a leaf, lift it out of the rooting medium. Typically, there should be a cluster of 1-in.- to 2-in.-long roots emerging from its base. If the roots are much shorter than this, carefully replace the cutting in the rooting medium and water it in.

123

Seedlings of sun-loving annuals like these (*Petunia integrifolio*, foreground, and *Cleome* 'Violet Queen', back) need bright light when started indoors. (Photo by Chris Curless; © The Taunton Press, Inc.)

Experience and notes from previous years will help you estimate how long a given type of cutting from a particular species or cultivar of annual will take to root. Once a cutting has rooted, and you have potted it into its own container, you should move the new plant into a spot where it will receive strong light but not direct sunlight. Even sun-loving species need a few days to recover from the shock of transplanting before you begin to gradually move them into bright full sun. During this period of convalescence, keep the new plant well watered: The soil in its pot should remain evenly moist but not waterlogged.

Wintering over

In the colder sections of North America, wherever winter inflicts prolonged, hard frosts and freezes the soil, division of annuals is a slightly more complicated process than in frost-free climates. Tender perennials need protection to survive the winter.

Actually, protecting plants from winter cold is easy. It depends on the same strategy you use yourself: When the weather gets frosty, the plants move indoors. When to do this varies with the species of plant.

Most tender perennials should be moved indoors before the cold can damage them. In fact, begonias, geraniums, heliotropes, lantanas, and some other super-sensitive species should come in even earlier (details on the over-wintering of particular species are included in the plant descriptions in The Essential Annuals). To protect them from the shock they will experience moving from the garden into the dry warmth of a centrally heated house, dig and move these plants before you turn on the heat in fall.

Your goal in wintering over plants is to keep them in a semidormant state, not to encourage growth that the dry air and low light levels of your house's interior cannot support. Do not feed the plants with nitrogen fertilizers during this period. Woody plants such as lantanas can even be moved into a frost-free corner of the garage for wintering over. To prepare them for this, first move them into pots and gradually reduce the amount of water you give them, in this way easing them into a dormant state.

Cannas and dahlias benefit from a frosting before they are moved into protection, as this helps push them into dormancy. Indeed, if their roots are dug and stored before they have been chilled in this manner, they tend to continue to grow and are likely to rot in their dark winter storage. When digging cannas and dahlias, be careful not to damage or break the tubers or rhizomes. Cut back the stems to 6 in., and clean the old soil from the tubers. Dry the clumps in the sun and store them upside down for a few days to drain any moisture from their stems. Then store the roots in bags of barely moistened, almost dry, peat moss, vermiculite, or perlite in a cool spot where the temperature stays within a range of 40° to 50°F. Don't store the roots in a humid area, or they may rot. Keep the soil around the rootstock just moist enough so that they do not shrivel.

Tropical plants that arise from tubers (tuberous begonias, caladiums, and colocasias, for example) must not be allowed to freeze before being brought inside for the winter. Instead, before the first frost, transplant them into pots, and then gradually, over a period of weeks, reduce the water you give the plants until the foliage starts to drop. Stop watering altogether when all of the foliage has yellowed or dropped, and store the pots in an area that is warm (60° to 75°F) and dry until next spring. Alternatively, you may opt for cleaning all the old soil, roots, and dried leaves off the tubers and then storing them in dry peat, vermiculite, sand, or perlite rather than keeping them in bulky pots.

MOVING TENDER PLANTS INDOORS

To winter over geraniums, coleus, alternanthera, or other tropical or subtropical plants, dig them out of the soil and then replant them into containers. Plants already growing in tubs or pots can be brought indoors as is, though if their top growth is expansive it should be cut back. Container plants that show signs of being pot-bound, with root tips emerging from the drainage holes in the pot or tub bottom, should be lifted out of the containers and should have their roots pruned back. Afterwards, repot them back into the same containers, since moving them into new containers might stimulate a burst of new growth.

Place the containers in a sunny and cool, but frost-free, location—a cool windowsill or a sun porch is ideal. Alternatively, you can root cuttings from these plants in August and winter these over indoors. Such rooted cuttings are easier to tend and take up less room than the parent plant.

Hibiscus, coleus, and other tender perennials will winter over indoors in pots. (Photo by Judi Rutz; © The Taunton Press, Inc.)

PLANTING and CARE

S UCCESS IS EASY TO COME BY when growing annuals, but often that success has more to do with the plants' tolerance than the gardener's skill. The fact is that these are adaptable plants, which as a group can survive in a wide range of conditions. Almost certainly they will flower, to some extent, if you plant them in your garden, but it may well be that they do this in spite of your care rather than because of it. That's fine. But do not forget that there is a big difference between merely surviving and truly thriving. To enjoy annuals at their best, to see them perform to their fullest potential, you have to do more than fail to kill the plants.

To see your annuals perform at their best, you must understand the handful of things that they really do need from their environment. The conditions that the

Violets combine beautifully with ferns in a moist, shaded spot. (Photo by Lee Anne White; © The Taunton Press, Inc.)

seed packets and the nursery labels recommend—"full sun," "partial shade," "a good loam"—have to be more than just words to you. You have to know what these terms mean, and how to satisfy them.

Assessing a Site

Some things that an annual plant needs for its best growth—a rich or poor supply of nutrients, lots of moisture, or dryish soil—you determine largely by the care you give to the plants. There are other factors, such as the amount of sunlight your plants will receive, the temperatures they will experience, or the amount of wind to which they will be exposed, which are largely outside your control, which are determined by the site, the spot in which you place the plants. In any case, to ensure that your plants get what they need, you must begin your gardening with a careful and accurate site assessment. You must know what nature will give the plants. Smart gardeners will then adjust their designs to include only plants that find their sites hospitable.

Sun or shade?

Sunlight is the fuel that drives your annuals' growth. Just as with your car, you have to deliver fuel at the right octane level, the right solar intensity, if the plants are to operate at peak capacity.

Gardeners traditionally describe the light level within the various parts of their plots as "sun" or "shade." The distinction seems obvious, but in fact, gardeners define these terms in their own way.

Full sun is the condition typically prescribed for sun-loving plants. As little as 5 hours of direct sunlight a day is enough to qualify a site for the full sun category, as long as that sunlight is received from just before midday through the early part of the afternoon, when the sunlight is at its most intense. Five hours of sunlight received during the early morning or late afternoon and evening, when the sun is low in the sky, does not qualify as full sun.

┌───┐
│ ── QUICK SOIL TEST ──   │
│   │
│ Determining which type of soil is found in your gar- │
│ den bed is easy. With a trowel, dig a hole a couple │
│ of inches deep and then scoop out of it a handful of │
│ soil. Moisten this slightly (just moisten it, don't soak it), │
│ and squeeze it into a ball in your hand. Then drop the │
│ soil from waist height onto a paved surface. A ball of │
│ sand will disintegrate when it hits the pavement. A ball │
│ of clay may crack, but will generally stick together. A │
│ ball of a good loam will shatter.   │
└───┘

A pot of petunias and scented geraniums make an elegant—and aromatic—accent on this wall. (Photo by Michael A. Ruggiero.)

northern gardens, you are likely to be able to grow in full sun plants that are usually considered to be for shade only.

The intense sunlight and heat found throughout most of the Deep South, the Southwest, and in summer at higher elevations of the mountainous West make some light shade in the early afternoon beneficial even for sun-loving plants. In seaside gardens, by contrast, you can safely locate shade-loving plants such as fuchsias into sunnier positions than you would normally allow them, because the ocean moderates air temperatures, keeping seaside gardens cool.

Soil

When you stand admiring a flower, it's easy to forget that what you see is only half the plant, and that in many respects, the more important part of the plant is underground. After all, it's on their roots that most plants must depend not only for water but also for nutrients. What you do for your plants before ever you sow a seed is often the most important factor in determining their success. Take care of the soil, and to a large extent the plants will take care of themselves.

By far the best soil for growing most annuals is a loam. This is a soil composed of different-sized particles—sand, clay, and silt—in a balance that naturally contains a healthy mixture of moisture and air. Loams are easy to dig and they offer the gardener the best of both worlds. Loams drain

Abundant water and fertilizer and an organic-enriched, well-drained soil have made a lush display of this border. From back to front: canna 'Pretoria', zinnia 'Red Sun', marigold 'Primrose Lady', and mealycup sage 'Victoria'. (Photo by Michael A. Ruggiero.)

well, yet they retain an abundance of nutrients and moisture for strong plant growth.

If your soil proves to be something other than the ideal loam, you can improve it. To a sandy soil you should add generous amounts of compost, leaf mold, or other organic material to help bind the soil together and increase its ability to absorb and hold water and retain nutrients.

Clay soils also can be improved by the addition of decomposed organic materials. Organic matter causes the tiny clay particles to clump together in larger crumbs so that pores are opened in the soil.

Another way to improve the structure of a clay soil is to dig in lime or gypsum; a dose of 2 lb. per 100 sq. ft. of soil surface is usually adequate. These calcium compounds also cause the clay particles to stick together into larger clumps, which allows water and soil to pass freely through the soil. Gypsum accomplishes this without changing the pH, whereas lime makes the soil more alkaline. Lime may be helpful if your soil is markedly acidic; an inexpensive pH testing kit, available at any garden center, will tell you if it is.

In general, however, soil pH is much less of a concern when growing annuals than when growing many other types of plants. Annuals, as a group, flourish in any pH from mildly acidic (pH 6.0) to a neutral or mildly alkaline soil (pH 7.2).

In other respects, though, annuals make extraordinary demands upon their soils. Because annuals make all their growth in a matter of weeks, they take heavy withdrawals of nutrients and other resources from the soil. For this reason, it is important to nourish and renew the soil in an annual bed with yearly doses of organic matter.

It is also important to prepare the soil deeply so that your annuals' roots will have a deep reservoir on which to draw. If your soil is naturally well drained and reasonably fertile, then you can get away with digging the planting area and mixing in organic matter only to a depth of 6 in. But excavating to 8 in. (the depth of a spade's blade) is better, and 12 in. is better yet. If your soil is poor, you might consider constructing a raised bed and filling it with a mixture of equal parts of bagged topsoil, sand, and compost. Or you can grow your annuals in containers.

A raised bed provides a near-ideal niche for annuals. (Photo by Michael A. Ruggiero.)

PLANTING CONTAINERS

When preparing a container for planting, take care to provide for adequate drainage. This is especially important when planting a large and deep container, as most annuals will not send their roots all the way to the bottom. If you fill the container entirely with potting soil, the bottom portion is likely to remain wet and so will sour.

To prevent this, fill the bottom third of the container with gravel, pot shards, or Styrofoam packing peanuts to ensure rapid drainage. Cap this drainage layer with a sheet of landscape fabric (permeable plastic mulch material sold at garden centers) before adding the potting soil. The landscape fabric barrier will allow water to pass through but will keep the soil from sifting down and clogging the drainage material.

Fertilization

In comparison to other plants, annuals live on an accelerated schedule. To complete their life cycle, they've got to produce a large quantity of foliage and flowers in a matter of weeks. To accomplish this, they need an abundant and more or less uninterrupted flow of resources. That's why it's so important to keep soil fertility at a high level when growing these plants.

Careful staking and meticulous care have turned a row of bronze-leaved dahlias into an annual hedge. (Photo by Michael A. Ruggiero.)

This is especially true if you buy seedlings at the local garden center. What you get there are greenhouse-grown plants that have been fed on a regular and frequent schedule. Such seedlings are usually rootbound by the time that you get them, and are not able to forage for their own food when you move them out into your garden. If you don't continue the program of fertilization that the nursery has established, the plants will suffer a traumatic shock and stop growing. Chances are, they'll never really recover from this experience.

As a group, annuals find any balanced, complete fertilizer formula acceptable. That is, the three numbers in the formula (which represent the percentage, by weight, of nitrogen, phosphorus, and potassium, respectively) should be approximately equal, as in a 20-20-20 fertilizer (a popular formula for the water-soluble types) or even 5-10-5 (a common formula for the granular fertilizers you find at the hardware store and garden center). There are a few exceptions, which are noted in The Essential Annuals, beginning on p. 152.

How much and how often to fertilize varies with the fertility of the soil, the type of plants you are growing, and the stage of growth your plants have reached.

Fertilization also depends on timing. Because of their smaller size, young seedlings should be given smaller doses of fertilizer than they will require when they become older and larger plants. In addition, seedlings grow better when fed with a plant-starter type of fertilizer. This is a fertilizer with a formula rich in phosphorus, such as 9-45-6, to help seedlings establish a good root system. Later on, as the seedlings grow, you can switch to a fertilizer with a balanced formula.

Fertilize before planting

The most traumatic event in the life of most annual plants is the move from a nursery container out into the garden. The plant needs all of its strength to cope with this transition. That's why you should take care that the transplant doesn't suffer from a lapse in fertilization; mix fertilizer with the soil in the bed before planting so that the nutrients will be available from the moment the transplant moves in.

One effective routine is to enrich the soil with a granular organic fertilizer when you are preparing the bed for planting, and then to feed the seedlings with a dose of a water-soluble starter fertilizer when you transplant them into the garden. The water-soluble fertilizer provides a quick boost. Then, as the transplants settle in, their roots will find the longer-lasting granular food. Follow up these initial feedings with periodic feedings of a water-soluble fertilizer with a balanced formula.

The frequency of application will depend on the product you use. Read the product label carefully, calculate how much fertilizer you should apply for a planting the size of the one you've created, and then apply less. Too heavy an application is harmful to the plants and the environment, and fertilizer manufacturers, not surprisingly, tend to err on the generous side in their recommendations.

An unstudied combination of diverse flowers can have a charm all its own. (Photo by M. C. Pindar.)

An old quarry provided the site for extraordinary annual displays in Butchart Gardens, Victoria, British Columbia. (Photo by Michael A. Ruggiero.)

temperature of approximately 70°F. This means that they provide no benefits to spring or fall plantings in the northern parts of the United States, and they are generally unsuitable for use with cool-season annuals. In addition, they are more expensive, pound for pound, than most other types of fertilizers.

Laying Out the Garden

Most of us garden on a budget, and common sense suggests that before buying annual transplants or even seeds, we should know precisely how many plants we need. Fortunately, it's easy to calculate ahead of time the number of plants you'll need to carry out any design that you may have planned. At least, it's easy if you've taken the time to draw on graph paper a to-scale plan of your design. If you haven't already done this, now is the time.

Keep in mind that your to-scale drawing doesn't have to be pretty, just more or less accurate. Get a sheet of 10-squares-to-the-inch graph paper and let the length or width of each square equal a set number of inches across the bed (2 in. per square is a good measure for an average-sized bed or border).

Using a pencil with a substantial eraser, rough in the outlines of the display you would like to create, indicating the space to be occupied by each type of plant. Then use the four-step formula that Mike Ruggiero has developed over his years of planting annual borders at the New York

Be sparing, but watch the plants: If their growth stalls, apply a bit more fertilizer. You can always make another application, but you cannot take back any fertilizer after it is applied. After all, you don't want to find yourself in the situation of the poor tailor, who complained that he had cut the cloth three times, and it was still too short.

An alternative way to ensure a gradual, consistent flow of nutrients to the plants is to mix one of the so-called timed-release fertilizers into the soil at planting time. Timed-release fertilizers are convenient to use and can work quite well in warm weather plantings. However, they do not release their nutrients until the soil reaches a

SAMPLE GRAPH PAPER PLAN

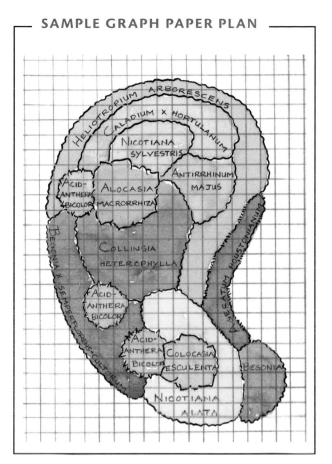

Botanical Garden The formula, given at right, converts the rough plan into an accurate plant count with little or no math anxiety. Then see p. 138 for an example of using the estimating formula.

Of course, calculating the number of plants becomes more complicated if your design includes areas devoted to different plants. And what if the areas you allot to the different kinds of plants are not regularly geometrical in outline, but instead follow flowing, irregular lines? This is

when having drawn the plan on graph paper really pays off.

Calculate the area represented by each of the graph paper's squares; if you have drawn to a scale in which each square equals 2 in. of garden space, then the amount of actual planting area represented by each square on the graph paper is 4 sq. in. (2 in. by 2 in.). Next, count the number of squares included in the space you have allotted to

PLANT-ESTIMATING FORMULA

Here's how to calculate about how many plants you'll need to fill the garden.

STEP 1 Determine the number of square feet in the area to be planted.
* For rectangular areas, multiply the length times the width
* For circular areas, measure the radius (the distance from the center to the perimeter). Multiply this number by itself and then multiply the result by 3.14.
* For areas that are oval in shape, figure out the average radius (a rough guess is adequate!). Multiply this number by itself and then multiply the result by 3.14.
* For triangular areas, multiply half the base times the height.

STEP 2 Determine the number of square inches in the area to be planted by multiplying the number of square feet by 144 (the number of square inches in a square foot).

STEP 3 Determine the number of square inches a mature plant will occupy. This can be accomplished by taking the spacing between a plant and its neighbor, as specified in every entry in The Essentials Annuals, and then multiplying this number by itself.

STEP 4 Divide the number of square inches in the planting area by the number of square inches required for each plant. The result will be the total number of plants required to fill that planting area.

THE FORMULA IN ACTION

STEP 1 You have decided to plant a square-shaped bed of wax begonias. You measure the sides of the bed and find the width to be 4 ft., and the length to be 4 ft. also.

   4 ft. x 4 ft. = 16 sq. ft.

STEP 2 Multiply the square footage by 144 to find the area in square inches.

   16 sq. ft. x 144 = 2,304 sq. in.

STEP 3 You look up *Begonia semperflorens-cultorum* in The Essential Annuals and learn that the suggested spacing for this plant is 8 in. to 10 in.

- Planted 8 in. apart, the plants will each occupy 64 sq. in. (8 in. x 8 in.).
- Planted 9 in. apart, the plants will each occupy 81 sq. in. (9 in. x 9 in.).
- Planted 10 in. apart, the plants will each occupy 100 sq. in. (10 in. x 10 in.).

Note: The middle of the suggested range (9 in.) is usually the recommended spacing, but if you are anxious for the plants to merge into a solid sheet of foliage and flowers more quickly, you should plant them at the closer spacing. If you plant at the widest spacing, and the vigor of the plant growth is for some reason less than the best (perhaps the summer is unusually cold and wet), then the begonias will not cover the bed completely.

STEP 4 Having decided that you'll plant at the safe spacing of 9 in., you divide the area of the bed (2,304 sq. in.) by the area required for each plant.

- Planted on 9-in. centers, 2,304 sq. in. divided by 81 sq. in. equals 28.44 (or 29) plants.

Note: If your calculations come out to a fraction such as 28.6, round up to the nearest full number, here 29. Don't be cheap and round down when you should round up. The single plant may not seem significant, and in fact you may not notice the difference in the bed at planting time. But the lack of that last plant may later be enough to prevent the mature plants from filling in to cover the bed completely.

each kind of plant and multiply those numbers by 4 to figure out the respective planting areas in square inches.

If you didn't draft your plan on graph paper, you can still figure out the planting areas for different plants by using a grid. You can draw the grid right onto your plan using nothing more than a pencil and a ruler.

Laying out the design in the garden

Once you've drafted your design and calculated the numbers of plants needed to fill it, it's time to transfer the design from paper onto the soil.

In doing this, your most important tool will be a tape measure. Begin by measuring out and marking with stakes and string the perimeter of your bed. Then, with more stakes (represented on Drawing C by the light-colored circles) and strings, you locate and mark on the bed the crossed lines of the grid you drew over your design plan. Finally, by referring to the plan, you establish where the edges of the various planting areas cross the grid lines, and you mark these points with more stakes (represented on Drawing C by the black circles).

Play "connect the dots" with this last set of stakes, and you'll have the boundaries of the different planting areas completely outlined on the flower bed. You can connect the marker stakes (the black circles on Drawing C) with string, but if the outlines of the planting areas are supposed to curve (as they do here), you'll achieve better results with lengths of garden hose or rope. You can lay these down over the bed, running them from marker stake to marker stake, and then pull and push them until you create pleasing, smooth curves that mimic the ones you drew on the paper plan.

A GRID TO CALCULATE PLANTING AREAS

In the sample plan on p. 137, we sketched a rectangular bed 20 ft. long and 4 ft. wide. We divided it into a grid of blocks, each 2 ft. by 5 ft. with an area of 10 sq. ft.

A. Basic grid

B. Grid with planting areas indicated and color-coded

C. Grid with stakes indicated

Next, we sketched in the outlines of our planting scheme and color coded the different areas so that we'll know which areas are to be planted with each kind of annual.

The areas we outlined in this fashion are not exactly regular, but they can easily be converted into triangles, squares, and rectangles, as we have done in Drawing C. Using the four-step formula outlined on p. 137, you can calculate the area of each of these scraps of planting area and add the various pieces of each color together to figure out the total planting area for each kind of annual.

A

B

C

STAKES AND STRING IN THE GARDEN

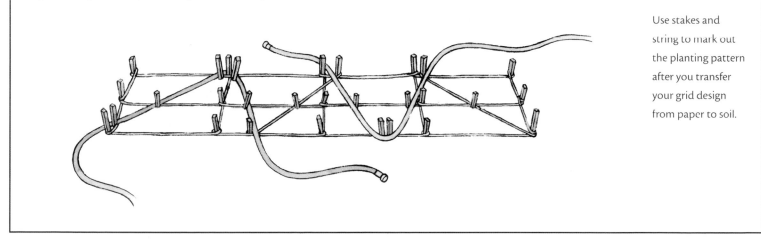

Use stakes and string to mark out the planting pattern after you transfer your grid design from paper to soil.

This tub of coleus is attractive, but it would have been more lush if it had included plants to spill over the edge. (Photo by Michael A. Ruggiero.)

Counting plants for container plantings

To calculate the number of annuals needed for planting a window box, pot, urn, tub, or any other container, use the same four-step formula that you used for calculating the plant needs of your bed. Then adjust the results. If you plant exactly the number of plants needed to fill the planting area, you'll create a planting that runs out to the edge of the container and then abruptly stops. This will give the planting an awkward, tuftlike look.

A far more pleasing look is one in which the plants seem to spill out and over the container's lip. You achieve this by adding extra plants around the periphery of the planting space. In general, you increase the total number of plants by 25 percent over the formula.

If, for example, you have calculated that 16 plants are needed to fill your tub, you increase that number to 20. The extra plants should have flexible stems that fall easily into a cascading form, such as petunias, scaevolas, or narrow-leaved zinnias.

Transplanting Techniques

The key to success in planting annual seedlings into the garden is simple. With most species, just set the transplants into the soil of the garden bed at the same depth as they rested in the potting mixture in their pots, cell packs, or plugs. A few species, such as cosmos and marigolds, can sprout roots from the lower part of their stems. Such plants are set 1 in. deeper into the soil than they rested in their pots, to encourage the transplants to form a deeper, stronger root system that makes them more stable as adults. These exceptions are noted in the plant descriptions in The Essential Annuals.

Transplanting is a traumatic experience for seedlings because the finer roots are inevitably damaged. Usually, the roots regrow quickly but until they do, the seedlings may have trouble drawing from the soil the moisture they need.

Doing your transplanting on a cloudy day will ease the transition, because your seedlings will need less water then. If you can't wait for a cloudy day, then at least postpone transplanting until after the hottest part of the day has passed. Another precaution is to water the seedlings well on the night before or in the early morning of the transplanting day, so that they will be full of moisture when you make the transfer. Water them again immediately after you finish transplanting.

When, in preparation for transplanting, you slip the seedlings out of their containers, inspect the roots. Gently loosen or tease out any that have entirely circled the bottom of the pot or cell pack. This will encourage new root growth to reach outward into the soil, rather than just confining itself to the area of the original mass.

Some authorities recommend slicing through or snipping off these encircling roots, but such drastic treatment is unnecessary, and will increase the amount of root loss that transplanting causes. The more roots you can preserve intact, the faster the young plants will recover and resume normal growth.

UNTANGLING ROOTS BEFORE PLANTING

Before planting a pot-bound plant, gently untangle some of the outer roots to encourage them to grow out into the soil.

PROTECTING NEW TRANSPLANTS

If the weather is hot and sunny on the day following your transplanting, fashion an awning of newspaper one sheet thick over the transplants with garden stakes. This won't entirely block the sun, but it will reflect and filter out some of its rays so that the transplants are less likely to overheat and dehydrate.

Weed Prevention

Pulling weeds shouldn't be a major chore for the annual gardener. If you are managing your plantings properly, weeds won't get a foothold. In general, the techniques you use to keep annual beds weed free are the same as those you'd use in any other kind of garden. However, annual gardeners have an advantage. Weeds entrench themselves among perennials or shrubs, infiltrating their roots among those of the desirable plants so that you cannot remove the invaders entirely. Whenever annual gardeners clear their beds to prepare for replanting, they also eliminate existing weeds.

Focus on prevention

When you prepare the soil for planting, remove not only the top growth of any weeds, but also extract all the roots from the soil. If you can leave the bed vacant for a while, consider "solarizing" it at this time. Water it well, then cover it with a sheet of clear plastic, burying the edges of the plastic around the bed's perimeter. Left in place for four weeks, the plastic acts as a solar energy collector, causing the sun to heat up the soil beneath and cook all the weed seeds contained in it.

Many gardeners rely on pre-emergence herbicides to keep their annual beds weed free. These chemicals are applied to the soil (usually in granular form) to prevent seeds from germinating for a period of weeks or months. Used according to the directions on the product label, pre-emergence herbicides will keep new weeds from sprouting, but they are equally effective at preventing the germination of annual flower seeds. If you use this method of weed prevention, you will have to create your displays with transplants purchased as seedlings at the nursery or started indoors.

Annual flowers may exhibit a graceful airiness, as in this cluster of cleomes 'Rose Queen'. (Photo by Steve Silk; © The Taunton Press, Inc.)

Tucking in your annuals with a layer of some organic mulch also inhibits weed growth by smothering any seeds that have fallen onto the surface of the beds and by keeping any new arrivals from coming in contact with the soil. Don't overdo it, though. A 1 in. deep layer of mulch is sufficient; a deeper layer encourages crown rot, a disease that attacks the bases of the annuals' stems.

Organic mulches can be raked aside when you need to work the soil in a bed, and then afterwards redistributed. Most types provide similar benefits, and you can make your choice on the basis of price. Check with local suppliers to find out what sort of organic mulch is cheapest in your area. Usually, you'll get a far better price if you buy it by the cubic yard rather than by the bag.

Watering

Proper watering is perhaps the hardest of the gardener's skills to learn, and expertness in irrigation is usually the determining factor in whose garden is a success and whose is not. Most of us begin our gardening careers looking for an easy formula that will tell us when to water, and how much. Unfortunately, there's no such rule. What experience teaches is that when and how you should water varies with a couple of factors.

If your soil contains lots of organic matter, it will absorb water easily, drain well, and retain moisture well. That will allow you to irrigate

Flowers of tuberous begonias can be large and colorful. (Photo by Michael A. Ruggiero.)

deeply but less often. It will also help your soil make more efficient use of rain and snow.

Mulching can also reduce a garden's need for water. And how often you water will be determined partly by what you choose to grow. Cosmos thrive in a dryish soil, while cannas need a moist one.

Another important factor in determining watering needs is the age of the plants. The roots of newly planted seedlings or transplants don't reach far into the surrounding soil, and they need more frequent irrigation than they will a few weeks later when they have rooted into their new homes.

HOW WATER MOVES THROUGH SOIL

Water moves primarily up and down through the soil, not from side to side. So when you water (and when it rains), the water entering the soil moves almost directly downward. Later, as evaporation pulls water from the soil surface, it may, through capillary action, rise back up. But there is little lateral movement.

As a rule, plants can draw only on the water that passes by their root systems, so if the roots don't extend far from the base of the plant (as in the case of newly transplanted seedlings), they don't have access to most of the water in the soil. Later, as their roots spread, they can tap a far greater reservoir of soil moisture. In the period right after transplanting, though, seedlings can die of thirst in the midst of abundance. Consequently, annuals commonly need more frequent watering in the spring, while they are still small, than they will in late summer, when they are far larger.

Weather also affects your watering. In years when rainfall is greater than the norm, you'll water less often. And during the spring and fall, because the temperatures are cooler, your annuals will transpire—"sweat"—less water and so need less irrigation. In most areas of the United States, spring and fall are also rainier seasons than midsummer, which further decreases the need for irrigation during those seasons.

Finally, the means by which you deliver water will also affect the frequency and extent of your irrigation. Drip irrigation uses water most efficiently, but drip systems are better adapted to irrigating trees and shrubs.

Sprinklers are the traditional irrigation technology, and the portable kind require no installation at all. They are extravagant in their use of water, though. You can reduce this waste considerably by purchasing a sprinkler suited to the geometry of your garden. An oscillating sprinkler, for example, is the most efficient model for watering rectangular areas, while a perforated ring sprinkler—the "whirlybird" kind—is more efficient at watering circular areas.

Watering by hand is time consuming and so is usually not a practical way of irrigating large expanses of plants. You may find it the most effective way to supply the water needs of newly transplanted seedlings, but once the plants have rooted in, you'll probably want to enlist the help of a sprinkler or drip system. Hand watering is also useful for giving that extra drink to an especially thirsty plant—the canna planted amid cosmos, for instance.

Whatever method of irrigation you choose to adopt, temper your use of it with a bit of ordinary common sense. When planning a design for any area of the garden, try to use plants that share

MAKING MULCH

You can make your own mulch. Fall leaves, raked into a heap and then shredded with a rotary lawn mower or an electric leaf shredder, make an effective and reasonably attractive mulch. A few hours' work every fall can yield enough mulch to keep your garden tucked in for a whole year, and the shredded leaves can be stored in plastic bags until you need them.

similar needs for water—that will greatly simplify the job of irrigation.

Pinching and Deadheading

Many popular annuals are self-branching. That is, their stems sprout branches spontaneously, so that the mature plants naturally grow into a bushy, compact form. Petunias and marigolds, for example, branch freely and without encouragement from the early stages of their development. However, other annuals do not. Zinnias, catharanthus, and heliotrope (among others) need some pinching if their central stems are to branch.

Nemesia 'KLM' is an outstanding cool season annual for a northern spring or a southern winter garden. (Photo by Michael A. Ruggiero.)

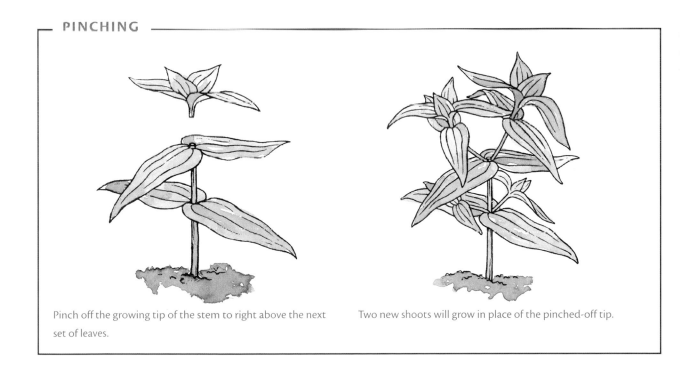

PINCHING

Pinch off the growing tip of the stem to right above the next set of leaves.

Two new shoots will grow in place of the pinched-off tip.

With timely pinching, garden mums make a carpet of color in fall and a strong contrast for ornamental cabbages. (Photo by Michael A. Ruggiero.)

The simplest form of pinching is the one you practice on annuals, such as zinnias, that tend toward dominant central stems. The goal of pinching is to make the zinnia branch earlier, lower down on the central stem, so that it will direct more of its strength into these branches and the multitude of flowers they bear. As soon as the young zinnia has borne two or three pairs of leaves, with your thumb and forefinger pinch off the top of the stem just above the topmost pair of leaves (you can also use a pair of sharp shears for this operation).

You can also use pinching to keep some vigorous annuals in bounds. The garden mum (Chrysanthemum x grandiflorum), a perennial that we normally grow as an annual, begs for this treatment. If left unpinched, the stems of most cultivars grow long and soft, eventually flopping over. Staking the plant with twigs will help it keep its shape, but you should also encourage compact growth by periodically pinching back the branch tips (for specific instructions, see individual entries in The Essential Annuals). Pinching will reduce the number of flowers the plant bears, but the blossoms will be larger and better looking.

Pinching can rejuvenate plants that have become overgrown and leggy. Petunias, for instance, tend to flower mostly at the ends of their stems, and after a few months in the garden, the plants are likely to be bearing all their blossoms at the end of long, ratty stems. Pinching each stem back by two-thirds, to a leaf, will encourage the plant to sprout new shoots with better looking blossoms.

Deadheading

One of the first rules of gardening is to never allow a plant to go to seed, unless the seeds are

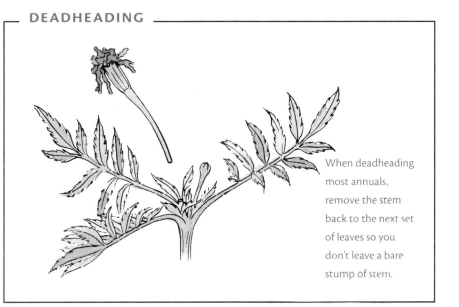

DEADHEADING

When deadheading most annuals, remove the stem back to the next set of leaves so you don't leave a bare stump of stem.

ornamental or you want them for future propagation. Seed production requires an enormous investment of energy, and it weakens the plant. In the case of true annuals, seed production actually kills the plant.

Deadheading is the timely removal, either by pinching or snipping, of spent blossoms before they bear seeds. Removing the knots of wilted, fading petals keeps a plant looking better, but more importantly, it frustrates the plant. The plant responds by making more flowers, trying again to set seed. We watch and wait, and at the proper time deadhead those, too, so that the cycle may begin once more.

As with all else in the world of gardening, there are exceptions. Some plants, such as many cultivated forms of impatiens, typically self-deadhead, aborting and shedding their flowers before seeds

Actually a frost-sensitive perennial, dusty miller 'Silver Lace' (front) doesn't bloom in its first year of growth, so requires no deadheading when grown as an annual. (Photo by Michael A. Ruggiero.)

Staking is essential support for many heavy-headed flowers such as dahlias. (Photo by Michael A. Ruggiero.)

can form. Cleomes will set seed if not deadheaded, but the bean-like pods, which reach out like a spider's legs, don't appreciably affect the plant's commitment to producing more flowers. If allowed to set seed, cleomes will self-sow around the garden and may develop into a minor weed the following year. If you don't want your garden to bristle with such volunteers, be sure to deadhead.

Staking

Generally, staking is only necessary for annuals with a tall, central stem or cluster of stems such as the 3-ft.- to 4-ft.-tall 'Monarch' snapdragons. Often, by selecting dwarf cultivars of the same plant (such as the 9-in.-tall 'Tom Thumb' snapdragons), you can eliminate the need for staking.

HOW TO MAKE STAKES INVISIBLE

Short stakes linked with string support cosmos unobtrusively.

One way to make stakes invisible is to use flexible supports so that the plants can drape themselves in more natural postures. For instance, to keep a mass of cosmos from tumbling forward, you can slip a series of shorter stakes in among their front stems and then tie a loose cordon of soft string or twine from stake to stake. Use the green cotton string you'll find at any garden center, as it will blend visually with the plants it is supporting, and let the stakes stand no more than half to two-thirds the height of the plants. As the cosmos lean forward against the string, they'll envelop and hide the stakes.

Alternatively, you could hide the stakes by planting some shorter, bushier annuals in front of the cosmos.

In other cases, as with zinnias, pinching the young plants to bushier, stronger growth can reduce or eliminate the need for staking. Putting tall-growing annuals in a spot where they are sheltered from the wind also reduces the need for this sort of support. But if you want the dramatic effects that only soaring flowers can provide, then you will have to do at least some staking.

The best type of stake is the one that does the job unobtrusively. A giant sunflower lashed to a 2x4 is secure, but it's not nearly as attractive as one supported from behind by a half-hidden, slender but strong bamboo stake. Keeping your stakes from becoming the center of attention is easy enough—the eye will naturally jump to the more colorful flowers, if you give it a chance.

Be careful not to accidentally injure your plants when you push the stakes into the soil. Tuberous-rooted plants such as dahlias are especially vulnerable in this respect. To avoid skewering their tubers, insert the stakes right at planting time. If you wait until later, when the soil has settled back in over the tubers and the tubers themselves have grown longer, you won't know where you can insert the stakes safely.

Most garden centers sell a variety of plastic, wooden, bamboo, and metal stakes, some linked together to make loose chains of support, others welded to hoops. Often, however, the supports you make yourself from string and twigs are the best. For crude though these may look, they are the easiest to hide.

BRUSH STAKES

Another near-invisible sort of support, one that works especially well with the bushier sorts of annuals, is that provided by brush stakes. You can cut these yourself, pruning off branches from such twiggy weed trees as wild cherries or birches. Cut the branches while the trees are still dormant so that you won't have to strip them of foliage, and store them in a cool, dark place such as the corner of the garage.

Then, as soon as your annual seedlings have established themselves in their beds and started to expand, shorten the branches so that they measure no more than two-thirds the height to which you expect the plants to grow. Poke the butts of the brush stakes firmly into the soil just outside the perimeter of the annuals' branches or even in among them. As the plants grow, they'll sprawl over the dull colored brush, hiding it from view entirely.

Brush stakes are ideal for bushy, branching plants.

THE ESSENTIAL

PART THREE

ANNUALS

Blue pansies 'Universal True Blue' and white lily-flowered tulip 'White Triumphator'. (Photo by Michael A. Ruggiero.)

YOU'VE STUDIED THE TECHNIQUES AND SKILLS, the tools that you need to garden successfully with annuals, and now it's time for the last step. You must learn the material you work with—the plants. Getting to know the different annual flowers need not be difficult, and it will make your gardening easier and more rewarding.

Each species of flower grows best within a certain set of conditions, and a plant in harmony with its environment is likely to be healthy and trouble-free. Put a plant in a site that doesn't suit it, and all the nurturing you give it will be a waste of time. Research has proven that a plant that finds its environment stressful is not only more prone to disease, but also more attractive to insect pests. Plant your garden intelligently, and you'll spend less time spraying and dusting.

Usually, more than one annual will succeed in any given spot. There are alternatives, and the more alternatives you know, the more interesting your garden will be. In the following pages you'll find descriptions of more than 90 essential plants. They are the best of the annuals—versatile, adaptable, and striking. These plants are not only easy to grow, they will also make an extraordinary impact in your garden.

All of the plants are especially rewarding. There are old favorites as well as exciting new introductions to the market. Just as important, the plants in this group will provide all the colors, textures, and profiles most gardeners are likely to need.

What's more, among these plants you will find species and hybrids to fill all the environments found in most American gardens.

But the most important feature of this gallery is that we've designed it to do the hard work of developing a personal plant palette for you. We have structured the gallery to make it easy for you to refine the plant list even further, to sort out the handful of plants you will want at any one time.

To make it easy to look up plants that catch your eye in a catalog or nursery, the plants in this gallery are arranged alphabetically. In addition, the names under which they are listed are the botanical names. Many gardeners are put off by Latin names, but these names have the advantage of precision. In many cases, a common name is shared by several plants, whereas a Latin name applies to only one plant. That's why the better nurseries and mail-order catalogs list their plants by the Latin botanical names. If you want to purchase plants from them, you have to use the botanical names. Readers who prefer to use common names first will find them included in the index at the back of the book.

Even the scientific nomenclature isn't foolproof, however, for occasionally botanists change the botanical name of a plant. Coleus, for example, has been recently reclassified as Solenostemon. Because the name Coleus is still the one by which most gardeners (and nurserymen) know this plant, we've chosen to list it as such, though we've also noted the new name.

Lantana trained as a standard underplanted with celosia. (Photo by Mobee Weinstein.)

In other words, convenience has been our guide here, too. Where there are different botanical names for a plant, you'll find them listed as synonyms at the entry head. The primary listing is always the more familiar one.

Alongside the name at the beginning of each plant entry, you'll find a photograph, so that you can see what the plant looks like. In most cases, the photograph shows the plant not as an isolated individual, but in the midst of a garden setting, so you can see how the featured specimen

Hot colors from canna 'Pietoria', zinnia 'Red Sun', and African marigold 'Primrose Lady'. (Photo by Michael A. Ruggiero.)

Scatter these seeds evenly over the surface of the moist potting medium, then press them gently into the soil with your hand.

The main body of each plant entry highlights what makes each plant special—the most striking characteristics of the flowers and leaves. You will find tips on the most effective ways to use the plant in the garden, whether in beds and borders or containers. We'll also tell you how to grow it, in a section on Culture. We've noted the special needs of each plant, the type of soil it prefers, the amount of sunlight it requires, and its needs for water and fertilizer. Finally, the section headed Gardener's Choice is a connoisseur's checklist of the choicest cultivars, and Pests and Diseases warns of the most common problems.

interacts with other garden plants and with the design as a whole.

Nothing is more annoying than sifting through a page of text to extract the one or two facts that interest you. That's why we've pulled out the plant facts and set them down in a table right at the beginning of each entry. The height to which a plant grows, and its spread, are here, along with basic propagation tips—how to start the plant from seeds, cuttings, or other means.

In some cases, you will find a direction to "soak seeds until they sink." This means you should soak the seeds in a container of water until they sink to the bottom before you plant them. In other cases, you will be directed not to cover the seeds with soil when you plant them. Some seeds need to be exposed to light in order to germinate.

The plants included in this gallery are all commonly available at better local nurseries. But though commonly available, these are by no means common plants. Some are relatively unknown as yet, the favorites of the future. Many more belong to species and strains that are familiar to almost everyone, such as pansies, marigolds, and zinnias. Don't let familiarity discourage you from taking a second look, however. The most talented designers are those who have the courage to reinvent the familiar, for a familiar plant used in an unfamiliar way can have a startling effect. Great designers listen not to popular prejudices, but only to their imaginations. And that is a step within the reach of all of us.

✜ **In southeast Asia,** its land of origin, the sunset hibiscus is grown as a food crop, but North American gardeners cultivate this relative of the okra for its flamboyant blossoms. Sunset hibiscus bears large, disc-like flowers common to the hibiscuses. These blossoms are pale in color, ranging from white to sulfur yellow. They are usually borne singly along the stem, which can grow 6 ft. to 7 ft. high. Each flower lasts only one day, and the plants usually do not begin blooming until mid or late summer. However, once flowering does begin, it usually carries on steadily into fall.

SOW Indoors, 6 to 8 weeks before last frost. Soak the seeds until they sink before sowing. Sow in individual cell packs, or 2 in. pots. Germination occurs in 15 to 21 days at 75° to 80°F; keep seedlings warm. Outdoors, sow after the soil temp has reached 70°F.

GARDEN USES An excellent plant for the back of the border. The outsized, palmately lobed leaves can reach 1½ ft. long and are attractive, adding a tropical note to the summer garden.

CULTURE As you would expect of a plant with tropical origins, the sunset hibiscus needs warm weather to thrive, and full sun. It prefers evenly moist but well-drained soil rich in organic matter. Waterlogging is bad for this plant, but the soil should never be allowed to dry out completely, either.

GARDENER'S CHOICE The most commonly available cultivar is 'Cream Cup'—its flowers are a soft primrose yellow with a deep purple base.

Musk mallow (*A. moschatus*), a related species, resembles the sunset hibiscus but is more compact, growing 12 in. to 18 in. tall. The musk mallow's flowers are even more flamboyant, though, for they resemble those of tropical hibiscus. Each blossom lasts only one day, but the flowers are so profuse that the plants seem to be perpetually in bloom. Once it finally begins flowering, the musk mallow blooms more or less continuously until frost. The most commonly available cultivars are 'Oriental Red' and 'Oriental Pink', which are practically indistinguishable from 'Red Mischief' and 'Pink Mischief'.

PESTS AND DISEASES Slugs may attack young plants; whiteflies and aphids like the underside of the hairy leaves.

✜ **As is often the case,** the botanical name of this plant offers a clue to one of its outstanding characteristics. Ageratum is derived from a pair of Greek roots, a, which means "not," and geras, which means "old," and this seems to refer to the fact that the blossoms of this plant are slow to age, keeping their color for an exceptionally long time.

SOW For best results, sow indoors 6 to 8 weeks before the last spring frost. Seeds will germinate in 7 to 10 days at 65° to 70°F. Or sow outdoors after all danger of frost has passed. Do not cover seeds when sowing.

GARDEN USES Traditionally, flossflower has served as an edging for the front of the border. Recently, taller cultivars have begun to appear and can serve as an accent in the middle or back of the border for an old-fashioned look. Because they have stronger stems, these taller-growing flossflowers have also become staples of the cutting garden.

Abelmoschus manihot
sunset hibiscus
Malvaceae—**mallow family**
height: 5 ft. to 7 ft.; spacing: 16 in. to 24 in.

Abelnoshchos' outsized, dramatic foliage makes a handsome backdrop for more compact annual flowers. (Photo by Michael A. Ruggiero.)

Ageratum houstonianum
Flossflower
Asteraceae—**daisy family**
height: 4 in. to 36 in.; spacing: 6 in. to 12 in.

The fine, flossy texture of the blossoms gives this popular edging plant its common name. (Photo by Judi Rutz; © The Taunton Press, Inc.)

CULTURE The ideal spot offers full sun and well-drained soil. But flossflower also performs well in light shade and in evenly moist soil, especially in regions that are extremely hot in the summer.

Pinch plants when they are small to promote branching. Feed monthly with a complete fertilizer. Deadhead blooming plants regularly, snapping off spent flowers. This is especially important with the lower-growing cultivars, which burst into bloom all over the plant at the same time, and which then, if neglected, as promptly go to seed and die. Deadheading is also especially important for white-flowered cultivars, on which the faded flowers are especially noticeable and unattractive.

Because the seedlings are small and easily overrun by weeds, they are best sown indoors. As soon as they are up, move them to a cool spot where temperatures stay at 50° to 55°F during the night, and rise just 5 to 10 additional degrees during the day. These cooler temperatures help to keep the plants from getting lanky and weak.

GARDENER´S CHOICE 'Blue Hawaii' is an earlier compact form than the old standby 'Blue Danube' (or 'Blue Puffs'). 'Madison' (or 'Blue Triomphe'), a best-seller, is 8 in. to 9 in. high and bears larger flowers than most other compact forms. 'White Hawaii Improved' is the most popular white-flowering form. 'Blue Horizon' is weather tolerant and free flowering, with abundant mid-blue flowers on sturdy 30-in. to 36-in. stems that can be cut continuously. The powder blue and white bicolor cultivars 'Bavaria' and 'Capri' grow 15 in. to 20 in. tall and can be cut and brought into the house.

PESTS AND ĐISEASES Be on the lookout for whiteflies, which are attracted to the hairy leaves.

Alternanthera **spp.**
alternanthera
Amaranthaceae—**amaranth family**
height: 10 in. or more; spacing: variable

❧ **Small and pallid,** the flowers of alternanthera could never win this plant a spot in the garden. Instead, alternanthera earns its keep with its vivid leaves, which are as brilliant as a parrot's feathers. The cultivated plants in this large genus belong mainly to two species, Alternanthera ficoidea and A. dentata, which are the parents of a range of diverse cultivars.

SOW Seedlings vary in vigor and appearance, so choice plants are usually propagated by cutting or division.

GARDEN USES Dwarf cultivars are very effective when massed in carpet-bedding displays; they can also be sheared to fill the sections of a parterre with sheets of color, or to edge a bed or border. Other varieties are useful in baskets, containers, or raised beds, where their colorful foliage will hang gracefully among flowering annuals.

Interplanting petunias with maroon-leaved alternantheras will furnish a dramatic background for the petunia flowers, and the durable alternanthera foliage will also help mask the petunia leaves, which grow shabby by midsummer.

CULTURE You can grow alternanthera from seeds started indoors in February or March at 55° to 64°F. However, because such seedlings are variable in appearance and vigor, named cultivars are usually propagated by division or cuttings. Take cuttings in late summer or late winter, and root them in a peat/perlite, peat/sand, or peat/vermiculite mixture. Those taken in late summer can be potted in a fairly organic, well-drained potting soil and then overwintered in a sunny window.

If you keep the soil evenly moist and feed lightly each month with a complete fertilizer, alternantheras make excellent and attractive houseplants.

Outdoors, any spot with full sun to partial shade, and well-drained but rich organic soil, satisfies the basic needs of alternanthera. Setting plants out in the garden too early in the season, before the soil has warmed, or in a too-shady spot, will lead to plants with poor foliage color.

GARDENER´S CHOICE Parrot leaf (A. ficoidea var. amoena) is a low-growing plant whose green leaves are interestingly marked with red, orange, purple, and yellow. Its cultivar 'Aurea Nana' is pale yellow, 'Rosea Nana' is rose colored, and 'Sessilis' is pale green to purple. All are valuable in carpet bedding displays or as edging plants.

A. dentata 'Rubiginosa' (sometimes called indoor clover) has deep maroon leaves and a more open habit of growth. Its branches can grow 2 ft. to 3 ft. in a single season. It is excellent in baskets, containers, or anywhere a loose ground cover is needed. This species flowers in midwinter, and if the flowers are allowed to mature and set seed, the plants will self-sow. Most of the seedlings produced in this fashion "come true." Lean the flowering branches over trays of soil so that when the seeds are ripe they will fall onto the trays and germinate without much trouble.

PESTS AND DISEASES Generally pest and disease free.

Dark-leaved *Alternanthera dentata* 'Rubiginosa' poses a strong contrast to the lush green foliage of its neighbors. (Photo by Michael A. Ruggiero.)

❧ **The genus *Amaranthus*** is a substantial one that includes about 60 species of annuals or short-lived perennials. Many are grown as food crops, for seeds that may be ground into a nutritious flour, or for foliage, which is eaten as a salad green.

SOW Indoors 3 to 4 weeks before last frost date. Germination occurs in 10 to 14 days at 70°F. Grow seedlings at 60°F until they can be planted outdoors after last frost.

GARDEN USES A few of the amaranths offer ornamental flowers or colorful foliage and are useful in beds and borders. A hint of another attraction is hidden in the name: Amaranthus derives from two Greek roots—a, "without," and marian, "to wither," and it refers to the long-lasting nature of the flowers, which can also be dried for floral arrangements.

CULTURE Amaranths can be started outdoors from seeds sown after any chance of frost has passed. For early or large plants, start seeds indoors. Keep the containers of seeds and seed starting mix at 70°F. Transplant seedlings out into the garden while they are still small. Compact transplants will be able to support themselves unaided, but large ones will need staking.

Amaranths are tropical plants that need hot weather to thrive, so wait to set out seedlings until it's time to plant tomatoes. They thrive in almost any type of soil as long as it is well drained and does not remain soggy. Even in poor soil, they don't need regular fertilization. They also tolerate heat and drought. Although they may survive in an area of light-to-partial shade, they need full sun to perform well.

Amaranthus spp.
tampala, St. Joseph's coat,
love-lies-bleeding

Amaranthaceae—amaranth family
height: 1 ft. to 4 ft. or more; spread:
12 in. to 24 in.

Amaranath 'Illumination' glows when contrasted with tall vervain. (Photo by Michael A. Ruggiero.)

GARDENER'S CHOICE Undoubtedly, the best known species is love-lies-bleeding (A. caudatus), an old-fashioned garden favorite that grows 3 ft. to 5 ft. tall and bears many tassel-like, drooping clusters of red flowers atop a contrasting arrangement of green, purple, or red stems and light green leaves. The cultivar 'Green Thumb' is a dwarfish plant (12 in. to 15 in.) that bears upright green plumes. 'Pygmy Torch' produces upright red flowers on a 12-in. to 18-in. plant.

Tampala (A. tricolor), a native of China and India, is very variable and has some of the more interesting cultivars. 'Early Splendor', sometimes called summer poinsettia, has bronze lower leaves and red upper leaves. 'Illumination' has green-bronze lower leaves and red and gold upper leaves, and 'St. Joseph's Coat' has upper leaves that are a mixture of yellow, green, and red. All tricolor cultivars are known for their colorful foliage and insignificant, not very showy flowers.

PESTS AND DISEASES Aphids, red spider mites, and root rot caused by poor drainage can be problems.

Antirrhinum majus
common snapdragon

Scrophulariaceae—**figwort family**
height: 6 in. to 48 in.; spread: 6 in. to 12 in.

Yellow snapdragons with swan-river daisies.
(Photo by Michael A. Ruggiero.)

❧ **Besides their sheer usefulness,** snapdragons possess an irresistible nostalgic appeal. Who can look at one without remembering a childhood moment of pinching the two-lipped blossoms to watch them yawn open and then snap shut? This, apparently, has been a favorite activity since ancient times, for the Romans called this plant the lion's snap. This name was later changed to dragon's snap by English gardeners, and eventually softened to the less threatening snapdragon of today.

Snapdragons come in a variety of heights, with flowers of lavender, white, red, pink, yellow, orange, and bronze, and bicolors.

SOW Indoors, 6 to 8 weeks before last frost date. Germination takes place in 10 to 14 days at 65° to 72°F. Seeds are small and should not be covered. Keep seedlings at 45° to 50°F at night, and 55° to 60°F during the day.

GARDEN USES Snapdragons are versatile plants that are rewarding whether grown by themselves in bedding displays, or in mixed borders with other annuals and perennials, or in the cutting garden and greenhouse as a source of cut flowers. Use dwarf cultivars in bedding displays, intermediate cultivars in mixed borders and for cut flowers, and tall types as spectacular focal points or in the back of the border.

CULTURE Start snapdragons indoors in a sterile medium (snapdragon seedlings are extremely prone to damping off), and sow seeds thinly. Later, make sure that there is ample air circulation around the seedlings, and keep their foliage dry by watering from the bottom.

Plant snapdragons in full sun to light shade, in sharply drained, slightly acid to alkaline soil rich in organic matter. Plant tall varieties out of the wind and stake them if necessary. Pinch young plants to promote branching and bushiness. Timely deadheading keeps plants blooming all season.

Space tall cultivars 12 in. apart, dwarf cultivars 6 in. to 8 in. apart.

GARDENER'S CHOICE There are dozens of fine cultivars and more appear every year. They fall into three categories: dwarfs, such as the extra early 'Floral Showers' (6 in. to 8 in. high), which top out at 12 in.; intermediate cultivars, such as 'Liberty' (18 in. to 22 in. high), which reach a height of 24 in.; and large cultivars, such as 'Rocket' (36 in.), which can reach 4 ft. under ideal growing conditions.

PESTS AND DISEASES Root, stem, and crown rot will be a problem in poorly drained soil. Whiteflies, aphids, and mites can sometimes be troublesome.

✎ **This plant is a real workhorse**—undemanding, reliable, handsome, and versatile. The flowers, though modest in size, are cheerfully bright (in pink, red, rose, white, and bicolors) and are abundantly borne throughout the summer and into fall. But many gardeners would argue that the foliage is this plant's greatest attraction. Glossy green, succulent, and dense, it makes a lush setting for the flowers, and in some cultivars it is colorful as well, red-tinged or splashed with white.

START Best to buy transplants; starting plants from seed requires 15 to 20 weeks of indoor growing.

GARDEN USES Wax begonias make reliable, pleasing filler for window boxes, containers, and mass plantings. Their neat, uniform growth also makes them ideal for carpet bedding, where rows of cushionlike begonias are often used to sketch in the outlines of a design.

CULTURE Though not spectacular, wax begonias are exceptionally easy to grow. They flourish in full sun or light shade and adapt easily to any well-drained soil that has been enriched with organic matter.

Few home gardeners start wax begonias from seed, since raising them to transplantable size can take 20 weeks, and equivalent plants can be found at any garden center. Remarkably, these slow-growing plants usually cost no more than zinnias or marigolds, which the nurseryman produces in less than half the time.

Cold soil will stunt wax begonias, so wait until the beds have warmed up, then plant in humusy soil that retains moisture. Water during periods of drought, preferably in the early morning (water droplets remaining on the leaves when the hottest sun arrives in midafternoon can cause them to spot). Fertilize monthly with a complete fertilizer, or spread timed-release fertilizer (14-14-14) once in the early summer.

GARDENER'S CHOICE Good green-leaved cultivars include Ambassador series, 8 in. to 10 in. tall, in pink, salmon, white, coral, scarlet, rose, and bicolors; Olympia series (6 in. to 8 in. tall), in pink, red, white, salmon-orange, and starlet (red and white); 'Linda', 6 in. to 8 in. tall, with pink-rose flowers; 'Scarlanda', 6 in. to 8 in. tall, with intense red flowers; 'Stara', 14 in. tall, in deep rose, white, or light pink; 'Viva', 6 in. to 8 in. tall, in white.

There are good bronze-leaved cultivars in the Cocktail series, with 6-in.- to 8-in.-tall plants in the following colors: 'Brandy', light pink; 'Gin', clear pink; 'Rum', white with rose edge;

Begonia semperflorens-cultorum
wax begonia

Begoniaceae—**begonia family**
height: 6 in. to 12 in.; spread: 8 in. to 10 in.

Wax begonias (rear) serve as ground cover around a compact, pink-flowered shrub rose. (Photo by Michael A. Ruggiero.)

'Whiskey', pure white; and 'Vodka', scarlet. Plants in the Senator series grow 8 in. to 10 in. tall, with pink, rose, salmon, scarlet, or white flowers, and those in the Danica series are 10 in. to 12 in. tall in rose or scarlet.

PESTS AND DISEASES Fungal diseases are the worst threat in poorly drained soil: Wax begonias are likely to suffer stem rot, botrytis, and damping off. Watch for slugs, especially on plants growing in the shade.

Begonia Tuberhybrida Hybrids
tuberous begonia

Begoniaceae—begonia family
height: 8 in. to 18 in.; spread: 12 in. to 15 in.

Tuberous begonias. (Photo by Michael A. Ruggiero.)

✍ **Though not as trouble free** as the wax begonias, tuberous begonias offer more spectacular blossoms in assorted warm colors, and a greater diversity of foliages and patterns of growth.

START For summer bloom in beds, plant tubers directly outside, 1 in. to 2 in. deep, as soon as the soil has warmed. For earlier bloom, start tubers indoors in individual 6-in. pots, 6 to 12 weeks before last spring frost.

GARDEN USES Cultivars with pendulous branches are invaluable for hanging baskets, planters, and window boxes, while others bloom on sturdy upright stems and are excellent for bedding.

CULTURE Although some types can be started from seed, for the most part it is easier and more successful to raise these plants from tubers. You can purchase new tubers each spring, or you can harvest tubers from existing plants in the fall, store them over the winter, and replant them the following spring (more on this technique later).

Plant tubers with the concave side facing upward, in humusy, moist but well-drained soil. Tubers started indoors can be potted as individual specimens, or three or four can be planted together in a hanging basket. Use potting soil rich in organic matter, and do not pack it tightly—the roots of tuberous begonias love a loose-textured growing medium. Keep the soil moist but not soggy, and do not let it dry out totally between waterings.

Feed plants with a half-strength complete fertilizer every 2 weeks during the flowering season. Deadhead regularly, pinching off aging flowers as soon as they start to discolor. Deadheading keeps the plants looking more attractive, and it also prevents decaying petals from dropping onto the leaves and causing them to rot.

Tuberous begonias are actually frost-sensitive perennials. To preserve plants from year to year, wait until after the first light frost of fall, and then carefully lift the tubers from their beds or containers. Wash off the soil and leave them to dry in the sun for a day. If the weather is too cold or too damp to dry them outdoors, spread them out in an air-conditioned room. Store the dry tubers in a cool (40° to 45°F), well-ventilated area and check frequently. Discard any that develop soft spots or show any signs of rot.

Propagate tubers in the spring by division; each division should have at least one healthy bud per section. Or, take 4-in. stem cuttings from healthy new growth. Snip off half of each leaf: Reducing the foliage area reduces the amount of water lost through leaves and protects the cuttings from dehydration.

GARDENER'S CHOICE The low-growing Non Stop cultivars produce continuous 2-in. to 4-in. double blooms, on compact 8-in. to 12-in. plants that start flowering very early and continue freely until fall. The Camellia types bear large, 4-in. to 6-in. flowers that resemble camellias. Pinch off all but the terminal bud from each stem to produce fewer but larger blossoms. The Lace cultivars have overlapping layers of petals and a finely ruffled look. The pendulous Panorama and Musical series are outstanding in containers.

PESTS AND DISEASES Slugs, whiteflies, and leaf spots are the main problems. Planting in poorly drained soil encourages bacterial and fungal rots.

❧ **Botanically, ornamental cabbage** and kale belong to the same species—Brassica oleracea—as those kitchen garden standbys, the common edible cabbage, kale, Brussels sprouts, cauliflower, broccoli, and collards. Practically speaking, however, the ornamental plants are quite distinct. Whereas their relatives in the vegetable patch have been bred for edible leaves and flowers, the ornamental strains have been selected to emphasize the colors of their foliage. In fact, the ornamental kales often do see use in the kitchen, but even there their role is primarily decorative: The smaller and more tender of the vivid, ruffled leaves are used to dress up salads.

SOW For best results, sow seed indoors in late June or early July for transplanting into the garden in fall. May also be sown directly into the garden. Cover seed lightly at planting time; germination occurs in 3 to 10 days at 70°F.

The ornamental cabbages and kales are cool-weather plants, and although they flourish as a spring crop, they are outshone by the many more spectacular flowers of that season. Reserve them for fall plantings. Cool weather intensifies their leaf color, so that the leaves grow progressively more vivid as they mature. They peak just as most other garden plants are failing. In particular, ornamental cabbages and kales make useful replacements for warm-weather annuals, which flag with the arrival of autumn.

GARDEN USES The dramatic foliage of these plants makes a striking setting for other fall flowers such as hardy mums or pansies, and it shows up brilliantly against the russets and golds of ornamental grasses. They also provide an attractive and offbeat planting for window boxes or tubs. Above all, though, they can withstand temperatures as low as 10°F, or even lower, and in mild locations they carry on the garden display well into winter. Few plants are as effective in shortening the winter hiatus, and in their season, few plants are as welcome.

CULTURE Sow seeds from late June to mid July either directly in the garden or indoors in pots. Thin the garden plantings or transplant indoor sowings into individual pots or packs when the seedlings show their first true leaves. When transplanting, bury seedlings to the level of the lowermost leaves (the cotyledons), to encourage stronger, straighter stems and stockier plants.

Plant in full sun in rich, organic, well-drained soil. To ensure the best color, feed with a complete fertilizer that is low in nitrogen. Fertilizers rich in nitrogen encourage fast leaf growth, but the foliage will have a less intense color. Keep plants evenly moist: Drought will stunt them while overwatering can cause stem rot.

Brassica oleracea **Acephala group**
flowering kale, flowering cabbage
Brassicaceae—**mustard family**
height: 10 in. to 15 in.; spread: 1 ft. to 2 ft.

Cabbage 'Tokyo White' with chrysanthemums. (Photo by Michael A. Ruggiero.)

161

GARDENER'S CHOICE The Osaka series cabbages are 12 in. high, with blue-green lower leaves and colorful white, pink, or rose centers. The Tokyo series offers the same range of colors but on slightly more compact, 10-in. plants. The Nagoya kales are 8 in. high and 12 in. to 14 in. wide, with very ruffled crowns of red, rose, or white leaves. 'Red Chidori' is one of the more uniformly growing cultivars, with a deep rose crown that covers almost the entire plant. 'Flamingo Plumes' and 'White Peacock' or 'Red Peacock' are more upright cultivars that reach a height of up to 18 in. Their deeply lobed leaves weep at the tips, which gives the plants a vase shape.

PESTS AND DISEASES Be on the lookout for slugs, snails, and cabbage loopers.

Browallia speciosa
bush violet, sapphire flower
Solanaceae—**nightshade family**
height: 12 in. to 18 in.; spread: 8 in. to 10 in.

Bush violet, *Browallia speciosa,* is a superb planting for any sort of planter. (Photo by Michael A. Ruggiero.)

☙ **A native of Columbia,** the bush violet (Browallia) was named in honor of John Browall, a Swedish bishop who was also a botanist and a staunch defender of his countryman Linnaeus's system for the naming of plants and animals. Although there are about six species of Browallia, only about three are used in the garden, and of these B. speciosa is the most popular.

SOW Indoors, sow at any time of the year; do not cover seeds. In the North, sow 15 to 16 weeks before planting out into the garden, 11 weeks in the South (where the sun is stronger and growth quicker). Seeds germinate in 7 to 15 days at 65° to 75°F. Keep seedlings on the dry side. Or sow outdoors, or use tip cuttings.

GARDEN USES This species makes a loose, bushy plant that looks particularly fine in baskets, window boxes, or any other kind of container that lets its stems spill over in a cascade. However, browallia is a versatile plant that grows well in full sun or partial shade, and that is useful for shady beds and borders.

CULTURE You can sow browallia seed either indoors or out, though indoor sowing is generally more successful. The small seeds should not be covered with soil after sowing, which leaves them at the mercy of the elements outdoors. If you sow outdoors, do so 6 to 8 weeks before the last frost date. Seedlings started indoors should be moved out into the garden only when the danger of frost is past.

You can also start new plants in early spring with tip cuttings taken from plants brought in from the garden the previous fall and overwintered indoors. Keep indoor plants—seedlings or rooted cuttings—in diffuse sunlight with an evenly moist soil.

Outdoors, browallia performs best in a deep, fertile, well-drained soil rich in organic matter, that remains evenly moist but not wet.

GARDENER'S CHOICE The Troll series cultivars bloom in blue or white; these plants are naturally compact (to 10 in.) but benefit from a light pinching to promote bushiness. The taller Bells series (10-in.- to 12-in.-high) cultivars have blue, white, or lavender flowers; pinch plants two or three times in the course of a season. They are better suited to cultivation in baskets and containers than in beds and borders. 'Amethyst' has deep purple flowers with a contrasting white eye at the center; this cultivar is somewhat more weather resistant and maintenance free than most other browallias.

PESTS AND DISEASES When growing browallias in the shade, be on the lookout for slugs. Indoors, this plant is a magnet for whiteflies and mites.

❧ **To give a flamboyantly tropical flavor** to the summer garden, no annuals are more effective—or easier—than caladiums. Their showy, colorful leaves are the main attraction; the caladium flowers are pleasant but unimpressive. You'll find caladiums as potted plants at local garden centers, at florist shops, or even on a supermarket shelf. A greater selection of cultivars is available as dormant tubers offered by mail-order nurseries.

Even the name of this plant is tropical: Caladium is merely a Latin version of kaladi, which is the local Amazonian name for this South American native. The modern fancy-leaved caladium, Caladium x hortulanum, is a blending of different species, which accounts in part for the diversity of the foliage from cultivar to cultivar.

START Plant tubers indoors in April, in peat/sand mix, and keep at 75° to 85°F. When shoots emerge, transplant the tubers to containers filled with rich organic loam, or plant them into the garden when nighttime temperatures stay above 60°F.

GARDEN USES Always showy, caladium leaves can lend drama to a bed or border, and a bold texture to a container planting.

CULTURE In the warmest areas of the country, caladium tubers may be planted directly into the garden. The plants thrive only when nighttime temperatures remain above 65°F and the soil temperature in the garden has risen to 65° to 70°F. So, through most of North America, caladiums need a head start to develop fully. Purchase container-grown plants from a greenhouse, or start tubers yourself indoors.

Caladiums love hot weather and humusy, evenly moist but well-drained soil. They are greedy feeders. Fertilize regularly; twice-monthly feedings with a balanced, water-soluble fertilizer are generally adequate. These are plants of the jungle floor, and they generally prefer light to medium shade. Some of the paler-leaved cultivars, such as 'Candidum', however, can be grown in the open sun.

To start caladiums outdoors, plant the tubers about 2 in. deep. Keep the surrounding soil moist, and after the first new growth appears, begin fertilizing. Indoors, plant tubers 1 in. deep in shallow pots of peat or a peat/sand mix. Water well, then place the pots in a warm location, such as on top of a horticultural heating pad. When leaf shoots start to emerge from the pots, usually in 2 to 3 weeks, transplant the tubers into containers of rich loamy soil, or into a warm garden bed.

Plant a caladium tuber with its "eyes" facing downward, and additional new eyes will develop. This slows the emergence of the leaves but ultimately encourages bushier growth. Planting caladium tubers with the eyes facing upward encourages faster foliage growth but usually results in a less bushy plant.

Another way to produce a bushier plant is to examine the tuber before planting and locate the dominant eye. This eye is markedly larger than the other eyes, and if left intact it will bear leaves that are larger than those that sprout from the other eyes. Use a knife or spoon to make

Caladium x *hortulanum*
(*Caladium bicolor*)
fancy-leaved caladium

Araceae—arum family
height: 6 in. to 3 ft.; spread: 1 ft. to 3 ft.

Fancy-leaved caladiums (center) combine with New Zealand flax (top), fan palm (right), and white impatiens (bottom). (Photo by Michael A. Ruggiero.)

163

a shallow slice and scoop out the dominant eye; this will enhance the growth of the other, secondary eyes and increase the total quantity of foliage.

To carry over caladiums from one growing season to the next, dig the whole plants in the fall, pot them up and bring them inside. Gradually decrease the amount of water you give them until all their leaves turn yellow or drop off. Then store the tubers in their pots, or dig them up and pack them in dry peat, sand, perlite, or vermiculite. Keep dormant caladiums in a warm (60° to 65°F), dry spot.

GARDENER´S CHOICE Popular cultivars include 'Aaron', creamy white with green edges; 'Candidum', large white leaves with green veining; 'Fannie Munson', pink with red veins and green edge; 'Freda Hemple', dwarf, red with green band on edge; 'Carolyn Whorton', rose leaves, dark red veins, irregular green edge; and 'Miss Muffet', cream with red dots.

PESTS AND ÐISEASES Few serious problems afflict caladiums, and those that do are easily avoided. Chilly or damp storage can cause the tubers to rot. Starting tubers or growing them under conditions that are too cool can cause erratic or weak growth. Inadequate watering can cause the foliage to "burn" or brown around the edges.

Calendula officinalis
pot marigold

Asteraceae—daisy family
height: 6 in. to 24 in.; spacing: 10 in. to 15 in.

Calendulas mix with cabbages in this kitchen garden. (Photo by Michael A. Ruggiero.)

❧ **The pot marigold** has a long history in the garden, where it has been cultivated both for the ornamental qualities of the flowers and for their culinary and medicinal uses. The generic name Calendula is derived from the Latin calendae, "calendar." This is an allusion to the ancient Roman fancy that the plant's golden flowers resembled the golden coins that had to be paid as interest on debts on the first day of each calendar month. The common name, pot marigold, refers in part to the ease with which this plant is grown in a pot; marigold is a corruption of Mary's gold, for this plant was believed particularly dear to the Virgin Mary.

SOW Outdoors in spring after last frost date, or indoors 8 to 12 weeks before last frost date. Sow seeds in pots in late summer for midwinter flowers indoors. Seeds germinate in 7 to 10 days at 65° to 70°F. Cover seeds completely with soil after sowing; darkness is essential for germination.

GARDEN USES In northern gardens, calendulas are an asset all summer long, as neat edging for a bed or as compact, middle-of-the-border plants. They thrive in containers. Pick buds just as they begin to color for long-lasting cut flowers. Calendulas also are most appropriate in the kitchen garden, for their petals may be used fresh in salads and when dried and ground can be used like saffron to color rice, or to thicken soups and flavor stews.

CULTURE Calendulas are well worth growing, if only because their needs are so easily satisfied. They prefer full sun but cope well with average to poor soils, as long as they are well drained. They prefer cool summers with low humidity, and if deadheaded conscientiously they will bloom right through a northern summer. As a rule, calendulas don't last a whole southern summer, but they make valuable spring bedding plants and may also be grown on a windowsill to brighten the southern winter.

For best results, sow seeds indoors. When seedlings emerge, reduce the temperature to 50° to 55°F—a cooler environment keeps them sturdy and compact. Water the seedlings with warm water, however, for cold water will spot their hairy leaves.

GARDENER´S CHOICE The Bon Bon series is a strain of dwarf (12-in.) cultivars highly recommended for pots. They bear flowers of apricot, light yellow, orange, or gold. 'Fiesta' is more vigorous and performs better as a bedding plant, while the Pacific Beauty series include taller (18-in.) cultivars that make outstanding cut flowers ranging in color from orange and yellow to apricot and red.

PESTS AND DISEASES Leaf spotting can be a serious problem, weakening the plants while disfiguring the foliage. Irrigate with warm water to reduce the danger. Be on the lookout, too, for powdery mildew, slugs, whiteflies, and aphids.

᙭ **Garden hybrids** bred from natives of tropical and subtropical America, cannas are assertive plants with a strong visual character. The leaves are big and bold, sometimes maroon or variegated, and flowers come in a range of hot colors. Cannas tend to provoke strong likes and dislikes, and over the last century they have cycled from a high degree of popularity through periods of almost complete neglect. Cannas were all the rage in Victorian bedding designs, but more recently they have hung on mainly as a dooryard planting in the rural South.

START Rhizomes, in pots indoors, 4 weeks before last frost date; or plant directly into the garden after the last frost date.

GARDEN USES Today's gardeners are rediscovering the appeal of garden canna's exuberance and are using them in all types of annual plantings: in beds, borders, containers, and water gardens, and as accents in perennial displays.

Canna flowers are attractive, but as a rule they are less of a presence in the garden than the lush foliage. Many of the taller varieties work well when massed at the back of a bed or border, while dwarf varieties fit in up front. A spire of canna makes an authentic centerpiece for a Victorian-inspired circular bed, and cannas strike a strong tropical note in a large container.

CULTURE Cannas are among the easiest of annuals to grow, if they get heat, sun, regular fertilization, and a soil that stays evenly moist. Add extra organic material to the soil before planting the rhizomes. Don't plant cannas in the garden until the soil has warmed, when you set out peppers and eggplants. If you mulch the plants, wait until genuinely hot weather has settled in and the soil is very warm. As cannas produce a large volume of tall stems and broad leaves in a relatively short period of time, they need regular applications of a balanced fertilizer.

Water cannas regularly during periods of dry weather. Remember: It's hard to give them too much water—they thrive when planted in tubs and sunk into the water garden.

Cannas are usually propagated by dividing and replanting in spring the clumps of rhizomes saved from the previous year's plants. Cut the clumps into pieces approximately 2 in. to 3 in. long, making sure that each piece has one or two "eyes," or buds. In USDA Zones 9 to 10, plant these divisions directly in the garden, setting them 4 in. to 6 in. deep. Gardeners elsewhere

Canna x generalis
common garden canna

Cannaceae—**canna family**
height: 2 ft. to 7 ft.; spread: 2 ft. to 3 ft.

Canna 'Pretorio' makes a striking background to zinnia 'Red Sun'. (Photo by Michael A. Ruggiero.)

should pot up the divisions 4 weeks prior to the time when the soil has warmed up and they may be moved outdoors. To ensure that these divisions get off to a good start, set the rhizomes 1 in. deep in pots of humusy soil, and keep them indoors at a temperature of 75°F.

A few canna cultivars, such as 'Tropical Rose', can be grown from seed. Sow 10 to 13 weeks before the last frost date, and soak the seeds in water for 48 hours prior to planting to soften the hard seed coat. After sowing, keep the seed containers at a temperature of 75° to 85°F until germination occurs, usually about 8 to 12 days. After the seedlings emerge, grow them at 65° to 70°F until they are ready to transplant into the garden.

In the Deep South, cannas may be left in the ground through the winter months, but north of Zone 8, they should be lifted and stored indoors (see p. 125).

GARDENER´S CHOICE Popular cultivars include 'Red King Humbert', red flowers, 6-ft. to 7-ft. stems, maroon leaves; 'Wyoming', orange flowers, 4-ft. stems, maroon leaves; 'Pretoria', orange flowers, 4-ft. stems, variegated yellow and green leaves; 'Richard Wallace', yellow flowers, 3-ft. to 4-ft. stems, green foliage; 'Stadt Fellbach', orange flowers, 3-ft. to $3^{1}/_{2}$-ft. stems, green foliage; 'The President', red flowers 3-ft. stems, green foliage; 'Futurity Pink', rose-pink flowers, 3-ft. stems, burgundy leaves; Pfitzer's varieties, red, coral, pink, or yellow flowers, 2-ft. stems, green foliage.

PESTS AND DISEASES Snails, slugs, and Japanese beetles can be troublesome.

Celosia argentea var. *cristata*
common cockscomb

Amaranthaceae—amaranth family
height: 6 in. to 36 in.; spread: 6 in. to 18 in.

Golden flowered cockscomb (front) combined with yucca 'Gold Sword'. (Photo by Mobee Weinstein.)

The clue to this flower lies in its botanical name: Celosia derives from the Greek word for "burning," and the vivid, bunched flowers of the plumosa cultivars do lick upward like a candle flame. In contrast, the squat, crested flower heads of the childsii types look more like the comb on a rooster's head—a cockscomb.

SOW Indoors, sow plumosa and childsii groups 2 to 4 weeks before last frost date. Sow spicata group 4 to 5 weeks before last frost. Germination should take place in 10 to 12 days at 70°F for plumosa and childsii types; 10 to 14 days at 75° to 80°F for the spicata group. Cover seeds lightly and keep on the moist side until germination occurs. Grow all types at 70°F.

GARDEN USES Celosias make dramatic and durable bedding plants, they flourish in containers, and they provide brilliant-hued cut flowers. Spicata celosias are excellent for the back of the border or as cut and dried flowers.

CULTURE All three groups are easy to grow, given a spot with full sun and well-drained soil that stays evenly moist. The celosias are extremely tolerant of heat, humidity, and drought, which makes them a natural for city gardens. They are less forgiving of dry, cold conditions, and setting seedlings out too early, or neglecting the watering, is likely to stunt plants.

Sowing the seeds too early in the spring encourages the plants to start flowering while still in their pots, and this changes the hormonal balance within the plants so that they will not grow bushy when set out in the garden.

GARDENER´S CHOICE The plumosa group bears plumy or featherlike flowers of vivid colors. Popular cultivars include 'Kimono', dwarf, 8 in. high, uniform habit, red, orange, scarlet, yellow, pink; 'Apricot Brandy', 12-in., compact, apricot-orange plumes; the Castle series, 12-in. plants that are exceptionally maintenance free, scarlet, pink, or yellow; and 'New Look', 15 in. tall with large glowing red plumes and deep bronze foliage.

The childsii group: Jewel Box series, super dwarf (4 in. to 6 in.), red, carmine, yellow, deep salmon, orange; 'Jewel Box Red', with bronze foliage (all other childsii types have green leaves); 'Fireglow', 20-in. plants and a bright orange-carmine inflorescence; and 'Chief', 30 in. to 40 in. high, red, rose, gold, carmine, persimmon, bicolors, with single, very strong stems that make outstanding cut flowers.

The spicata cultivars ("wheat" or "foxtail" celosias) bear smaller inflorescences on 36-in. to 40-in. stems. The leaves are feathery. 'Flamingo Purple' has deep rose-purple plumes with dark green leaves and stems; 'Rose Tassels', silvery rose plumes with bronzy leaves and stems; and 'Pink Tassels', silvery pink plumes with green leaves and stems.

PESTS AND DISEASES During wet or cool summers, celosia is prone to leaf spots. Mites and southern root knot nematode can be troublesome in the South.

❧ **The white marguerite,** or the marguerite daisy as it is sometimes called, is a native of the Canary Islands, and it is what botanists define as a subshrub. Although it doesn't attain the stature of a true shrub, it does produce woody stems, and in a mild climate it behaves like an evergreen perennial. It cannot tolerate the winters of most regions of North America, and in our gardens it is commonly replanted every spring.

START From seeds or cuttings. Sow seeds indoors 6 to 8 weeks before last spring frost. Take cuttings in fall or early spring from new growth at stem tips.

GARDEN USES Most gardeners admire this plant for its daisylike flowers, but the white marguerite also furnishes a handsome mass of deeply cut, blue-gray foliage. It can be used effectively in bedding and container displays, especially when mixed with deep blue, purple, or other dark-colored annuals. The marguerite's yellow-centered blossoms also make attractive cut flowers and will last as long as 2 weeks in an arrangement.

In regions with cool springs and summers, this plant flowers over a prolonged season; where the weather is hot and steamy, use it as a foliage plant. Because it makes woody stems, the white marguerite is ideal for training into a standard, and it makes a fine focal point in a large container or a bedding display.

CULTURE Plant marguerites in well-drained, moderately fertile to poorish soil. They prefer full sun but will tolerate light shade. However, less sunlight will result in fewer flowers, and too much shade will cause weak, floppy stems.

This plant is a perennial in areas with frost-free winters, but you can take cuttings in fall and overwinter them.

PESTS AND DISEASES White marguerites usually remain insect and disease free. Occasionally, chrysanthemum leaf miner and aphids may become a problem, and crown gall may infest older plants.

Chrysanthemum frutescens
white marguerite, marguerite daisy
***Asteraceae*—daisy family**
height: to 36 in.; spread: 15 in. to 24 in.

The fine, bluish foliage and white, daisy-like flowers of marguerites make a simple but perfect planting for a terra-cotta pot. (Photo by Michael A. Ruggiero.)

Chrysanthemum x *grandiflorum*
(*Chrysanthemum* x *morifolium*)
garden chrysanthemum

Asteraceae—daisy family
height: 1 ft. to 5 ft.; spread: 1½ ft.
to 3 ft.

Garden chrysanthemums flanking ornamental cabbages in a fall display. (Photo by Michael A. Ruggiero.)

☙ **There are lots of "spring" flowers** (the crocus, the daffodil, etc.), but in public estimation, there's really only one fall blossom, and that is the "mum," the garden chrysanthemum. Of course, there are many other flowers that bloom during autumn (even a fall-blooming crocus), but it is the garden chrysanthemum that for gardeners and nongardeners alike symbolizes the season.

The curious part about this attitude is that the garden mum is actually a fairly recent creation: The flower as we know it today dates back only to the 1930s. There had been chrysanthemums before that time, but they were essentially florists' flowers. They demanded highly artificial methods of cultivation and were happiest in a pot in the greenhouse.

Then, in 1932, a Connecticut gardener named Alex Cummings crossed finicky florist mums with ultra-hardy chrysanthemums from Korea. The result was a nurseryman's dream: offspring that shared the best qualities of both parents. They were dubbed garden chrysanthemums to distinguish them from their hothouse relatives.

The botanical name of the genus, Chrysanthemum, is a spelling bee nightmare, but its meaning is quite simple. It derives from the joining of two Greek words, *chrysos*, which means gold, and *anthos*, which means flower. It refers to the fact that many of the wild species bear golden-hued blossoms.

SOW Indoors, in early spring. Germination occurs in 7 to 10 days at 70°F. Or take cuttings in late spring from overwintered plants and root in a peat and perlite mix, or in pure perlite or sand.

GARDEN USES Mums bring classic autumn colors to containers and fall bedding displays.

CULTURE Chrysanthemums are hardy perennials, but they are widely grown as annuals, started in a nursery bed and transplanted into the garden just as their flower buds begin to open in fall. Depending on the cultivar you select, you can have mums in bloom as early as August or as late as November. Most gardeners enjoy the flowers, and then uproot the plants and consign them to the compost heap. But overwintered plants can serve as parents for a new crop the following year.

To accomplish this, dig up and pot a plant when it has finished flowering. Plunge the pot into the bottom of a cold frame so that the lip of the pot is almost even with the soil surface. Cover plants with straw or salt hay after the first heavy frost. You can also overwinter potted mums in an attached garage.

In early spring, divide the overwintered mums and plant the divisions back into the garden or a suitable nursery bed. Or leave the potted plants in the cold frame until late April, then make cuttings, each with no more than five leaves, from the strongest of the new shoots, and root them.

When the rooted, potted cuttings have begun to grow, and each has a total of four to five leaves, pinch off the growing tip of the cutting, pinching back to a point just above the third leaf. As soon as each side branch has sprouted its fourth or fifth leaf, pinch it back in the same manner. Continue this treatment, which involves consistency but not much work, until early July for early-flowering cultivars, and until early August for October and November bloomers.

Garden mums thrive in any sunny location that offers a well-drained but moisture-retentive soil rich in organic matter. Fertilize and water as you would other annuals.

GARDENER'S CHOICE There is a bewildering variety of chrysanthemum cultivars on the market, but you won't go wrong if you stick to selections from the Prophet series. New, improved cultivars are added to this series each year, but the older standbys are available as well.

PESTS AND DISEASES Chrysanthemums are not trouble-free plants: They are susceptible to leaf spots, wilt, mildews, rust, aphids, leafminers, mites, and thrips. Discard infested plants after they bloom and replace the following year with new, clean stock. Rabbits and deer relish chrysanthemums, but timely fencing should keep them at bay.

Spider flower is one of the most carefree and rewarding of the tall-growing annuals. The name may seem unappealing for such an attractive plant, but it is descriptive. Sprouting from the cleome's flower heads are long, threadlike stamens that really do resemble the legs of a daddy longlegs.

SOW Indoors, 4 to 6 weeks before the last spring frost. Germination takes place in 10 to 14 days, with no special requirements. Grow seedlings at 70°F.

GARDEN USES Cleome is perfect for the back of a border. Because it continues to bloom without deadheading, it's also a good centerpiece for a bed that's too broad to allow easy pinching of the flowers in the center. When planted in a mass, its graceful arching branches have a fountainlike effect that few other annuals can equal.

Cleomes also work well in large containers. They hold up reasonably well as cut flowers, but because the flowers have a pungent smell, don't mass too many together in a small, closed room.

CULTURE Grow cleomes in full sun in moderately fertile but well-drained soil. They perform better in soils that are sandy than in heavy, sticky clay soils. They are fairly drought tolerant and will not need regular irrigation except in times of prolonged drought.

Seeds may also be sown outdoors after the soil has warmed, but germination may be erratic and a more consistent display will result from planting with seedlings started indoors.

This flower self-sows freely and it may spread beyond its allotted space to become a weed.

GARDENER'S CHOICE There are a number of named cultivars of cleomes, but in fact there seem to be only three colors: white ('Alba' or 'Helen Campbell'), pink ('Rose Queen' is somewhat deeper in hue than 'Pink Queen'), and purple ('Purple Queen' and 'Lavender Queen' bear flowers of the same shade of lavender).

PESTS AND DISEASES In wet growing seasons, cleomes may be attacked by three forms of fungus, all of which cause spots to appear on the leaves. Just remove the affected leaves to control the infection. Root rot may kill plants grown in poorly drained soils.

Cleome hasslerana
spider flower

Capparidaceae—**caper family**
height: 3 ft. to 6 ft.; spread: 1½ ft. to 3 ft.

Spider flower self-sows and once planted, returns year after year. (Photo by Michael A. Ruggiero.)

Coleus x *hybridus*
(*Solenostemon scutellarioides*)
coleus, flame nettle

Lamiaceae—mint family
height: 6 in. to 36 in.; spread: 6 in.
to 18 in.

Coleus offers a near-infinite variety of leaf colors, sizes, and shapes. (Photo by Michael A. Ruggiero.)

❧ **Wherever you want color fast,** that's a spot for coleus. A small transplant turns into a lush mound of brilliant foliage in a matter of weeks, delivering almost any hue you could want, from near black to an incandescent chartreuse, in splashes, streaks, and solids.

SOW Indoors, 6 to 8 weeks before last spring frost date, and 8 to 10 weeks before transplanting into the garden. Do not cover seeds. Germination should occur in 10 to 15 days at 65° to 75°F. Preserve choice plants by taking cuttings in fall and overwintering them indoors. Or take 2-in.- to 4-in.-long cuttings from the stem tips of potted stock plants in March to have new plants ready for bedding out in May.

GARDEN USES Coleuses are ideal plants for any garden situation. They can be used in beds, borders, containers, baskets, or anywhere else you need exotically colored foliage. Most types can tolerate either full sun or shade, although the colorful foliage of some cultivars will bleach when grown in full sun.

CULTURE Most types of coleus are easily grown from seeds sown in early spring. Do not cover the seeds. Water with lukewarm water, then keep humidity high around the seeds by placing a piece of clear glass or plastic over the pot. Set the pot in a semishaded area until the seedlings begin to appear, then move it into full sun.

Approximately 2 weeks after germination, the seedlings will be big enough to transplant into cell packs or 2-in. pots. Feed them every other week with a water-soluble fertilizer diluted to half the recommended strength.

Typically, coleus raised from seed are highly variable in appearance, so a gardener in quest of a particular leaf color or form must purchase it as an already-started plant. To acquire more transplants less expensively, you can buy one plant and take cuttings from it. Cut tips no longer than 4 in. from strong, healthy stems; bigger cuttings are slower to root and generally make weak plants. After your cuttings have rooted, pinch off the growing tips to produce bushier plants.

Plant coleus in an organic-enriched soil that drains well but remains evenly moist. Wet soil can cause plants to rot, while soils that are too sandy and fast-draining may not hold enough moisture to keep plants adequately supplied with water. Pinch off flower spikes as they appear, to keep the plants neat and bushy.

GARDENER'S CHOICE Two popular strains that may be raised from seed are the 10-in.-high Wizard series and the 18-in.-high Rainbow cultivars. Both offer a wide range of foliage colors. There are also hundreds of named cultivars available as rooted cuttings from specialist growers, in a fantastic assortment of leaf sizes from tiny to huge, and colors ranging from palest greens and white to purples, reds, golds, and virtual blacks.

PESTS AND DISEASES Watch for slugs in shady locations and mites in sunny ones. Seedlings are highly susceptible to damping off.

❧ **As its common name suggests,** the dwarf morning glory (*Convolvulus tricolor*) is a more mannerly version of the familiar common morning glory (*Ipomea purpurea*). Unlike the common morning glory, which will climb or sprawl to 8 ft. or 9 ft., the dwarf morning glory rarely extends its stems more than 20 in. The flowers are similar, except that those of the dwarf morning glory have distinct yellow throats encircled with a zone of white.

SOW Indoors, 6 to 8 weeks before last frost date. To aid germination, nick seeds and soak in warm water for 24 hours before sowing. Germination should occur in 5 to 7 days at 68° to 80°F. Grow seedlings at 60° to 65°F. Outdoors, sow in spring from upper South and northward, or in fall where winters are mild (Deep South and low-altitude Southwest). Sow seeds where the plants are to bloom, and thin seedlings to 12 in. apart.

GARDEN USES This plant is excellent for seaside and coastal gardens. Use it in the front of beds and borders, and in window boxes or baskets that allow its stems to trail gracefully. The individual blossoms last only a day, but the plant continues to bear them throughout the growing season.

CULTURE Native from Portugal to Greece and northern Africa, the dwarf morning glory grows best in full sun but will tolerate light shade if all other growing conditions are perfect. It prefers soil that is sandy, dryish, and acutely well drained. Unlike so many other annuals, dwarf morning glories don't benefit from a rich, humusy soil, although you should give them a light dose of slow-release fertilizer at planting time.

GARDENER'S CHOICE 'Royal Ensign' is the best known and most frequently grown cultivar. It has spectacular, 2-in. wide, royal blue flowers that cover its dense, 1-ft. mound of foliage. Other cultivars in the Ensign series are rose or white.

The Enchantment series offers plants with slightly taller (14-in.) stems, and flowers similar to those of the Ensigns, except that the Enchantment series includes a red-flowered cultivar.

PESTS AND DISEASES Root and stem rots are common problems of dwarf morning glories grown in wet soils.

Convolvulus tricolor
dwarf morning glory

Convolvulaceae—**morning glory family**
height: 10 in. to 14 in.; spread: to 20 in.

Ipomoea 'Tricolor' softens the hard surface of a trellis or fence. (Photo by Judi Rutz; © The Taunton Press, Inc.)

❧ **The name *Cosmos*** comes from the Greek word Kosmos, which means "beautiful thing." It's an apt description of the common cosmos, whose daisylike flowers hover on tall stalks above a cloud of finely cut, soft, and fernlike foliage. The flowers come in pink, white, red, rose, or bicolors.

SOW Indoors, 5 to 7 weeks before last spring frost date, or outdoors after last frost date. Germination comes in 6 to 10 days at 68° to 75°F.

GARDEN USES These fresh and simple flowers are excellent for bedding displays and mixed borders. The dwarf cultivars adapt well to large containers.

CULTURE Common cosmos is easy to grow, as long as you give it a spot with full sun and average garden soil that is very well drained. Persistently wet soil is likely to cause roots and stems to rot. The best soil is sandy, or at least somewhat poor in organic matter and nutrients. Exposure to abundant levels of nutrients, particularly nitrogen, will result in plants with lush foliage but few flowers.

Sow seeds directly into the garden after the last spring frost date, as soon as the soil temperature has warmed to 60°F. Sow three to four seeds together, spacing your planting spots about

Cosmos bipinnatus
cosmos

Asteraceae—**daisy family**
height: 1 ft. to 7 ft.; spread: 9 in. to 24 in.

One cosmos is enough to soften the silhouette of this picket fence. (Photo by Michael A. Ruggiero.)

15 in. apart. After the seedlings have sprouted their second set of true leaves, pinch out all but the strongest individual from each group.

For earlier bloom, sow seeds indoors 5 to 7 weeks before the last spring frost date. Keep the seed pots at a temperature of 68° to 75°F, and germination should take place within 6 to 10 days. As soon as the seedlings have produced those two sets of true leaves, separate and transplant them to 2-in. pots or cell packs.

When transplanting the seedlings, bury the stems up to the base of the seed leaves to encourage the seedlings to sprout roots from along the stems, producing stronger-stemmed plants. Even with this encouragement, the stems of taller-growing cosmos may need staking. In rich soil, even short cultivars may need support.

Deadhead regularly to keep the plants producing flowers and looking neat. Water infrequently but deeply. Usually, fertilization is unnecessary, though in very sandy soils you may need a light dose of a complete fertilizer.

GARDENER'S CHOICE Popular cultivars include the 4-ft.-tall 'Picotee', which bears rosy pink flowers with deep rose centers; the 3-ft.-tall, deep crimson–flowered 'Dazzler'; and the 20-in.- to 24-in.-high Sonata series, which includes cultivars in white, pink, red, rose, and bicolors.

The closely related yellow cosmos (C. sulphureus) grows 10 in. to 18 in. high, with a spread of 12 in. to 20 in., and single, semidouble, or double flowers of yellow, gold, orange, and red. Its culture and uses in the garden are similar to those of common cosmos. The Ladybird and Sunny series are the most commonly available strains. Both offer cultivars with yellow, red, orange-red, and golden flowers. The Ladybirds are more compact, growing to a height of just 10 in. to 14 in. The Sunny cultivars are similar but grow 2 in. to 6 in. taller.

PESTS AND DISEASES Root rot and mites sometimes attack cosmos. Where they are abundant, deer, which devour both the foliage and flowers, are the most serious threat.

Dahlia spp.
dahlia

Asteraceae—daisy family
height: 1 ft. to 7 ft.; spread: 1 ft. to 3 ft.

❧ **Among the annuals,** only garden mums rival dahlias in the diversity of their flower sizes, shapes, and range of colors. The differences between dahlias can be truly striking: The flowers of some cultivars grow as large as dinner plates and may seem to have little in common with the dahlia next door whose blossom is as small and round as a Ping-Pong ball. Dahlias also vary widely in stature: Individual plants may reach a height of 5 ft. or never grow taller than 1 ft.; most cultivars grow to 1 ft. to 3 ft.

The diversity of garden dahlias stems from the genetic diversity of their wild ancestors. There are about 27 species of dahlia, all of which are native to Mexico and Central America. From these, hybridizers have bred over 20,000 cultivars.

Technically, none of these are true annuals. Dahlias produce fleshy underground storage roots or tubers, and in regions where the ground doesn't freeze, the tubers can be left in the soil to overwinter outdoors and sprout new roots and stems in the spring. In all other regions, however, dahlias will behave like annuals unless the tubers are dug up in the fall and overwintered in a sheltered, frost-free spot.

START Plant stored or purchased tubers in pots, 4 weeks before last frost date, deep enough so "eyes" are 2 in. to 4 in. deep.

GARDEN USES Dwarf dahlias make excellent bedding or edging plants, while the taller types are very effective for adding color and mass to a border. Dahlias may be at their best, though, as cut flowers. Take the blossoms in the cool of the morning. Condition the flowers by inserting the cut ends of the stems into a bucket of lukewarm (100°F) water, then store the bucket in a shaded, cool place for several hours before arranging the flowers in a vase.

CULTURE Dahlias are sun lovers, and for the best flowers you should grow them out in the open, away from shade cast by buildings, fences, or other plants. An airy spot, where breezes keep the air circulating around the plants, will help protect your dahlias from diseases and keep them blooming from midsummer on.

Dahlia 'Park Princess' is an outstanding cultivar for bedding displays. (Photo by Michael A. Ruggiero.)

These plants prefer rich soil. Before planting (ideally, the previous autumn), dig generous amounts of well-rotted manure or compost into the bed. If possible, dig the soil to a depth of 2 ft. to 3 ft., but you can cultivate dahlias successfully in shallower soils, too, as long as the drainage is good. Dahlias won't tolerate wet feet! Although some cultivars can be grown from seed, it is easier to start with tubers, which you can purchase new or take as divisions from overwintered clumps. Plants grown from tubers grow faster and bigger, bloom earlier, and bear many more flowers than do plants started from seeds.

If your tubers are still fully dormant and have shown no symptoms of new growth, you may plant them in early spring. Look for the "eyes," the prominent buds from which the new growth will sprout, and take care to set the tubers so that the eyes are buried 2 in. to 4 in. deep.

If the eyes on your dahlia tubers have begun to sprout, or your local springs tend to be very wet and cold, then you may prefer to start your tubers indoors in pots.

To start from seed, sow indoors 12 to 14 weeks before the last spring frost date in the North, and 10 weeks before the last frost in the South. Germination occurs in 5 to 10 days at 68° to 86°F.

Potted dahlias and those that you have started from seed should stay inside, in shelter, and move out into the garden only after all danger of frost has passed and the soil has warmed. When planting pot-raised dahlias into the garden, set the plants at the same height in the soil as they have been in the pots.

To encourage bushy, many-stemmed plants that will bear lots of flowers, pinch off the topmost bud on each dahlia stem as soon as it has borne three to four sets of leaves. If, on the other hand, you would prefer to have a few blossoms of extraordinary size and quality, leave the topmost buds intact but pinch off all the side buds that sprout from the bases of the leaves.

Dahlias are heavy feeders and require biweekly applications of a water-soluble, balanced fertilizer from midsummer until early fall. During periods of dry weather, water your dahlias regularly, at least twice a week if the weather is hot, for drought ensures poor growth and bloom.

Cover the soil with a couple of inches of organic mulch to keep the soil moist and cool and to suppress competition from weeds.

You'll probably have to stake the taller "exhibition" cultivars; shorter cultivars and dwarf "bedding" dahlias need no staking.

To store dahlias over the winter, wait until the first fall frosts have blackened the tops of the plants. Then dig up the tubers and cut back the stems that sprout from them to a length of 6 in. Clean the old soil off the tubers, taking care not to injure them. Store them upside down in a cool, dry place for a few days to drain any moisture from the stems. Afterwards, store the tubers in peat moss or Styrofoam packing peanuts in a cool (38° to 50°F), dry area.

To propagate more plants from old tubers, pot the dormant tubers into containers of peat and coarse sand in late winter. Keep the potting mix moist, and when the tubers' eyes start to swell, divide each clump of roots with a sharp knife, making sure that each piece you cut includes at least one eye. Alternatively, you can simply grow the old tubers in pots and take cuttings of the new growth after the shoots have reached a length of 6 in. (see p. 125).

GARDENER'S CHOICE The American Dahlia Society classifies dahlias into 12 divisions according to the form of the flowers. Classifications of dahlias are as follows:

1 Single	5 Formal decorative	9 Incurved cactus
2 Anemone	6 Informal decorative	10 Straight cactus
3 Collarette	7 Ball	11 Semicactus
4 Peony-flowered	8 Pompom	12 Orchid-flowered

Additional classification within these categories is made by flower size:

Size A—Large: over 8 in. in diameter	Size Ball: over 3 in.
Size B—Medium: 6 in. to 8 in.	Size Miniature ball: 2 in. to $3^1/_2$ in.
Size BB: 4 in. to 6 in.	Size Pompom: not over 2 in.
Size M: not more than 4 in.	

This system of classification may seem overly technical, and unless you become a dahlia devotee and begin exhibiting your flowers at shows, you are unlikely to use these categorizations in your daily gardening. But this information comes in handy when ordering tubers or divisions from catalogs—nurserymen rely on these code words to describe their stock.

PESTS AND DISEASES Aphids, slugs, borers, leafhoppers, mites, and thrips are common pests. In heavy, poorly drained soils, watch for botrytis, mosaic virus, smut, and rot.

Dianthus chinensis
China pink

Caryophyllaceae—**pink family**
height: 6 in. to 18 in.; spread: 6 in. to 12 in.

❧ **The China pink,** as the common name suggests, is a native of China. It is also called the rainbow pink, in honor of the many colors of the flowers. "Pink," in this instance, does not refer to color, but to the fringed edges of the petals—the blossoms look as if they had been trimmed with a seamstress's pinking shears.

China pinks are biennials, but gardeners generally treat them as half-hardy annuals, starting plants early in spring to force them into bloom during their first growing season.

SOW Indoors, 8 to 11 weeks before last frost. Cover seeds lightly and place in the light to germinate; germination should occur in 8 to 10 days at 70° to 75°F. Outdoors, sow in spring after the soil is workable.

GARDEN USES They make excellent flowers for the front of a bed or border. In addition, they slip easily into a rock garden or container, and they thrive if planted into a crevice in a stone retaining wall or other sunny spot where the soil drainage is good.

CULTURE China pinks have very definite requirements, but if you satisfy these, you will find the plants easy to grow. They need a neutral to alkaline soil that is not too rich.

Unlike most other annuals, which tend to be heavy feeders, China pinks prefer sparing applications of fertilizer. Feed them at half the rate recommended for flowers on the fertilizer label, and use a low-nitrogen formula. Read the list of ingredients to make sure that the type of nitrogen in the fertilizer comes from ammonia rather than nitrates or urea.

Space the plants 6 in. to 12 in. apart in the garden—the exact distance depends on the vigor of the cultivar—and deadhead conscientiously to keep your China pinks blooming well until frost. They do not perform well where the summers are overly hot and humid.

GARDENER'S CHOICE The weather-tolerant Telstar cultivars are dwarf, growing 4 in. to 6 in. high and 10 in. wide, and early flowering, commonly blooming about 8 to 9 weeks after seeds are sown. They may overwinter, as well, to bloom again the following year.

Ideal is another weather-tolerant series of cultivars that reach a height of 12 in. to 14 in. The flowers of 'Snowfire', an old favorite, have a deep red center with a fringed white edge. The Carpet series cultivars cover the whole range of China pink flower colors, bearing blossoms that are $1^{3}/_{4}$ in. wide on 8-in. plants.

PESTS AND DISEASES Plants grown in poorly drained soil are susceptible to root rot and several different fungal diseases. Otherwise, China pinks are rarely bothered by pests or diseases.

Planted in mass, red-flowered China pinks make a splash. (Photo by Michael A. Ruggiero.)

❧ **The hyacinth bean** is a cosmopolitan plant. A native of tropical Africa, it is cultivated in India and southeast Asia for its edible pods, and it has escaped from gardens to become a wildflower in the southeastern United States. It thrives as an annual vine in the North, too, and is well worth growing for its fragrant white or purple flowers and the beanlike pods, which, depending on the plant, vary in color from greenish purple to purple.

Inside the pods are edible beans that correspond in color to the flowers: White-flowered cultivars usually produce white seeds, while the purplish-flowered ones make purple seeds. The pods, incidentally, are the source of the botanical name Dolichos, which means "long" in Greek.

SOW Indoors, 4 to 6 weeks before last frost. Soak seeds for 24 hours in warm water prior to sowing. Germination occurs in 5 to 14 days at 65° to 70°F. In the Deep South and warmer regions of the Southwest, sow directly into the garden in hills 12 in. apart, planting 2 to 4 seeds per hill.

*Lablab purpureus (**Dolichos lablab**)*
hyacinth bean

Fabaceae—**bean family**
height: vining to 10 ft., higher in warm climates

A vigorous climber, hyacinth bean will screen a porch or embroider a fence in a matter of weeks. (Photo by Michael A. Ruggiero.)

GARDEN USES This enthusiastic vine makes a colorful and fast-growing cover for an arch or arbor, or an unusual screen with which to enclose a porch.

CULTURE Grow these trouble-free plants in full sun and rich, humusy, well-drained soil. Take care not to set out plants or seeds in the garden until the soil has warmed in spring—exposure to cold will stunt the lablab. A good rule of thumb is to wait until the local planting time for tomatoes. Northern gardeners who want to give their plants a head start (and thus produce longer vines) can start seeds indoors, as much as 6 weeks before the average date of the last spring frost.

Actually, you can plant your hyacinth beans even earlier, but if you do, you'll complicate the job of moving the plant out into the garden. Because this is a vine, you must provide some sort of trellis for the indoor seedlings to climb, and then, if the stems become too long, it'll be hard to tease them off this support so they may be trained onto the structure in the garden. Some idea of this plant's growth rate can be gathered from the fact that it needs weekly feedings while still in a pot.

GARDENER´S CHOICE Seeds sold by catalogs and nurseries include a wide range of types, and some produce markedly more attractive plants with more vibrantly colored flowers, leaves, and pods. The best way to secure these superior strains is to collect seeds from your own best plants and use them as planting stock the next spring.

PESTS AND DISEASES Trouble-free.

Fuchsia x *hybrida*
fuchsia, lady's eardrops

Onagraceae—evening primrose family
height and spread: vinelike, hanging growth with 1-ft.- to 3-ft.-long branches

🌜 **"Lady's eardrops" is a somewhat fanciful name** for a flower, but then these are decidedly fanciful blossoms. Indeed, a fuchsia bush all hung with blooms looks more like the creation of a Victorian jeweler than Mother Nature.

START Propagate from cuttings taken in the early spring; this is the only way to perpetuate superior cultivars.

GARDEN USES Striking and colorful, fuchsias are plants to be displayed as specimens, in hanging baskets and window boxes, or trained with a trunk to make miniature trees, or standards. Actually, in the wild, many fuchsias are trees. This genus includes about 100 species, and all are woody plants, either shrubs or trees. As such, they are of course perennials. But because of their sensitivity to cold, in most parts of North America they are grown as annuals.

In frost-free regions with moist, temperate summers, such as are found in coastal regions of the Pacific Northwest, fuchsias can be planted as landscape shrubs, and elsewhere, ambitious gardeners may choose to dig favorite plants from their containers and overwinter them in a sheltered spot.

CULTURE Fuchsias are at their best in cool, airy, partially shaded locations. Where summers are hot and dry, they are unlikely to thrive. In the Deep South, fuchsias are best cultivated only as winter annuals. In the North, especially in coastal areas, fuchsias flourish as summertime plantings.

Soil for fuchsias should be well drained and rich in organic material, so that the roots find themselves in an environment that is moist but not wet. Pay particular attention to watering during the hottest part of your growing season. Drought can easily kill fuchsias, and even the survivors will wilt, drop leaves, and slack off in the production of new flowers.

Fuchsias are robust feeders, so fertilize them on a regular basis whenever they are actively growing and flowering. Biweekly applications of a water-soluble, complete fertilizer with a balanced formula, such as 20-20-20 or 5-10-5, will keep your plants healthy, although you can also apply a topdressing of slow-release fertilizer at planting time.

Deadhead to keep your fuchsias flowering, and pinch back the new growth periodically to encourage bushier growth. Gently spray the foliage with water to keep it clean and increase the humidity around the plant.

To overwinter plants, dig them before the first killing frost of fall, and move them to a cool, shady location where the temperature will remain at about 40°F through the winter months. Throughout this period of semidormancy, give the plants only enough water to keep the stems from dying.

In February or early March, bring the plants back into a sunny, warm spot and increase the watering to more normal levels to return them to a state of active growth. If the regrowth is vigorous, you may be able to nurse the overwintered plants back to an attractive state and return them to the garden after all danger of frost has passed. Pinching new shoots back to the second or third set of leaves will encourage branching and denser regrowth.

If the renewed growth on your overwintered plants is uneven, you may do better to take tip cuttings from the new shoots that do appear (see p. 119) and grow these cuttings into new plants.

Most garden fuchsias are hybrids and must be grown from cuttings if the offspring are to come true (i.e., be identical to the parent plants). There are a few named strains, such as 'Florabelle', that may be grown from seed. Sow seeds indoors, 13 to 14 weeks before transplants are needed. Do not cover seeds. Germination occurs in 21 to 28 days at 70° to 75°F. Grow at 50° to 55°F in a shaded location.

However, because fuchsia plants take so long to raise from seed, most gardeners find seed-grown plants more trouble to start at home than they are worth. In particular, the seedlings do not thrive unless given supplementary lighting for at least 13 hours a day from January through March.

GARDENER'S CHOICE 'Jack Shanan', single pink flowers; 'Gartenmeister Bonstedt', upright, firecracker-shaped red flowers; 'Lena', double purple-and-white flowers; 'Swingtime', double red-and-white flowers; 'Double Indian Maid', double red-and-purple flowers; and 'Florabelle', semidouble purple-and-red flowered plants that branch spontaneously and need no pinching.

PESTS AND DISEASES Wilt, blight, and virus diseases may infect fuchsias; also watch for aphids, Japanese beetles, whiteflies, and mealybugs.

Fuchsia 'Gartenmeister Bonstead' is an upright cultivar with outstanding heat tolerance. (Photo by Judi Rutz; © The Taunton Press, Inc.)

Gazania rigens
treasure flower

Asteraceae—daisy family
height: 6 in. to 15 in.; spread: 8 in. to 12 in.

A perennial in frost-free regions, *Gazania* is grown as an annual throughout most of North America. (Photo by Michael A. Ruggiero.)

❧ **In its native South Africa,** the treasure flower is a perennial, and it also persists from year to year in frost-free regions of North America. Throughout most of the United States, however, it must be dug out of its garden bed in the fall and moved indoors in a pot if it is to survive the winter. For this reason, most gardeners choose to grow it as an annual, although if you keep a favorite specimen on a cool and sunny windowsill it may last until spring, when you can return the plant to the garden.

Although the treasure flower cannot stand cold, it does tolerate drought and heat, which makes it particularly valuable wherever summers are long and intense.

SOW Indoors, 6 to 8 weeks before planting outside, when danger of frost is past. Germination comes in 8 to 14 days at 58° to 62°F. Cover seeds. Grow seedlings at 60°F. Or sow outdoors after all danger of frost.

GARDEN USES Use gazanias as edging for beds and borders, or grow them in planters. Where the soil is light and sandy and the sun is full, you can mass them as a flowering ground cover.

Unfortunately, the colorful blossoms do not make satisfactory cut flowers, because they close in rainy or cloudy weather and at night.

CULTURE For the best results in the colder sections of North America, give gazanias a head start by sowing the seeds indoors 6 to 8 weeks before the weather warms and the danger of frost ends. In regions with long, warm growing seasons, you can sow the seed directly into the garden. In either case, when sowing the seeds, it's important to cover them completely, because total darkness is necessary for germination.

GARDENER´S CHOICE The Daybreak series, compact plants that bloom about 3 weeks earlier than other gazanias, in orange, yellow, or golden orange. Depending on the cultivar, plants and seeds are often sold as a mixture, which expands the color range to include bronze, white, and pink.

Mini-Star series bears short-stemmed (8-in.-tall) flowers in a wide range of colors: excellent for baskets, containers, beds, borders, or rock gardens. Harlequin hybrids, 15-in. high, bloom in red and ruby as well as the typical range of yellows and oranges. Sundance hybrids are prolific bloomers, and some of this strain's cultivars bear striped flowers.

PESTS AND DISEASES Overwatering leads to crown rot, especially in heavy, poorly drained soils. Mites can be a problem.

Gomphrena spp.
globe amaranth

Amaranthaceae—amaranth family
height: 9 in. to 30 in.; spread: 10 in. to 15 in.

❧ **Southerners call this plant gomphrena** or bachelor's button; elsewhere, it is better known as globe amaranth. As the wealth of common names suggests, this is a plant with a long history in our gardens. Thomas Jefferson made a note in his garden diary of having sown it at Monticello in 1767, and by the middle of the nineteenth century it was a standard in flower seed catalogs. Its popularity only increases with time, no doubt because it is so easy to grow, so dependable, and so versatile.

A native of tropical Panama and Guatemala, this flower blooms in a wide range of vivid colors, including purple, lavender, white, pink, orange, and yellow. It grows from 9 in. to 30 in., depending on the cultivar.

SOW Indoors, 8 to 10 weeks before last frost date. Germination comes in 15 to 20 days at 70° to 75°F. Soak seeds in water for 3 to 4 days before sowing, and cover completely when planting. Outdoors, sow after the last frost date.

GARDEN USES At home in bedding displays and at the front and middle of borders, globe amaranth also adapts well to containers. In addition, you can cut the flowers and enjoy them in fresh arrangements, or you can preserve them for use in dried arrangements.

To dry the flowers, cut the stems before the blossoms have quite fully opened, bundle the stems, and hang them upside down in a cool, dry spot. The blossoms open as they dry and despite dehydration keep their vivid coloration for years.

CULTURE Globe amaranth thrives in almost any well-drained soil, and it tolerates both heat and drought. It prefers a location with full sun, where it will bloom from early summer until the first frost.

Its seeds germinate poorly, so to make sure you get the quantity of plants you want, you should order two to three times as much seed as you think you need. Do not overwater seedlings—they are especially prone to damping off.

GARDENER'S CHOICE 'Buddy', intense violet-purple flower heads; the Gnome series, 8-in.- to 10-in.-high, mounding plants, 1¹/₂-in. to 2-in. white, rose, pink, or purple flowers.

A close relative, the Haage amaranth (Gomphrena haageana), is native to the southwestern United States and Mexico. It differs in that it can grow to 30 in. high. It gave us the red-flowering cultivars, such as 'Strawberry Fields' (or 'Strawberry Fayre'), as well as 'Lavender Lady', which bears pale lavender-pink flower heads on 2-ft. stems. The Woodcreek series of haageana cultivars runs the entire range of colors on 18-in. plants.

PESTS AND DISEASES Globe amaranths are especially attractive to whiteflies.

⚘ **Say "sunflower" and you instantly summon images** of a towering stem capped with a soup-bowl-sized yellow blossom. This, of course, is the generic type of common sunflower that is grown for its edible seeds, and it is a memorable sight. There are, however, many other annual sunflowers, and they vary dramatically in height and in the color and size of the blossoms. Some cultivars are just 1 ft. tall, while others tower to 15 ft. The flowers may be dark red, pale or golden yellow, or creamy white. In the so-called double sunflowers, the petal-like ray flowers that surround the central disc have been multiplied through breeding and mutations to give the flower heads a ruffled, more dahlialike look.

The botanical and common names of this native North American flower are synonyms: Helianthus is actually a compound of two Greek words, helios, meaning sun, and anthos, which means flower.

If cut and dried, globe amaranth provides a year-round show. (Photo © Michael Gertley.)

Helianthus annuus
common sunflower

Asteraceae—**daisy family**
height: 1 ft. to 15 ft.; spread: 1 ft. to 1¹/₂ ft.

Few annuals make as strong a statement as sunflowers. (Photo by Michael A. Ruggiero.)

SOW Directly into the garden after the last frost date, or indoors 10 days before seedlings are needed. Seeds started indoors should be sown into individual pots. Germination occurs in 5 to 10 days at 68° to 86°F.

GARDEN USES In the flower garden, tall sunflower cultivars can serve as a screen for the back of a border, or as a source of cut flowers.

In its natural state, the common sunflower has an unbranched stem, but the stems of many of the cultivated types spontaneously divide into branches. This is especially true of the shorter cultivars, which tend to be bushier. Their self-branching habit makes them easier to integrate into the garden than their giraffelike relatives, and they are just as valuable as a source of cut flowers. They can also be grown without staking, a kind of support the taller cultivars are likely to need, especially when grown on a windy site.

CULTURE Sunflowers need a spot with full sun—over the course of a day, the blossoms actually turn to track the sun as it crosses the sky. They are less choosy about soils, demanding only that the drainage be good. In fact, they may suffer in very rich soil because an abundance of nutrients encourages weak, floppy growth and few flowers.

Sunflowers do not respond well to transplanting, and it's best to sow them directly in the garden whenever possible. If you start them indoors, plant out the seedlings while they are still quite small. Larger seedlings might seem to offer a head start, but in fact, the bottoms of their stems may not thicken as the plants grow, even as the tops of the stems increase in diameter, and this creates a weak spot and a likely breaking point.

For the best cut flowers, snip the stems when the flower buds are just beginning to show color. Cut in the early morning or late evening to reduce the danger that the flowers will wilt. Remove any leaves from the bottom of the cut stems, and stand the flowers in water that has been mixed with a floral preservative. Then condition the flowers by storing them in a cool, dark place for several hours before moving them to the spot where you intend to display them. If handled carefully in this fashion, your cut sunflowers may last as long as 3 weeks.

GARDENER'S CHOICE 'Russian Giant' is one of the tallest sunflowers, growing to 10 ft. or more, with single yellow blooms 10 in. to 12 in. across, on strong, thick stems. At the other end of the scale, 'Big Smile' has 6-in.-wide flowers on 12-in. to 15-in. stems.

Other cultivars include 'Goldburst', 6 ft. high, with fully double, 5-in. to 7-in. golden flowers with no center disc; 'Valentine', 5 ft. high, primrose yellow, 4-in. to 6-in. flowers with a dark disc; 'Floristan', 3½ ft. high, 4-in.- to 5-in.-wide reddish flowers with yellow tips, on branching stems; 'Velvet Queen', 5 ft. high, 4-in.- to 5-in.-wide, deep velvet red flowers; and 'Teddy Bear', 2 ft. high, double, 6-in. golden yellow flowers.

The cucumberleaf sunflower, (Helianthus debilis subsp. cucumerifolius) grows 4 ft. to 5 ft. high and bears 3-in.-wide single yellow or creamy white ray flowers with red-purple centers. 'Italian White' is a fairly new cultivar that produces 4-in.-wide flowers that are creamy white to pale yellow with a dark disc, atop 5-ft.-high stems.

PESTS AND DISEASES Leaf spots, mildew, wilt, stem rot, aphids, and beetles can be problems.

Helichrysum bracteatum
(*Bracteantha bracteata*)
strawflower

Asteraceae—daisy family
height: 12 in. to 30 in.; spread: 9 in.
to 15 in.

Strawflowers are handsome in the garden and
even more welcome in wintertime in dry arrangements. (Photo by Michael A. Ruggiero.)

Heliotropium arborescens
(*Heliotropium peruvianum*)
heliotrope, cherry pie

Boraginaceae—borage family
height: 8 in. to 30 in.; spread: 12 in.
to 15 in.

❧ **The great virtue of this Australian native** lies not in the display it makes in the garden, but rather in the one its flowers make after they are dead. If the blossoms are cut before they are fully open and then hung upside down in a cool, dry spot, they will keep their vivid coloring even when dried to a strawlike texture.

Strictly speaking, though, it is not the flowers that are the attractive part of these blossoms, for in fact, these are small and inconspicuous. The color is in the enlarged bracts, or modified leaves, which cluster protectively around the flowers.

SOW Indoors, 4 to 6 weeks before last frost; do not cover seeds. Germination comes in 7 to 10 days at 70°F. Outdoors, sow after last frost date.

CULTURE Strawflowers need full sun and very well drained soil. They perform best where summers are long and hot, and they are exceptionally tolerant of drought.

A moderately fertile soil is ideal, and a poor one acceptable. Avoid soil rich in organic matter it will cause your strawflowers to shoot up into gangling plants with lots of leaves and few flowers.

GARDENER'S CHOICE 'Bright Bikinis' is low growing (12 in. high), with fully double flowers in a mixture of colors just 12 weeks after seeds are sown. 'Monstrosum', actually a strain of cultivars, bears larger flowers on taller plants (30 in. to 40 in. high) and can be purchased (as seed) in a mixture of colors or as individual cultivars bearing flowers of a single color.

PESTS AND DISEASES Stem rot may attack strawflowers grown in heavy, wet soils, and mildew can become a problem, especially later in the growing season when the days are still warm but the nights are cool.

❧ **In its native Peru,** the heliotrope grows into a woody shrub, but its extreme sensitivity to frost makes it an annual throughout most of North America. The small tubular flowers of this plant are colorful and pretty, but their real distinction lies in their perfume. Depending on the nose, this may suggest vanilla or a cherry pie, and it is one of the sweetest, strongest fragrances found in an annual flower.

The plant's botanical name comes from a marriage of two Greek words, helios, which means sun, and trope, which means turn. It originates in an old myth that the flower heads actually turned to face the sun.

SOW Indoors, 10 to 12 weeks before the last frost date. Germination should come in 7 to 14 days at 75°F. Or start new plants with tip cuttings taken from overwintered stock.

GARDEN USES Heliotrope is a very useful and rewarding plant for bedding displays, window boxes, containers, and baskets, and its woody stems make it an obvious choice for training into a tree form, or standard. Heliotrope flowers are also a favorite of butterflies and bees.

CULTURE This plant is a sun lover, and it grows best in full sunlight and well-drained soil. It hates cold and will not tolerate even a touch of frost. If, when spring rolls around, you are in doubt about when to move your heliotrope out into the garden, wait: A little late is much better than a little too early.

Purple heliotrope makes a striking contrast to a variegated flowering maple (*Abutilon*). (Photo by Michael A. Ruggiero.)

Hibiscus acetosella (*Hibiscus eetveldeanus*)
coppertone mallow

Malvaceae—mallow family
height: 3 ft. to 5 ft.; spread: 2 ft. to 3 ft.

Coppery foliage inspired this mallow's common name. (Photo by Michael A. Ruggiero.)

When you do plant out your heliotrope, take a minute to pinch back the shoots' growing tips to promote compact, bushier growth. Fertilize your plants every second week, and deadhead fading blossoms promptly to keep the plants blooming right into fall.

Before the first autumn frost, cut back the plants, dig them and pot them up, and bring them indoors to overwinter on a sunny, cool windowsill. When the new growth sprouts early the following spring, you can take cuttings and root them to increase your stock.

GARDENER´S CHOICE The most popular and available cultivars include 'Marine', which bears 6-in.-wide, deep violet-blue flowerheads on 18-in. stems. 'Mini-marine' bears blossoms similar in color and size to those of 'Marine', but on 8-in.- to 10-in.-tall plants that are excellent for edging. The Marine Lemoine strain is also similar to 'Marine' but slightly taller, to 24 in. 'Blue Wonder' is the earliest of the heliotropes to flower. 'White Lady' sports compact white flowers on 12-in. plants.

PESTS AND DISEASES Whiteflies are the most serious pest.

Unlike most other members of the mallow family, the coppertone mallow is not grown primarily for its flowers. Instead, it is prized for its deeply lobed, maroon-colored leaves. Actually, where the growing season is short, the coppertone mallow may not flower at all. In warmer regions and when grown indoors, this plant will bear pinkish red hibiscus-type blossoms. The plant flowers lavishly, but each blossom lasts just a single day.

SOW Indoors, 8 to 12 weeks before plants will be needed for transplanting into the garden after danger of frost has passed. For best results, before planting, scarify seeds or soak them in lukewarm water until they sink. Sow seeds in individual pots; germination usually occurs in 10 to 30 days at 70°F. Grow seedlings in warm conditions, at 65° to 70°F. Or, take cuttings from tips of new shoots of plants overwintered indoors. Root the cuttings under lights in a mixture of peat and sand.

GARDEN USES Because it is fast growing and tall, the coppertone mallow makes an imposing specimen plant and is also useful as a background for other plants. Its rapid growth also makes it a good candidate for training into a standard or tree-form.

The coppertone mallow adapts well to life in containers as well as in a garden bed or border.

CULTURE Plant coppertone mallow in shade or sun, but keep in mind that in the shade its leaf color is less vibrant. The plant prospers in well-drained, fertile soil that has been enriched with organic material.

If grown in a container, it can be wintered over in a greenhouse or a large, sunny but cool window. In early spring, just as the new growth is starting, prune such overwintered plants back hard, leaving just a skeleton of the main stems. This treatment forces vigorous new growth; an unpruned plant's growth is likely to be weak in its second year.

Early spring is also the time to start new plants. There are two ways to accomplish this, and each has its advantages. Plants grown from seed are the most vigorous, but their appearance is variable. Some will bear deeply cut leaves with three to five lobes, while others will bear only shallowly lobed or unlobed leaves.

Plants grown from cuttings will be uniform in appearance if all the cuttings are taken from a single plant, and you can select a parent plant with foliage of the sort that pleases you. However, cutting-grown plants are generally less vigorous than seed-grown ones.

PESTS AND DISEASES Whiteflies are the most common and serious pest of this plant, although aphids and mealybugs may also infest specimens grown indoors.

❧ **No flower brightens a shady yard** like garden impatiens, with its combination of brilliant flowers and rich, often colorful, foliage. Descended from an African wildflower that ranges naturally from Tanzania to Mozambique, the garden impatiens employs a particularly exotic means of seed dispersal. The plant's generic name derives from the Latin word for impatient, and impatiens can react explosively to a touch. When the plant's seed capsules are ripe, any disturbance may cause them to split, with the sections of the casing coiling back like stretched springs to spray the seeds over the surrounding soil.

SOW Indoors, 10 to 12 weeks before last frost date if planting outdoors; plants intended for indoor use may be sown at any time of year. Do not cover seeds. Germination comes in 7 to 18 days at 70° to 75°F.

GARDEN USES Garden impatiens are excellent for beds, borders, window boxes, containers, and hanging baskets. The range of flower colors is broad and continually increasing, as hybridizers introduce new cultivars. The blossoms of double-flowered forms are especially appealing, resembling tiny roses.

CULTURE Full to partial shade is this plant's natural element, but in cloudy climates it will tolerate stronger sunlight, especially if it is given the rich soil it prefers. Mix organic matter into the soil so that it absorbs water readily, yet also drains well. In hot weather, garden impatiens needs frequent watering, but poorly drained, soggy soil will soon make your plants rot.

Although garden impatiens can be grown from seed, it's a long process. Most gardeners prefer to buy their impatiens as ready-to-plant seedlings, or to start new plants for spring by overwintering a few of last season's impatiens indoors. Take cuttings from these about 8 weeks before the date of the last spring frost, which is when the young impatiens may be planted outside.

GARDENER'S CHOICE The most popular series is Accent, with over 25 named color forms. Flowers are $1^1/_2$ in. across and they appear on 8-in. plants in 60 days from sowing. Super Elfin—another very commonly grown series—has well over 20 cultivars that flower on 8-in. to 10-in., self-branching plants. Deco cultivars offer bronze foliage that contrasts nicely with the burgundy, orange, pink, red, rose, salmon, or white flowers. Tempo flowers early, and the 8-in. to 10-in. plants bear larger blossoms than either the Accent or Super Elfin types. There are over 25 Tempo cultivars; some are unusual in that a single flower may show three different colors. The Confection series boasts fully double flowers. The plants grow 2 in. taller and bloom 2 weeks later than most single-flowered garden impatiens, and they are ideally suited to pots and baskets. Blitz is taller (14 in.) than most other garden impatiens and bears larger (2-in.- to $2^1/_2$-in.-wide) flowers, making these cultivars ideal for the middle of the border.

Impatiens wallerana
busy lizzie, patience, garden impatiens
Balsaminaceae—**balsam family**
height: 6 in. to 18 in.; spread: 10 in. to 15 in.

Shade-tolerant impatiens offers flowers in every hue. (Photo by Michael A. Ruggiero.)

A related species, garden balsam (I. balsamina), grows 12 in. to 36 in. tall, with a spread of 8 in. to 18 in. Depending on the cultivar, its flowers may be single or double. The double types are particularly showy, with blossoms that look like tiny camellias or roses. Unlike most other types of impatiens, which bear their flowers on the ends of their branches, the garden balsam bears its blossoms in clusters around the succulent stems. Garden balsam is eye-catching if planted in a mass, and it works well in bedding displays or as filler to tuck between spring flowering shrubs for summer color.

PESTS AND DISEASES Be on the lookout for slugs, especially during extended periods of wet weather. During extended periods of dry weather, mites may become a problem.

Impatiens spp.
New Guinea hybrid impatiens
Balsaminaceae—balsam family
height: 12 in. to 24 in.; spread: 12 in. to 24 in.

Outsized flowers and flamboyant foliage make New Guinea impatiens a strong presence in a shady garden. (Photo by Michael A. Ruggiero.)

❧ **Plants collected on the island of New Guinea** and the nearby Solomon islands provided the stock from which these plants were bred. The resulting cultivars are similar to other impatiens in that they love heat and tolerate shade. But the flowers of the New Guinea impatiens easily outclass those of all their relatives: The New Guinea blossoms measure 2 in. to 3 in. in diameter.

The foliage colors flaunted by the New Guinea impatiens are far more flamboyant, too. Many cultivars bear foliage that is bronze, red, or variegated in combinations of green, red, bronze, or yellow, so the leaves may be as attractive as the flowers.

START Propagate from stem cuttings taken in early spring or summer. Root them in sand, perlite, or vermiculite, with bottom heat of 75°F, in a plastic-enclosed environment. Seeds of selected series will germinate indoors in 10 to 14 days at 78° to 80°F. Sow 14 to 16 weeks before last frost date. Do not cover seeds. Grow seedlings warm, at 70° to 80°F.

GARDEN USES With their outsized flowers and brilliant foliage, New Guinea impatiens turn a window box, planter, pot, or basket into a real eye-catcher. They are also useful as edging plants.

CULTURE The degree of sun you give this strain of impatiens depends on your region and the season. In cool and cloudy northern gardens, plant New Guinea impatiens in full sun or light shade. This kind of exposure is also appropriate for southern plantings made in fall or spring, when the sunlight is naturally less intense.

Throughout most of the United States, however, and especially in the South, summertime plantings of most New Guinea impatiens need heavier shade. However, there are some varieties that thrive only in full sun, and if the plant label or seed packet specifies this treatment, pay attention. Such full-sun varieties are not recommended for summer plantings in the Deep South and Southwest.

New Guinea impatiens also prefer a soil that has been enriched with copious amounts of organic material, so that it drains well and yet retains moisture. They do best when they are not allowed to dry out, but they do not like to be soggy. They are moderate feeders and benefit from regular applications of a complete fertilizer such as 20-20-20 or 14-14-14. The need for fertilizer increases as the plants mature.

GARDENER´S CHOICE The bright orange-flowered 'Tango Improved' and the pink, rose, red, salmon, and fuchsia Spectra hybrids can be grown from seed. Most other cultivars must be propagated by cuttings.

The popular Paradise series offers a wide range of colorful hybrids named for exotic island paradises, such as the violet-flowering 'Bora-Bora', white 'Moorea', scarlet 'Antigua', or the red-on-pink bicolor 'Pago-Pago'.

PESTS AND DISEASES Aphids, mites, and slugs are common pests. Watch out for tarnished plant bugs. In regions with high humidity, New Guinea impatiens are prone to damping off and bacterial stem rot.

Ipomoea spp.
sweet potato vine, moonflower, morning glory

Convolvulaceae—**bindweed family**
height and spread: vining plants with stems 3 ft. to 20 ft. long

❧ **The phrase "strange bed fellows"** takes on new meaning when you start experimenting with the annuals of this group. The genus Ipomoea includes not only the familiar morning glories, with their extravagant blossoms, but also the newly introduced ornamental sweet potatoes, whose principal attraction lies in their leaves, as well as one of the most exquisite of the night-blooming flowers, the moonflower. However, all of these diverse ipomoeas have a certain family resemblance, at least with respect to their cultural needs.

The one ipomoea that almost every gardener knows is the common morning glory, I. purpurea. Its 2-in.- to 3-in.-wide flowers may be blue, pink, or white, depending on the cultivar. The blossoms open in the morning, when the air is fresh, and then close with the onset of the afternoon heat. Though the vines may grow to a length of 15 ft. to 20 ft. in a 2- to 3-month growing season, they don't branch much, and if you want a curtain of foliage and flowers, you must plant your common morning glories in a mass.

Ipomoea tricolor is somewhat less vigorous, climbing to a height of just 8 ft. to 10 ft., but, as if compensating for its lesser stature, it bears larger blossoms. These flowers open to a diameter of 4 in. and, depending on the cultivar, may be blue, purplish blue, or white.

Ipomoea alba, commonly called moonflower, opens its pure white flowers, which measure 6 in. long and wide, in the late afternoon to spread fragrance through the night air. A perennial in frost-free climates, it reaches a height of 8 ft. to 10 ft. in most North American gardens.

Ipomoea 'Nil' is the imperial Japanese morning glory. Its three-lobed leaves are attractively variegated in green and white, and it bears showy 4-in.-wide flowers of violet, purple, rose, chocolate, or blue with a thin white border or fringe. It reaches a height of 3 ft. to 4 ft.

Ipomoea quamoclit, the cypress vine or cardinal climber, can grow to a height of 20 ft. The leaves are finely cut into threadlike segments, making a soft foil for the brilliant scarlet flowers, which measure 1 in. to $1^1/_2$ in. across.

Ipomoea batatas, the sweet potato vine, until recently was grown only for its tuberous, potato-like roots. In recent years, however, a number of ornamental versions of this vine have begun appearing in nurseries. These feature attractively colored, lobed and cut leaves borne on twining stems.

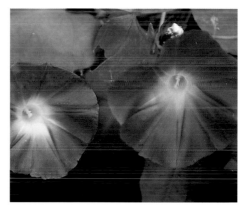

Depending on the species, *Ipomoea* may be showy flowers or dramatic foliage—and occasionally both. (Photo by Michael A. Ruggiero.)

Ipomœa lobata (Mina lobata), sometimes called flag-of-Spain, is a 20-ft.-tall climber that bears masses of small, tubular flowers that open scarlet, then fade to orange, then yellow, then white. As the season progresses, the vine becomes hung with flowers of varying ages, gradually assuming an intriguing, multicolored appearance.

SOW Indoors, sow seeds 6 to 8 weeks before planting out. Soak seeds in warm water for 24 to 48 hours or nick the hard seed coat with a file before planting. Germination occurs in 7 days at 70° to 85°F. Or sow outdoors after all chance of frost is past. Caution: All parts of the plant, including seeds, are poisonous.

GARDEN USES Common morning glory is a familiar sight, twining up fences and arbors and over garden walls. Ornamental sweet potato vines are excellent choices for hanging baskets and make an unusual and handsome ground cover for a sandy, sunny spot.

CULTURE All the ipomoeas grow best when given a spot with full sun and a soil that is well drained and not overly rich—fertile soil prompts overly vigorous growth that is characterized by abundant leaves and few flowers, and which is liable to attract insect pests.

GARDENER´S CHOICE Ipomœa batatas 'Blackie', one of the new ornamental sweet potatoes, bears deeply lobed black leaves that make a striking background against which to display the flowers of other annuals. Its trailing habit makes 'Blackie' a natural for window boxes and other containers.

Ipomœa 'Margarita' ('Margarite') is another ornamental sweet potato, with heart-shaped or rounded leaves that measure up to 6 in. across and are chartreuse in color.

Ipomœa tricolor 'Heavenly Blue' is probably the most popular of the morning glories, and it has earned that distinction with its sky blue, 4-in.- to 5-in.-wide flowers.

PESTS AND DISEASES For the most part, the ipomoeas are trouble free, but the sweet potatoes may attract potato beetles and slugs.

Kochia scoparia **forma** *trichophylla (Bassia scoparia* **forma** *trichophylla)*
summer cypress, burning bush

Chenopodiaceae—**goosefoot family**
height: 24 in. to 36 in.; spread: 18 in. to 24 in.

❧ **You'll find that the name** you call this plant changes with the season. From spring through the end of summer, the combination of a neat, upright profile and green, needlelike foliage really does give it the look of a miniature evergreen, a "summer cypress." But with the arrival of fall's cooler nights, the feathery leaves turn a fiery red or purple-red, and you cannot imagine this plant being anything other than a "burning bush."

SOW Indoors, 6 to 8 weeks before last frost date; do not cover seeds. Germination should occur in 7 to 10 days at 65° to 75°F. Outdoors, sow after all danger of frost has passed.

GARDEN USES This relatively fast-growing annual is effective in the back of the border, and it also works well as a focal point at the center of a circular bed. In addition, its coniferlike appearance makes summer cypress an ideal plant for a miniature instant hedge.

CULTURE This plant is most at home in soil that is well drained and even somewhat dry. It demands hot weather, and impatient gardeners must resist the urge to set it out too early in the spring while the nights are still chilly. Beware, too, of exposed sites where your summer cypress may be swept by strong winds that will snap off its brittle stems.

GARDENER'S CHOICE 'Acapulco Silver' is a 3-foot-tall cultivar whose leaves are silver tipped; its foliage turns scarlet in the fall. 'Evergreen' is 2 ft. to 3 ft. high, neater and more compact than the usual run of kochias. It remains green when other cultivars turn red, and its compactness makes it useful for containers.

PESTS AND DISEASES Seedlings are prone to damping off in wet soils. Kochia self-sows and can become something of a weed.

❧ **Lantanas are tropical shrubs** native to the West Indies that flourish in warm to hot weather. In frost-free areas they are woody perennials that may at times become weedy and need to be cut back severely to keep them in bounds. However, they cannot tolerate the winter temperatures experienced throughout most of North America and so must be grown as annuals. Otherwise, they are easygoing plants.

START From cuttings taken in summer and rooted in coarse sand, vermiculite, or perlite. Indoors, in late winter; germination is slow, taking about 8 weeks at 70° to 75°F.

GARDEN USES Yellow sage is a useful and versatile species that makes an effective and ornamental ground cover. It is also a rewarding bedding plant, and it adapts well to containers of all sorts—the long, trailing branches look especially fine spilling over the sides of a hanging basket. Patient training can convert one of this plant's woody stems into a trunk, to create a standard, or tree form.

CULTURE Lantanas not only tolerate gravelly or sandy soils but actually flower more prolifically in such nutrient-poor, well-drained sites. They flourish in the bright light and sandy soils of coastal gardens and are an excellent seaside plant. Although they thrive in full sun, you can also grow these plants in light shade. They'll survive even in moderate shade, although there they will flower poorly and the branches will grow spindly as they search for light.

Even under ideal conditions, yellow sage seeds germinate extremely slowly, and you will find it easier to propagate this plant by rooting softwood cuttings taken in summertime. Actually, most people find it easier simply to purchase new plants each spring.

GARDENER'S CHOICE There are several fine cultivated forms of yellow sage. 'Dallas Red' is an upright-growing form that bears red flowers. 'Alba' bears pure white flowers on 3-ft. trailing branches. 'Lady Oliva' bears bicolored flowers of lavender and pink, making it a striking choice for hanging baskets. 'Samantha' and 'Gold Mound' both have leaves that are variegated green and yellow, but the flowers of 'Gold Mound' are golden yellow, while those of 'Samantha' are primrose yellow.

The trailing lantana, Lantana montevidensis, is a related species with a vinelike habit, lilac-colored flowers with creamy centers, and smaller leaves. It is excellent for baskets, window boxes, and other containers, and it may also be trained up and around sphagnum-filled columns of wire mesh. Take care when choosing a planting site for trailing lantana. Its branches are very brittle and don't fare well in areas where they will be brushed against by passersby.

PESTS AND DISEASES Whiteflies and lantana aphids can be major pests.

Striking *Kochia* rises from a carpet of pink zinnias in a formal vignette. (Photo by Michael A. Ruggiero.)

Lantana camara
yellow sage
Verbenaceae—**vervain family**
height: to 4 ft., but usually less; spread: rangy, to 4 ft.

An exceptionally tolerant plant, yellow sage blooms better when grown in nutrient-poor soils. (Photo by Michael A. Ruggiero.)

Lobelia erinus
edging lobelia

Lobeliaceae—lobelia family
height: 4 in. to 8 in.; spread: 6 in.
to 12 in.

Although usually reserved for edging beds,
lobelia also looks spectacular cascading over the
lip of a pot. (Photo by Michael A. Ruggiero.)

❧ **The combination of rapid growth** with a neat, compact profile and generous, prolonged bloom makes the edging lobelia a most useful plant. In addition, its flowers supply some of the clearest, truest blues to be found in the garden.

SOW Indoors, 11 to 12 weeks before last frost date in the North, 10 weeks in the South. Do not cover seeds. Germination occurs in 14 to 21 days at 75° to 78°F. Sow individual pots, each with 5 to 10 seeds (seedlings do not transplant well).

GARDEN USES As its common name implies, this plant is useful as an edger, to define and finish off the perimeter of a flower bed or border. It also makes an attractive and durable planting for hanging baskets, window boxes, and all other sorts of containers. Its tolerance for shade also makes it a good choice for gardens overhung with trees.

CULTURE In hot southern gardens, partial shade is obligatory for edging lobelia. If the plants are to keep their looks through a southern summer, shear them back after the first flush of flowers and give them a light dose of fertilizer.

Farther north, where summer nights are cool, you can leave your lobelias unsheared, and you can grow them in full sun, as long as you give them a soil rich in organic matter that drains well but also holds moisture well.

Growing lobelias from seed is tricky, because the seedlings are prone to damping off. Sow seeds in a sterile seed-starting mix, and drench with a fungicide that is recommended as effective against damping off disease.

Lobelia seedlings are sensitive to transplanting and may not recover from the trauma of pricking out. Avoid this problem by sowing the seeds in small clusters into small individual plastic, clay, or peat pots. When the time comes to plant the seedlings out into the garden, just slip them out of their pots and plant each pot-full as a clump.

GARDENER´S CHOICE There are many good cultivars. Superior types include 'Crystal Palace', dark blue flowers, one of the best in full sun in the North with its bronze foliage instead of the more typical green; 'Midnight Blue', similar to 'Crystal Palace' but earlier flowering; 'Cobalt Blue', dark blue flowers; 'Mrs. Clibran', dark blue flowers with a white eye; 'Cambridge Blue', light blue flowers; 'Rosamond', wine red flowers with a white eye; 'Riviera Blue Splash', picotee blue-and-white flowers; 'Snow Queen' and 'Snowball', white flowers.

Cultivars in the Cascade series have blue, lavender, rose, white, and red flowers and green leaves. Their cascading growth makes them an excellent choice for baskets and containers.

PESTS AND DISEASES Seedlings need protection against damping off. Otherwise, if its basic cultural requirements are satisfied, this is generally a pest- and problem-free plant.

Lobularia maritima
Sweet alyssum

Brassicaceae—mustard family
height: 4 in. to 8 in.; spread: 4 in.
to 10 in.

❧ **One of the most striking ways to grow** this ground-hugging plant is also the easiest. Sprinkle the seeds between the paving stones or bricks of a terrace, patio, or flight of steps, and the resulting plants will spill out across the adjoining pavement like billows of sweetly scented foam. Wherever you plant sweet alyssum, though, its appeal will be as much to the nose as the eye, for the flowers' perfume has an assertive, honeyed sweetness. This makes sweet alyssum particularly appealing as a living mulch. Scratch the seeds into the soil across a bed of tulips, perennials, or roses, and you'll create a softly colored setting for the more permanent plants that also endows them with the perfume they may be lacking. At the same time, by covering the soil, you eliminate an opportunity for weeds. And because sweet alyssum is shallow rooted, it won't compete with deeper-rooted permanent plantings.

SOW Indoors, 6 to 8 weeks before plants are needed, in individual pots. Scatter 10 to 20 seeds per pot. Do not cover seeds. Germination occurs in 6 to 10 days at 75° to 82°F. Seedlings prefer to be cool (50°F) at night. Or sow outdoors in early spring, covering the seeds with ⅛ in. of soil.

GARDEN USES Its compact, low, and spreading growth makes sweet alyssum a good choice for edging a border or bed, and it has a most graceful appeal when planted so that it laps over the edge of a pot or window box, or cascades down the face of a dry-stone wall.

CULTURE To a great extent, the region in which you garden will dictate the spot for your sweet alyssum. In cooler areas, especially those with a cloudy climate such as the coastal Northwest, sweet alyssum benefits from full sun. However, in the South, where the sunlight is stronger, or in northern regions where summer heat is intense, such as in the Plains states, a spot with light shade will suit sweet alyssum better.

In any case, well-drained soil of average or even poor fertility is adequate. Sweet alyssum flourishes even in the sandy soils of seaside gardens, if just an inch of compost of some other organic matter is turned into the bed at planting time.

In most cases, sowing sweet alyssum seeds directly into the garden soil in which the plants are to grow is not only the easiest but also the most effective method of propagation. However, if you want an earlier display of flowers, or if you need plants with which to plant up a container, you may want to start your seeds indoors. Sow the plants in clumps, a pot-full at a time, because sweet alyssum makes a more effective display when grown in a mass, and because the tender young seedlings won't tolerate transplanting. When planting out, transplant the whole pot-full of seedlings as a unit.

In the cooler regions of the country, sow sweet alyssum in early spring. In hotter climates, make another sowing in mid to late summer, to guarantee a second flowering in fall or winter. Shear back the plants after the first flush of flowers fades, to encourage a more abundant and lengthy rebloom. When it finds a spot it likes, sweet alyssum will sow itself, providing an ongoing supply of "volunteers."

GARDENER'S CHOICE Plant breeders have developed many cultivars, and the following are outstanding. White-flowered cultivars include 'Carpet of Snow', extra-dwarf, 3 in. to 4 in. high; 'Snow Cloth', one of the earliest white-flowering cultivars, whose blossoms have no trace of green in their throats; and 'Snow Crystals', a tetraploid (having twice the number of chromosomes as ordinary sweet alyssum) with larger flowers, on 4-in.-tall plants.

'Oriental Night' is compact and early maturing, with violet-purple flowers. 'Wonderland Deep Rose' reaches a height of 3 in. and bears deep rose (almost red) flowers. 'Easter Bonnet', a compact tetraploid, grows to 3 in. and bears rose, violet, pink, or lavender flowers.

Billows of tiny white, pink, rose, or lavender blossoms are *Lobularia*'s gift to the garden. (Photo by Michael A. Ruggiero.)

PESTS AND DISEASES The seedlings are prone to damping off; watering with warm water often prevents it. Slugs and snails will attack sweet alyssum, especially those plants grown in partial shade.

Matthiola incana
common or Brompton stock

Brassicaceae—mustard family
height: 12 in. to 30 in.; spread: 12 in. to 15 in.

A clove fragrance and bright colors make stocks a strong choice for window boxes or cut flowers. (Photo by Michael A. Ruggiero.)

❧ **Though attractive and vividly colored,** stocks are not the most spectacular of flowers in appearance. But their fragrance, an intense, spicy perfume, is among the most memorable of any flower.

This plant's botanical name commemorates Pierandrea Mattioli, a medieval Italian physician and pioneering botanist. Stock is a southern European native. As such, it performs best in mild climates. It has escaped from gardens to become a wildflower in parts of California, and it flourishes as a biennial or perennial in England. Throughout most of North America, however, stock is best treated as a cool-season annual. It won't tolerate the heat and humidity that summer brings in so many parts of this country, and so American gardeners should save this flower for the spring or fall in the North and Midwest, and for the winter in the South.

SOW Indoors, 6 to 8 weeks before last frost. Germination in 10 to 14 days at 70°F. Do not cover seeds, and use sterilized soil to avoid damping off. Grow seedlings at cool temperatures: 50°F by night, 55°F by day.

GARDEN USES The unmistakable fragrance has made stocks a favorite cut flower and has won them enduring popularity as bedding, border, and container plants.

CULTURE When growing stocks from seed, it is important to keep the seedlings cool and to let the soil around their roots become partially dry between waterings. Because the seedlings are prone to fungal infections, it is best to water them in the morning, and on sunny days, so that the foliage will dry before nightfall. If the leaves stay damp overnight, they provide a perfect nursery for fungal spores.

Stock seedlings also do best in a potting mix that is well drained, a bit on the sandy side. They prefer a mix with a slightly alkaline to slightly acidic pH. If you plant seeds in a peat-based commercial seed-starting or potting mix, both of which tend to be strongly acidic, add $^{1}/_{4}$ cup of lime per 2-gallon bucket of the mix.

When planting common stock (Matthiola incana) in the garden, set the plants in a spot with full sun or light shade.

GARDENER'S CHOICE The 10-week stock (Matthiola incana 'Annua') is by far the most popular stock grown in North America—it flowers early in a wide range of colors. Choose cultivars that tend to bear double flowers, which are stronger both in stature and fragrance than single-flowered types.

Cultivars in the Frolic series are extra early and mostly double-flowering, and they bloom even at low temperatures. Frolic stocks bear 1-in.-long carmine, deep rose, pink, purple, or white flowers on $2^{1}/_{2}$-ft. plants. They are excellent for the cutting garden or for greenhouse growing.

The Midget series is the earliest of the bedding types to flower. Although they grow best in cool temperatures, the Midget cultivars are slightly more heat tolerant than other common stocks. They bear well-branched, fully double flowers on strong 8-in. to 10-in. stems, in shades of lavender, red, rose, pink, white, or violet.

A relative, the night-blooming stock (Matthiola longipetala) tolerates a bit more shade than common stock. Unlike the common stock, the night-blooming stock bears only single blossoms of a soft lilac hue. But when twilight teases the night-bloomers' blossoms open, they exhale a perfume that is even more powerful than that of their day-blooming relatives. If set alongside a door or under an open window, a handful of the night-bloomers will lure you out into the garden for many a moonlit stroll.

PESTS AND DISEASES Stock seedlings are prone to damping off, and zealous gardeners must take care not to overwater. In the garden, the plants are attractive to aphids and caterpillars.

Not many years ago, the blackfoot daisy rarely appeared in American gardens except in the Southwest, where it has long been admired for its tolerance of drought. Now it is common in nurseries nationwide. That's not surprising, for the blackfoot daisy is an easy plant to please.

This plant's name refers to the black stalks that support the blossoms—Melampodium is simply a translation into Greek of "blackfoot." Although sometimes sold as the "African zinnia," it is a native of the warmer regions of the Americas. Although there are a number of other Melampodium species in cultivation, M. paludosum is the only blackfoot daisy commonly grown as an annual.

SOW Indoors, 5 to 8 weeks before last frost date. Cover the seeds lightly; germination occurs in 7 to 10 days at 65° to 70°F. Or sow outdoors after all danger of frost is past.

GARDEN USES Blackfoot daisies provide a handsome display when planted in mass, or as edging plants around a bed of shrubs or taller flowers. They are also attractive when set out as single plants in a rock garden or in a container.

CULTURE Given full sun, Melampodium thrives in a wide range of well-drained soils, including those that are poor in organic matter and nutrients. Soils rich in nitrogen may provoke taller, bushier growth, but plants grown in those conditions bear fewer flowers. You'll have more compact plants, and enjoy an abundant crop of the yellow daisylike flowers from late spring until frost, if you set your blackfoot daisies into average garden soil and refrain from spoiling them with too much fertilizer.

Aside from its adaptation to unpromising sites, this plant is also remarkably self-sufficient. It is "self-branching," which means that it naturally makes a compact, dense plant, and there's no need to pinch back the plants while young. In addition, blackfoot daisy is self-cleaning, shedding its spent blossoms of its own accord and saving the gardener from the necessity of deadheading.

The blackfoot daisy does crave heat. Don't move it out into the garden until mid or late spring, when the soil has warmed to at least 60°F; planting young blackfoot daisies into cool soil is

Melampodium paludosum
blackfoot or butter daisy

*Asteraceae***—daisy family**
height: 8 in. to 24 in.; spread: 12 in. to 30 in.

A naturally compact plant, blackfoot daisy is an undemanding but very rewarding plant. (Photo by Michael A. Ruggiero.)

likely to stunt them. In areas with mild winters, blackfoot daisies may self-sow to return year after year as volunteers.

GARDENER´S CHOICE Cultivars include 'Derby', the earliest to bloom, 10-in.- to 12-in.-high globe-shaped plants; 'Showstar', 8-in.- to 10-in.-high plants that are superior for edging or container displays; and 'Medallion', the tallest cultivar, 15 in. to 18 in. high.

PESTS AND DISEASES Melampodium seedlings are susceptible to damping off. The mature plants are prone to spider mites and, when planted in the shade, slugs.

Moluccella laevis
bells of Ireland

Lamiaceae—mint family
height: 2 ft. to 3 ft.; spread: 12 in. to 15 in.

A novelty in the garden, bells of Ireland make distinctive cut flowers. (Photo by Michael A. Ruggiero.)

❧ **Though by no means a rarity,** this plant remains an intriguing novelty. The calyx, normally an unremarkable envelope that encloses the flower, has expanded in this case into a bell of vivid green to become the main show. The color, of course, is the reason for the supposed connection with Ireland. Actually, though, this plant is native to western Asia. The genus name, Moluccella, derives from a mistaken belief that its ancestors came from the Molucca Islands.

SOW Outdoors in early spring where plants are to grow. Or start indoors, 10 to 12 weeks before last frost. Chill seeds at 40° to 50°F for 5 to 10 days prior to sowing. Sow seeds individually in separate cell packs or peat pots: Seedlings' sensitive roots won't tolerate injury at transplanting time. Do not cover seeds. Keep seed containers at 75°F by day and 50°F by night; germination occurs in 20 to 35 days.

GARDEN USES Because bells of Ireland reaches a height of as much as 3 ft., you can set this plant in the middle or back of the border. Its usefulness in fresh or dried floral arrangements also earns it a berth in the cutting garden. Don't depend on bells of Ireland as a major source of garden color. Instead, view the flowers as a curiosity, something that will add a distinctive note to an arrangement of cut flowers.

CULTURE Give this plant full sun or light shade, and well-drained soil. Sandy soil is best, but bells of Ireland will tolerate a wide range of soils as long as they are well drained. The plants are relatively tolerant of drought, and they bloom late in the season.

Bells of Ireland resent being transplanted and are best sown directly into the spot where they are to grow outdoors. Sow in springtime, at about the time that corn is planted in your region. Gardeners in northern areas with short growing seasons can start seeds indoors 10 to 12 weeks before the last frost date.

Once it has put down roots, bells of Ireland is relatively undemanding. In a congenial location, it may even self-sow, providing the next year's crop.

When using bells of Ireland for cut flowers, be sure to cut the stems as soon as the green bells open, as the flowers don't last as long in the vase if cut at a later stage of development or when in seed.

PESTS AND DISEASES When grown in wet or poorly drained soil, bells of Ireland is prone to crown rot.

Nemesias are an outstanding cool-season annual, part of a group that has adapted to flourish in the cooler temperatures experienced in spring and fall in the North, and in winter in the Deep South and low-altitude Southwest. Such plants can furnish color at times of the year when most other plants are semidormant. As a rule, though, they cannot stand the heat and humidity that come with summer in most regions. So plant your nemesias early and enjoy them through the spring, then replace them with heat-loving annuals as summer settles in. Save some nemesia seed to start a new crop, in late summer in the North, or in mid fall in the South. In regions with particularly temperate climates, such as the Pacific Northwest, nemesias (and other cool-season annuals) may flower right through the summer.

The name Nemesia derives from nemesion, the name of a plant with medicinal value described almost 2,000 years ago by the ancient Greek physician Dioscorides. In fact, though, Dioscorides' plant was not the same as the modern nemesias, which he could not have known as they are South African in origin.

Most nemesias found in nursery yards and seed catalogs are hybrids, crosses of two wild species, N. strumosa and N. versicolor. Many of the blue flowering cultivars descend principally from N. strumosa, and they are likely to share its spurred and pouched blossoms. Its influence is seen in the multicolored strains of hybrids, and it has bequeathed to these strains flowers that are pouched but without spurs.

SOW Indoors, 12 to 13 weeks before planting out in mid to late spring. Cover seeds lightly, and place containers in total darkness; germination occurs in 14 to 25 days at 60° to 65°F. Grow seedlings at 50°F. Or sow outdoors in spring after all chance of frost is past; in mild climates, sow in fall for winter bloom.

GARDEN USES As a group, nemesia cultivars tend to be low and spreading or even floppy-stemmed plants, which makes them excellent for containers, baskets, and raised beds. In ordinary flower beds, however, they'll look better if you contain their growth by staking them with brush twigs.

CULTURE Nemesias grow well in full sun or partial shade, but they require a soil that is well drained, slightly moist, and of average fertility.

GARDENER´S CHOICE Superior cultivars include 'Blue Gem', 8-in.- to 10-in.-tall plants, forget-me-not blue flowers; 'KLM', 10 in. to 12 in. tall, blue upper and white lower petals; 'Mello Red & White', 8 in. to 10 in. tall, red upper and white lower petals; 'Mello White', 7 in. to 9 in. tall, pure white flowers; 'Tapestry', 10 in. tall, upright plants, flowers of mixed pastel colors; 'Funfair', 10 in. tall, bright yellows, reds, and oranges, but no blues; and 'Carnival', 10 in. to 12 in. tall, brightly colored flowers.

PESTS AND DISEASES Nemesia seedlings are prone to damping off in poorly drained soils. The adult plants are attractive to slugs.

Nemesia spp.
nemesia

Scrophulariaceae—**figwort family**
height: 7 in. to 12 in.; spread: 10 in. to 11 in.

Nemesia 'Carnival Lights' brings spring to a window garden. (Photo by Michael A. Ruggiero.)

Nicotiana x *sanderae*
(*Nicotiana alata*)
flowering tobacco

Solanaceae–nightshade family
height: 12 in. to 36 in.; spread: 12 in.
to 14 in.

Flowering tobacco 'Nicki Red' in a bedding
display. (Photo by Michael A. Ruggiero.)

This group of garden flowers is closely related to the plants that produce smoking and chewing tobaccos, a fact commemorated in the botanical name. Nicotiana was named for Jean Nicot, the man who brought seeds of tobacco back to France, although his interest in the plant was for its supposed medicinal value. The plants grown for garden display, the flowering tobaccos, include several species: Nicotiana x sanderae, the most popular of the garden types, actually originated in a cross of two of these, the South American wildflowers N. alata and N. forgetiana. Most of the popular groups of cultivated nicotianas, such as the Nicki hybrids, are Nicotiana x sanderae cultivars, although nurserymen often mislabel them as N. alata.

SOW Indoors, 8 to 10 weeks before last frost date. Do not cover seeds. Germination occurs in 7 to 12 days at 70°F. Grow seedlings at 60°F.

GARDEN USES Flowering tobaccos make a handsome show when massed in a bed or border. A small cluster will also serve to plug a gap in a perennial border or mixed floral display, and the compact cultivars are attractive as container plantings. The blooming stems also make elegant, though short-lived, cut flowers. The sweet fragrance of the blossoms varies with the cultivar and ranges from intense to undetectable.

CULTURE Throughout most of the United States, flowering tobaccos thrive in either full sun or partial shade, though in regions that experience intense heat and sunlight, such as the Central Plains and Southwest, they do best in partial shade. Protection from the full force of the sun also improves the appearance of the flowers: Blossoms tend to wilt during the heat of the day on plants set out in the open, while those in a lightly shaded spot remain fresh.

As a group, the flowering tobaccos prefer humusy, well-drained soil, but they perform reasonably well in a wide range of conditions. Timely deadheading is important to keep these plants in shape. Snip off the spent flower spikes, cutting back to a set of leaves just below the base of the old flower stem, and a new, though smaller, spike will sprout.

GARDENER'S CHOICE Nicotiana x sanderae is commonly sold in series of related cultivars. Typically, the individual cultivars vary in flower color, but those within each series are similar in size, habit of growth, and fragrance. Some of the most common series are Nicki hybrids, the most popular, $1^{1}/_{2}$-ft.- to 2-ft.-tall bushy plants bearing flowers of red, pink, white, lime green, or rose; Domino series, more compact than the Nicki cultivars, just 12 in. to 14 in. tall, and more heat and shade tolerant, with all the colors found in the Nickis plus salmon, purple, and bicolors; Metro series bloom 7 to 10 days earlier that the Nicki series and stand 12 in. to 14 in. tall, with white, red, rose, lime green, blush pink, or lilac flowers; 'Sensation Mix', tall plants from 24 in. to 36 in., with strongly scented flowers of white, red, purple, and shades of pink; 'Havana', two newer cultivars, both growing to 14 in., are 'Havana Lime Green' bearing flowers of chartreuse mixed with white, and 'Havana Appleblossom' with flowers that combine pastel rose-pink and white.

The tubular flowers of a related species, Nicotiana langsdorfii, are smaller than those of Nicotiana x sanderae and N. sylvestris (see the next entry) but are nevertheless intriguing. Their color is a rare pale yellowish to lime green. The contrast with the darker hued foliage is subtle, but set this flower by a bench, or a spot that you pass often, and you'll find yourself enjoying N. langsdorfii more and more.

PESTS AND DISEASES Slugs can be a problem, as can potato, cucumber, and Japanese beetles. Do not plant nicotiana near tomatoes, eggplant, potatoes, or any type of peppers—it can be a host of the tobacco mosaic virus, a pathogen that will devastate those crops.

✏ **This Argentine native** regularly reaches a height of 5 ft., which ranks it as one of the taller flowering tobaccos. Its drooping clusters of pure white flowers are fragrant at night. The leaves are large and coarse.

Nicotiana sylvestris is perennial in the warmer areas of North America, Zones 9 to 11, but it performs like an annual in the northern sections of the continent.

SOW Indoors, 4 to 6 weeks before last frost date. Do not cover seeds. Germination is in 7 to 12 days at 70°F.

GARDEN USES The boldness and size of Nicotiana sylvestris makes it a good choice for the back of a flower border or for the centerpiece of a bed.

CULTURE Although you can sow seeds directly into an outdoor bed, they are so fine that they are likely to wash or blow away. Play it safe and start the seeds indoors where they aren't at the mercy of the weather.

This species adapts well to full sun or partial shade, and when planted in sun its flowers do not wilt during the heat of the day as do the sanderae or alata cultivars. Take care, however, to plant Nicotiana sylvestris in a sheltered spot, because strong winds will shred its large leaves.

Deadhead promptly; don't wait until all the individual blossoms in a cluster have faded, for by that point the first blossoms that opened will already be making seeds. Instead, pinch off the whole cluster when two-thirds of the blossoms have withered. When removing flower clusters, do not pinch or snip back beyond the nearest leaf axil. If not deadheaded, plants will self-sow around the garden, so if you grow Nicotiana sylvestris one year, you are likely to find seedlings popping up spontaneously the next spring. Such "volunteers" closely resemble the parent plants, but they flower much later in the season than plants you start indoors.

PESTS AND DISEASES Aphids seem much more likely to attack Nicotiana sylvestris than other flowering tobaccos. Slugs can be a problem with plants grown in the shade. Otherwise, the relevant pests and diseases are the same as those found on N. sanderae.

✏ **The zonal geranium is among the most popular** of all annuals, and no wonder: It excels in a host of situations. In frost-free areas of California and the Southeast, these flowers are evergreen perennials, but in the rest of the country, they are annuals and are best reserved for the warm season.

If nothing else will persuade you to learn the Latin names of your plants, this flower should, for its common name leads to endless confusion and often disappointment. Although we commonly call it a geranium, this annual flower is, in fact, a pelargonium, as too many gardeners have learned to their sorrow after ordering geraniums from a nursery catalog and receiving modest-flowered plants that are suited only to the wildflower garden, or to a fairly minor role in the perennial garden.

Nicotiana sylvestris
flowering tobacco

Solanaceae—**nightshade family**
height: 4 ft. to 6 ft.; spread: 12 in. to 18 in.

Night-fragrant flowering tobacco self-sows readily to return year after year. (Photo by Michael A. Ruggiero.)

Pelargonium x hortorum
zonal or bedding geranium

Geraniaceae—**geranium family**
height: 12 in. to 24 in.; spread: 12 in. to 24 in.

A traditional favorite for containers and bedding, zonal geraniums can also move indoors in fall to overwinter on a sunny windowsill. (Photo by Michael A. Ruggiero.)

The pelargoniums that you should have ordered are hybrids, the results of crosses between two older species. Early Pelargonium hybrids usually bore simple kidney-shaped green leaves that were marked by dark, horseshoe-shaped or circular bands—the "zones" that gave this flower its name. (Pelargonium, incidentally, derives from the Greek word for stork, and the name was inspired by the supposed resemblance of the plant's seed capsules to a stork's bill.)

The leaves of today's cultivars, however, are as likely to be star- or oval-shaped, and they may be marked with various colors. There are cultivars with green and white leaves, or yellow-centered leaves edged with brown, orange, or green, as well as cultivars whose leaves are all chartreuse or yellow. In many of these modern cultivars, the foliage is so dramatic that the flowers, when they open, seem almost anticlimactic.

SOW Indoors, 12 to 14 weeks before last frost date. Seed companies usually scarify the seeds before they ship, but if they have not done so, run seeds across a sheet of fine sandpaper to scratch the outer coats before sowing. After planting, cover seeds with a fine dusting of potting mix that has been sieved, firm the soil, and keep moist. Keep seed pans and contents warm; 72°F is ideal. Germination is in 7 to 15 days.

GARDEN USES Zonal geraniums are outstanding in bedding displays, as well as in planters, containers, and window boxes. And zonal geraniums can do double duty: After a summer in the garden, you can dig them up in the fall and move them indoors to pass the winter as an attractive houseplant on a cool, sunny windowsill.

The fancy-leaved types show up best as specimens or accents in containers or window boxes, and they should not be lost in massed plantings or carpet beds.

CULTURE Pelargoniums are sun lovers, and they require well-drained soil that is rich in organic matter. They benefit from occasional feedings with a balanced fertilizer. Deadhead on a regular basis to keep the plants looking trim, and to maintain their production of new flowers.

Zonal geraniums raised from seed are preferred to those raised from cuttings, because the seed plants are sure to start life free from the virus diseases that may afflict cutting-grown plants. Many desirable cultivars, however, do not come true from seed and must be grown from stem cuttings.

If cut back severely in late winter, plants rescued from the garden in the fall will produce a flush of new shoots that are good material for stem cuttings. Take cuttings in late spring, 6 to 8 weeks before the last frost date, only from vigorous, healthy-looking plants. After the cuttings have rooted, plant them into individual pots and give the new plants as much sun as you can until they are ready to transplant into the garden. Keep both rooting cuttings and seedlings at 60° to 65°F by night, and provide as much light as possible during the day.

Many of the newer cultivars are self-branching, but older ones must be pinched to encourage an attractive branching form. Remove the tip of the stems while the plants are still small.

GARDENER´S CHOICE For bedding displays, it's hard to beat the Orbit series, which grows about 14 in. high and flowers throughout the season in a wide array of colors ranging from violet to salmon, red, rose, and hot pink, to white.

Multibloom cultivars are fairly new introductions with a good range of colors. They are more compact (to 12 in.) than many other series and flower 2 to 4 weeks earlier. The Maverick, Pinto, and Ringo 2000 series are popular and easy to find in local nurseries. 'Crystal Palace Gem' bears orange flowers but is grown mostly for its outstanding bright yellow foliage, as is 'Vancouver Centennial', which has golden yellow, star-shaped leaves marked with a bronze zone and bears salmon-colored flowers. 'Occold Shield' has golden yellow, kidney-shaped leaves with a bronze zone and bears orange flowers. 'Wilhelm Languth' has crimson flowers and white-and-green variegated foliage.

PESTS AND DISEASES Aphids, mealybugs, mites, whiteflies, and scale are the most common pests, and slugs for plants grown in shade. Diseases include root rot, stem rot, and leaf spot, as well as the viruses that eventually become endemic in populations propagated by cuttings.

❦ **As the common name suggests,** this plant's waxy, lobed leaves resemble those of English ivy. Its flowers are borne in huge masses and, generally speaking, the single-flowering forms are much heavier bloomers than the semidouble types.

The foliage and flowers are similar to those of zonal geraniums, but the ivy-leaved geranium's brittle stems grow as long as 4 ft. to 5 ft. (although 3 ft. is more typical).

START By cuttings taken from overwintered plants; plants started from seed require 15 to 20 weeks from sowing to flowering.

GARDEN USES The weeping growth habit makes the ivy-leaved geranium an excellent flower for a container, especially a hanging basket. If planted in an ordinary bed, ivy-leaved geraniums sprawl. They lack the precision needed for a formal bedding display, but they do make an attractive, informal ground cover.

CULTURE Ivy-leaved geraniums generally grow best where summer temperatures remain below 90°F, or in a spot where they are shaded during the hottest part of the day. Aside from their sensitivity to heat, these plants benefit from the same care as is preferred by the zonal geraniums.

Unlike the zonals, the ivy-leaved geraniums are best started from cuttings taken from overwintered plants 6 to 8 weeks before the last frost date. Take cuttings only from vigorous, healthy-looking plants. When rooted, move cuttings to individual pots and give them as much sun as you can until transplanting them into the garden.

GARDENER´S CHOICE The following cultivars are all propagated by seed, but they are widely available as ready-to-transplant seedlings at local garden centers and nurseries. The Balcon series (short for balcony) cultivars are highly resistant to heat and are good choices for a sunny window box. Tornado series cultivars bloom earlier than most other seed-grown ivy-leaved geraniums, bearing flowers of lilac, white, and carmine. They are naturally compact and branch without pinching, so they are relatively maintenance free. In the South and West, they make an excellent ground cover for the cooler months. 'Summer Showers' was the first true ivy-leaved geranium developed for propagation by seed (it and other seed-started cultivars are

Pelargonium peltatum
ivy-leaved geranium

Geraniaceae—**geranium family**
Height and spread: trailing stems, to about 3 ft. long

Excellent for hanging baskets and window boxes, ivy-leaved geraniums are too brittle-stemmed for use in bedding displays. (Photo by Michael A. Ruggiero.)

commonly available as plants at local nurseries or by mail order). The colors range from pink, red, lavender, magenta, and pink, to near white. The Breakaway series is named for the plants' habit of "breaking" (sprouting shoots from the base of the plants), which means that these cultivars branch without pinching. These cultivars are excellent in baskets, and 'Breakaway Salmon' and 'Breakaway Red' perform better at high temperatures than do most other ivy-leaved geraniums.

PESTS AND DISEASES See Pelargonium × hortorum.

Pennisetum setaceum 'Rubrum'
annual fountain grass

Poaceae—grass family
height: 2 ft. to 4 ft.; spread: 2 ft. to 4 ft.

A fountain of maroon foliage and arching flower stalks, this annual pennisetum contributes texture as well as color. (Photo by Mobee Weinstein.)

❧ **Unlike most of the other fountain grasses,** which are perennial throughout most of the United States, this species is perennial only in the warmest parts of the country (Zones 9 to 11), and an annual everywhere else. This vigorous pennisetum also differs from most of its relatives in that it flowers throughout the growing season, whereas the other, hardier species bloom only in late summer. Its foliage is outstanding, a beautiful maroon to reddish color.

Pennisetum setaceum is native to Africa. Although it adapts well to American gardens, it introduces a hint of the exotic with its vivid color, graceful mounded profile, and delicate, arching flower spikes.

START Easiest to start with nursery-grown plants. Thereafter, propagate by dividing over-wintered stock, in the spring.

GARDEN USES In a border or bed, annual fountain grass provides a striking contrast to the blossoms of other annuals. A mature plant has presence; it is large enough to assert itself in the back of the border or as the centerpiece of a bed, and it provides a startling vertical accent in a carpet bedding display. When cut and dried, it makes a handsome addition to dried flower arrangements.

Annual pennisetum also makes a great plant for a large container (it will quickly overwhelm a small pot).

CULTURE For the most intense color, plant annual fountain grass in full sun. In a lightly shaded spot, the plant's leaf color will not be as vibrant, and it will bear fewer flowers, but even so, it will be a standout. This plant prefers soil that is well drained but slightly moist.

Deadheading is optional. As the maroon to pink flower spikes fade, they change to a light brown. If you like this effect, you can leave the spikes intact. However, in regions where this grass is perennial, it tends to self-seed and may become a weed. In these areas, conscientious deadheading will save you much stooping and pulling later on.

You can preserve plants from year to year by digging them in the fall before the first heavy frost, potting them up (dividing them at this point if they are too large), and then overwintering them indoors in well-drained but moisture-retentive potting mix. Set the rescued plants into the sunniest location in your home and keep them warm. Indoors, the leaves of overwintering plants usually turn green and remain that way until you put them outside the following spring, when they will turn maroon again. You can divide these survivors when you plant them out (if you haven't already done so) to increase your stock.

Where Pennisetum setaceum is a perennial, treat it like any other perennial grass—lift plants in spring, divide, and replant them.

It's easiest to buy this grass in the form of young container-grown plants. Raising your own seedlings is a slow process, and the plants that result will not be uniform in appearance. However, if you wish to start from seed, sow indoors, 2 to 4 months before last frost. Seeds should germinate in 3 to 4 weeks at 70° to 75°F, but germination and seedling growth is slow—plants do not attain much size until their second year.

GARDENER´S CHOICE Pennisetum 'Burgundy Giant' is taller (to 6 ft.) and more upright than 'Rubrum', and its leaves are approximately twice as wide.

PESTS AND DISEASES Root rot may afflict plants grown on poorly drained soils. Otherwise, this grass is generally pest free.

Petunia x *hybrida*
hybrid petunia

Solanaceae—**nightshade family**
height: 10 in. to 18 in.; spread: 12 in. to 16 in.

Petunias of any kind make excellent container plants. (Photo by Michael A. Ruggiero.)

✂ **You'd be hard pressed to find** another annual as dependable and versatile as this one. Actually, in frost-free climates, petunias are perennial and bloom year-round, which makes them outstanding "virtual annuals" for the rest of us. The only annoying aspect of petunias is that the cultivars that catalogs describe as blue are actually purple. If you want a true blue, order cultivars that are advertised as light blue or sky blue.

The name petunia derives from petun, the Brazilian word for tobacco, and in fact the petunia is a member of the tobacco family and its leaves look like small tobacco leaves. The modern hybrids are believed to spring from crosses of several species, notably Petunia integrifolia and P. axillaris. Gardeners generally divide the hybrids into two classes: multifloras and grandifloras.

Multiflora petunias usually produce smaller blossoms than the grandiflora types but bear more flowers per plant. This, in combination with the multifloras' compact growth, makes them better adapted for bedding displays. Multifloras also tend to be more tolerant of wind and rain. In contrast, the grandifloras bear larger but fewer flowers, and the plants generally have a sprawling or cascading form, which makes them ideal for baskets, window boxes, and containers.

SOW Indoors, 10 to 12 weeks before last frost date. Seeds are extremely tiny; do not cover them. Mixing the seeds with fine sand will make sowing easier and distribution more uniform. Germination will occur in 7 to 12 days at 70° to 75°F.

GARDEN USES Petunias bloom extravagantly, whether planted in baskets, window boxes, containers, beds, or borders.

CULTURE These flowers tolerate a wide range of conditions, even the heat and polluted air of inner-city summers.

Petunia seeds are tiny and difficult to distribute evenly over the seed starting mix when sown. Often, seed companies "pellet" petunia seeds, coating them to make them easier to see and handle. If you should purchase a packet of unpelleted seed, use a salt shaker to sow it.

For best results, plant petunias in full sun to partial shade. They will grow in areas of deeper shade but won't bear enough flowers to make them an asset to the garden. Petunias require well-drained soil and will even tolerate sandy, poor soils.

Feed your petunias monthly with a balanced fertilizer, and deadhead regularly to keep them blooming continuously. Traditionally, petunia plants had to be pinched back while young to promote branching and a compact, attractive profile, but this pattern of growth is inherent in most of the newer cultivars. Even so, you may still need to practice this sort of pruning later on in the season.

By late summer, the stems are likely to grow lanky, flowering only at the tips. Cut such stems back by half to force the plants back into bushier growth with a renewed emphasis on flowering. You can also take a drastic approach and cut back all of a plant's stems at once. This treatment is effective, but it will leave that area of the garden looking rather stricken for a few days until the plants recover. Or, you can extend the process by cutting back a stem or two on each plant every few days. Such gradual pruning allows the plants to keep flowering through the pruning process, but it slows the rejuvenation.

You can also opt to avoid pruning altogether, and instead plan for your petunias' degeneration by interplanting vining annuals among them when you first install the display. The foliage of the spreading vines will gradually cover the ratty petunia stems but still allow the petunia blossoms to peep through.

As a last option, you can grow one of the new petunia cultivars that are naturally compact and never need deadheading or pinching back.

GARDENER´S CHOICE The number of petunia cultivars is overwhelming, but the following are outstanding: The Wave series bears 3-in. pink, rose, purple, or lilac flowers on branches that rise to a height of just 6 in. and spread 3 ft. to 4 ft. without any pinching or deadheading. These cultivars perform well in every situation but are ideal for baskets. The Supercascade series bears large, 4-in.- to 5-in.-wide grandiflora flowers in a wide range of colors. The plants are more compact than most other basket or window box types. Storm series plants bear 3-in. to 4-in. flowers that bear up outstandingly well in rainy weather and rebound quickly after storms. The multiflora Carpet series offers flowers of all colors on heat-resistant plants. They are excellent for southern gardens. The Celebrity series cultivars bear $3^1/_2$-in. flowers of all colors on showy 8-in. to 10-in. plants that seem to bloom forever. 'Celebrity Sky Blue' is among the most fragrant of all petunias. 'Supertunias' and 'Surfinia' petunias are making an impact in American gardens with their superior vigor and their tendency to bloom continuously without much care. 'Million Bells' is a group of mini-flowered petunias that produce 1-in. to 2-in. blooms on matlike growth. These particular cultivars do not come true from seed and must be grown from cuttings.

PESTS AND DISEASES Botrytis and tobacco mosaic are the most common diseases; aphids and whiteflies are common insect pests. Slugs are likely to attack in a shady spot.

⚘ **This subtropical plant** was a favorite of Victorian carpet bedders and is winning renewed popularity in the annual garden with its striking and varied foliage effects. Depending on the cultivar, New Zealand flax ranges in height from 12 in. to as much as 15 ft.; all bear leaves that look like those of some giant iris. The foliage is the plant's real attraction; flowers rarely appear except on specimens that have been planted in the ground in a warm climate and left undisturbed for a period of years.

Phormium means "basket" in Latin, and it refers to the Maoris' (the native New Zealanders') use of the fibrous leaves for weaving those receptacles. A native of Australasia, phormium requires frost-free conditions, but as it does not thrive in the overwhelming heat of a truly tropical climate, it is considered a subtropical plant.

In the mildest regions of the southwestern United States, New Zealand flax develops almost treelike proportions. Elsewhere, it makes a striking bedding or container plant.

All except the most vigorous cultivars can be wintered over indoors, in a sunny, cool room. The fastest-growing phormiums, unfortunately, often become too large to accommodate in this fashion. Better nurseries are selling the dwarf cultivars now, and these are becoming a staple of container gardeners everywhere.

START Grow from purchased plants, or divide large plants in early spring.

GARDEN USES Phormiums' height and bold form make them unusually effective as visual punctuation in bedding designs and mixed borders.

CULTURE Outdoors, phormiums prefer a well-drained, porous soil that is also rich in organic material. Place the plants according to their foliage type: green- or darker-leaved cultivars thrive in full sun to partial shade, but variegated phormiums need a partially shaded spot, at least where summers are hot.

GARDENER'S CHOICE 'Atropurpurea' is a large cultivar with 2-in.- to 3-in.-wide, 6-ft.- to 9-ft.-long bronze-purple leaves. It forms a vase-shaped plant that is good for extremely large containers. 'Aureum' bears leaves marked with broad yellow stripes. 'Apricot Queen' has foliage that is striped green and yellow and touched with apricot; it grows 2 ft. to 3 ft. tall. 'Bronze Baby' is smaller, reaching a height of just 2 ft. to 4ft., and has burgundy foliage. 'Flamingo' is an excellent container plant, with foliage that is green and yellow, and pink on the inside. 'Yellow Wave' has leaves that are striped yellow and green, and are similar to those of 'Apricot Queen' but without the apricot coloration.

PESTS AND DISEASES None serious, but mealybugs may come indoors on overwintering plants and then spread to other houseplants.

⚘ **The portulaca's modest, warm-colored,** rose-like flowers are attractive, but not spectacular, and the individual blossoms are short-lived. But this plant compensates with an outstanding virtue: It thrives in spots where most other flowers won't grow at all. A native of the tropical portions of Brazil, Argentina, and Uruguay, portulaca relishes heat and sun. Its succulent leaves and stems, which really do spread into something like a mat of coarse moss, are a storehouse for moisture, so that portulaca flourishes even on dry, poor soils.

Phormium tenax
New Zealand flax

Agavaceae—agave family
height: to 15 ft.; spread: 1 ft. to 10 ft.

New Zealand flax makes a bold contrast to purple-leaved *Setcreasea* and green Tolmeia; all three are traditionally houseplants. (Photo by Michael A. Ruggiero.)

Portulaca grandiflora
rose moss

Portulacaceae—purslane family
height: 4 in. to 8 in.; spread: 12 in. to 14 in.

An excellent ground cover for hot, dry sites, portulaca also makes an outstanding living mulch. (Photo by Judi Rutz; © The Taunton Press.)

This plant's botanical name derives from the Latin word *portula*, which means "little gate." Linnaeus, the Swedish botanist who invented the scientific system for naming plants and animals, gave this name to the portulaca because the mouths of the seed capsules swing open as if hinged.

SOW Outdoors, after soil has warmed; mix seed with fine sand for more even distribution. Or sow indoors, 10 weeks before the last frost date in the North and 8 weeks in the South. Germination occurs in 7 to 10 days at 70° to 75°F. Sow in pots, packs, or plugs, depositing 20 to 25 seeds per pot. Do not cover seeds.

GARDEN USES Portulaca is an excellent plant for sandy seaside locations and for rock gardens. It is also one of the best annuals for sowing as a living mulch, to cover the earth beneath roses or other shrubs.

CULTURE Portulaca grows well in any well-drained, sunny spot. The blossoms are true sun worshippers—they close at the onset of rainy weather and in the evening as the sun goes down. If planted in the shade, the plant's vigor diminishes and though it may set flower buds, they won't open.

Portulaca's tiny, steel gray seeds look like iron filings. Before you sow them, mix them with clean sand to make even distribution easier. They can be sown directly where they are to grow outdoors, when the soil has warmed in spring. Sow portulacas when it's time to plant corn and peppers in your area.

If you start your portulacas indoors, sow the seeds into 3-in. pots, allowing 20 or so seeds per pot. A solitary seedling won't produce a substantial-looking plant, but many together make a more handsome tuft of "moss." Take care not to overwater the seedlings—they are prone to damping off.

Whether you start your portulacas indoors or out, one sowing is likely to be all you'll ever have to make. For these plants often self-sow, returning as volunteers year after year. Because portulaca roots are shallow, these self-sown seedlings aren't likely to compete with your other plants for soil, moisture, and nutrients.

GARDENER´S CHOICE Portulacas may be purchased as seed or as pots of ready-to-plant seedlings, and they are marketed both as individual cultivars that bear flowers of a single color and as mixtures that bear flowers of various hues.

Sundial cultivars bear flowers in a wide range of colors. They open earlier in the morning and stay open further into the evening than those of most other cultivars. Sundial portulacas also flower 2 weeks earlier, and in locations with less sunlight, than most other cultivars. 'Swanlake' doesn't exceed a height of 6 in. and bears pure white, fully double flowers. Sundance Mixed is a popular series of cultivars bearing fully double red, yellow, white, and orange flowers that, like Sundial, remain open well into the evening.

PESTS AND DISEASES Portulacas are basically pest free, but the plants may rot if grown in poorly drained soils.

❧ **Originally from tropical Africa,** the castor bean plant has long been valued for the medicinal properties of its seed, the source of castor oil, and it is also used in the manufacture of soap and varnish. Gardeners have come to admire it for its bold, striking foliage, and for the tropical effect it can give to a border or other planting.

This is a plant with presence. In its native habitat, it may form a 30- to 40-ft. tree. Even when grown as an annual in North America, castor bean is likely to tower above your head, though there are shorter cultivars that make good plants for containers.

SOW Indoors, 4 to 5 weeks before last frost date. Soak seeds in warm water for 24 hours or scarify with a file before sowing to aid germination. Sow in individual 3-in. pots; do not let plants get pot bound. Germination will occur in 10 to 20 days at 70° to 75°F. Outdoors, do not sow until well after the last frost date. Be careful when storing seeds—they are deadly poisonous.

GARDEN USES In containers or in the ground, castor beans draw the eye as a focal point; their height can be used to advantage for an effective, fast-growing screen.

CULTURE The castor oil plant requires full sun and well-drained (but slightly moist), fertile soil. It loves heat and moisture, and if given the right conditions, selected cultivars may grow to 15 ft. and bear leaves up to 3 ft. across.

The large leaves are cut into fingerlike lobes; those of some cultivars are tinted red, while other cultivars bear green leaves with white veins. The taller cultivars tend to shed their bottom leaves as they reach upward; interplanting cannas among the castor beans, or planting other tall annuals in front, will mask the unattractive bare stems.

The petal-less flowers may be creamy yellow or red. Borne in upright panicles, they open in succession from the bottom of the flower head to the top. The blossoms are replaced by spiny capsules, each of which contains three large seeds that look like mottled brown and tan beetles or ticks (the name Ricinus is the Latin word for tick).

The seeds are highly toxic and the seed capsules should not be left to ripen on the plant, for as they do, they split, ejecting the seeds with such force that they may sail 20 ft. from the plant. This scattering of poisonous "beans" can pose a real hazard to children.

GARDENER'S CHOICE 'Carmencita' reaches 5 ft. to 6 ft. and bears bronze leaves and bright red flower buds; 'Carmencita Pink' is similar but bears pinkish flowers and seed capsules; 'Sanguineus' reaches a height of 8 ft., and bears large, reddish, 1-ft. to 2-ft. leaves; 'Zanzibarensis' grows 10 ft. to 15 ft., with large, 3-ft. green leaves.

PESTS AND DISEASES Generally trouble-free.

❧ **The cultivated forms of the Texas sage** are fairly recent arrivals in the annual garden. In its native range, which stretches from South Carolina to Florida, and westward and south to Texas, Mexico, and the tropical Americas, this species is a perennial, but north of that region, it behaves like an annual.

Ricinus communis
castor oil plant, castor bean

Euphorbiaceae—**spurge family**
height: 5 ft. to 12 ft.; spread: 2 ft. to 4 ft.

No other plant has the exotic flamboyance of castor beans. (Photo by Michael A. Ruggiero.)

Salvia coccinea
Texas sage

Lamiaceae—**mint family**
height: 18 in. to 30 in.; spread: 12 in. to 18 in.

Texas sage's delicate appearance belies this plant's durability. (Photo by Michael A. Ruggiero.)

Texas sage differs from the more familiar scarlet sage (Salvia splendens) in that it produces a compact, well-branched plant that is bushy even without pinching. The Texas sage also blooms continuously from spring to frost, even when you forget to deadhead.

The name salvia derives from the Latin word salveo, which means "save," and it refers to the medicinal properties exhibited by some members of this genus.

SOW Indoors, 8 to 10 weeks before last frost date. Germination occurs in 10 to 15 days at 70° to 75°F. Do not cover seeds. After germination, grow seedlings at 60° to 65°F.

GARDEN USES Texas sage makes a colorful, carefree addition to beds, borders, and container plantings.

CULTURE Texas sage is easily grown from seed, or from plants purchased at local nurseries. The plant's open, lacy appearance gives the impression that it is delicate and finicky, but in fact it tolerates a wide range of conditions, thriving in sun or shade, drought and heat, and in all types of soils except extremely wet ones.

GARDENER'S CHOICE 'Lady in Red', the best red-flowered cultivar, bears deep scarlet flowers on 20-in. to 24-in. plants, and it blooms earlier in the season than most other cultivars. 'Cherry Blossom' and 'Coral Nymph' are sold as distinct cultivars but are in fact the same. They exhibit a habit of growth similar to that of 'Lady in Red', but they usually grow slightly taller, reaching a height of 24 in. to 26 in. The flowers have white upper lips and pink lower lips. 'Snow Nymph' and 'Lactea' are two names for the same white-flowered version of 'Cherry Blossom'. Unlike the white-flowered forms of the scarlet sage (Salvia splendens), whose blossoms are actually cream colored, the flowers of 'Snow Nymph' and 'Lactea' are a true, pure white.

PESTS AND DISEASES Seedlings are prone to damping off, and mildew may attack the foliage of mature plants. Aphids are the principal insect pest; slugs also relish Texas sage.

Salvia farinacea
mealycup sage

Lamiaceae—**mint family**
height: 12 in. to 36 in.; spread: 12 in. to 18 in.

The mealycup sage is a hardy perennial in its native range in Texas and New Mexico. In the rest of North America, however, it is better regarded as an unusually rewarding low-maintenance annual. An adaptable, tolerant plant, it flourishes in a wide range of soils and exposures, blooming continuously almost without care from early summer to the first fall frost.

SOW Indoors, 12 weeks before last frost date; do not cover seeds. Germination comes in 12 to 16 days at 70° to 75°F. Grow seedlings at 60° by day and 55°F by night. In areas where this plant is perennial, it may be propagated by taking 3-in. to 4-in. tip cuttings from the stems 6 weeks before plants are needed for the garden.

GARDEN USES Use this self-sufficient annual in both informal and formal bedding plans, in containers, and as a source of cut and dried flowers. Its blossoms attract butterflies, bees, and hummingbirds (the latter prefer its red-flowered relatives).

CULTURE An adaptable, tolerant plant, mealycup sage flourishes in a hot, sunny spot but also grows well in partial shade. It prefers well-drained soil with some organic content, but it also tolerates poorish, sandy soils.

Like the Texas sage, mealycup sage is self-branching, which means that you don't need to pinch it back when you plant it into the garden. Deadheading spent flowers will make the plant look neater, but it isn't a requirement.

Feed plants lightly with a balanced fertilizer, but avoid overfeeding or applying high-nitrogen fertilizers. This sort of mistaken kindness causes lanky growth with weak stems.

Where it is perennial, mealycup sage may self-seed. In areas where winters are marked by frost but are relatively brief, you may dig up your mealycup sage plants, cut them back and pot them up, and then replant them in the garden as the weather warms once again.

GARDENER'S CHOICE 'Argent' bears silvery white blossoms in 6-in. to 8-in. spikes on strong upright stems that reach a height of 20 in. to 26 in. 'Blue Bedder', reaching a height of 24 in. to 26 in., is the tallest of the blue cultivars, but it has become difficult to find, having been replaced in the nursery trade by the shorter, more colorful 'Victoria'. 'Cirrus', which grows to only 12 in. to 14 in., is the shortest of the pure-white flowered cultivars. Of the blue-flowered cultivars, 'Mina' (also sold as 'Rhea') is the shortest that is generally available. It grows about 12 in. to 14 in. high and bears spikes of brilliant blue blossoms. 'Strata' was a 1996 All-America Selection. It produces unusual two-toned flower spikes of white and blue on 18-in. to 24-in. stems. 'Victoria' remains the most popular and the most widely planted of the mealycup sages. It is hard to beat the intense, violet-blue of its flowers, which are borne plentifully from spring to frost on compact 18-in. to 20-in. plants. It is also the most weather tolerant of the named cultivars. 'White Porcelain', another white-flowered cultivar, grows to a height of 18 in., which makes it intermediate between the shorter 'Cirrus' and the taller 'Argent'.

PESTS AND DISEASES Seedlings are prone to damping off, mildew may attack the foliage of mature plants. Whiteflies and slugs are the most troublesome pests.

Rewarding and undemanding, mealycup sage is an invaluable addition to the annual garden. (Photo by Michael A. Ruggiero.)

Salvia leucantha
Mexican sage

Lamiaceae—**mint family**
height: 1 ft. to 3 ft.; spread: 2 ft. to 3 ft.

Mexican sage flowers in fall, providing contrast to chrysanthemums. (Photo by Michael A. Ruggiero.)

❧ **Like many of the sages,** this plant is a perennial in its native range, Mexico, actually forming a woody subshrub or shrub there. Because of its sensitivity to frost, however, Mexican sage is best grown as an annual in all except the warmest American gardens. It prefers a well-drained soil and full sun; satisfy these fairly minor requirements and this plant will bloom handsomely as the days grow shorter in the fall.

START Take tip cuttings from overwintered stock 1 to 3 months before time for planting out; root cuttings in peat and sand. Transplant rooted cuttings into individual pots, and pinch off growing tips to promote bushier plants.

GARDEN USES In the garden, Mexican sage makes an unusual and attractive edging plant if you keep pinching back the growing tips periodically until late summer. Interplanted among the fall chrysanthemums, Mexican sage adds height and contrast, relieving the mounded carpet that an unmixed planting of mums makes. Or, for a more spectacular show, pack the Mexican sages in together.

Mexican sage makes an excellent cut flower, and if the stems are hung up in a warm spot, they'll turn into wonderful dried flowers.

CULTURE Though Mexican sage normally grows to a height of 3 ft., it will reach 5 ft. or more if you set the plants less than 24 in. apart (measuring from center of plant to center of plant). Planted on centers of 12 in. to 16 in., they'll grow taller still but will probably need the support of a stake to remain upright.

To provide plants for next year's garden, dig one up before a hard frost, transfer it to a pot, cut it back to a height of 6 in. to 11 in., and put it in a cool (55° to 60°F), sunny location. It will bloom through the winter, and after a few weeks indoors, new shoots will sprout from the lower stems and the roots. Snip off the larger of these shoots to root as cuttings for next year's planting. When the danger of frost is past in the spring, transplant the original parent plant back into the garden and you may get a season of spring blooms from it, too.

GARDENER´S CHOICE There are two different varieties of Mexican sage. The one that bears flowers with violet calyces and white corollas is the more common. The other variety, which is harder to find, bears all-violet flowers.

PESTS AND DISEASES Generally trouble-free.

Salvia splendens
Scarlet sage

Lamiaceae—mint family
height: 6 in. to 36 in.; spread: 10 in. to 18 in.

Partial shade and rich, humusy soil are secrets to a truly splendid display of scarlet sage. (Photo by Michael A. Ruggiero.)

❧ **This is one of the most used**—and most abused—annual flowers. Almost invariably, gardeners set out their scarlet sage in a bedding display in the full, pitiless sun. By midsummer, the plants look very tired. As they age, the flowers fade, the sun bleaching the blossoms at the bottom of the spikes before the upper buds even open.Fortunately, this problem is easily remedied: Plant scarlet sage where it will receive partial shade, especially during the hottest part of the afternoon. Just transferring the plants from one part of the yard to another will help to keep the blossoms fresh far longer and preserve their naturally vibrant colors.

SOW Indoors, 6 to 8 weeks before last frost date. Do not cover seeds. Germination occurs in 10 to 14 days at 70° to 75°F. Keep seedlings warm, 60°F at night.

GARDEN USES Compact and neat in its growth, and often uncompromisingly bright in its blossom color, the scarlet sage is well suited to formal floral displays, especially carpet beds. Planted in smaller groupings, it can also blend into an informal border, and it is one of the rare annuals that performs well in the shade garden.

CULTURE For best results, give scarlet sage partial shade and rich, humusy, well-drained soil. Feed the plants once a month with a dilute, water-soluble, complete fertilizer. Pinch the seedlings before you plant them out into the garden to encourage basal branching for bushier plants.

Deadhead to keep the plants looking neat. For maximum flower production, remove each flower spike when two-thirds of the flowers on it have begun to wither. If you wait for the last blossom to pass away, the blossoms lower on the spike, the ones that opened first, will already have set seeds.

GARDENER´S CHOICE 'Van Houtteii' is unusually imposing—it grows to a height of 4 ft. and blooms freely from early summer to frost. It bears rosy red flowers set into burgundy calyces. The Sizzler series offers a wide range of colors, including white, pink, lavender, plum, purple, and salmon, as well as the classic red and bicolors. Plants grow a compact 10 in. to 12 in. and are earlier to bloom than most other scarlet sages. The Salsa series is a group of fast-growing and very weather-tolerant dwarf cultivars with flowers in shades of rose, salmon, and scarlet, including some bicolors. 'Flamingo' is a compact, 6-in. cultivar that bears flowers of an unusual coral/salmon, with pale edges. The heat-resistant Hotline series cultivars grow to 15 in. high and 10 in. across, with flowers in the usual range of colors. 'Bonfire' bears scarlet flowers on 24-in. plants.

PESTS AND DISEASES Whiteflies are attracted to scarlet sage, and plants grown in shady spots are prone to slug damage.

❧ **In one of the incongruities** typical of botanical nomenclature, this Mexican wildflower ended up with an Italian name, for its European discoverer named it in honor of Frederico Sanvitali, an eighteenth-century Professore. The common name, creeping zinnia, is equally misleading, for Sanvitalia procumbens is no more a zinnia than it is a paesan. The flowers are small but glorious: small purple discs, surrounded by coronets of golden, petallike rays. It is, however, low and trailing, growing just 6 in. to 8 in. high.

SOW Outdoors, after all danger of frost is past. Or sow indoors, 4 to 6 weeks before the last frost. Do not cover seeds. Germination comes in 7 to 14 days at 70°F. Sanvitalia resents transplanting, so do that while seedlings are still quite young.

GARDEN USES Creeping zinnia makes an excellent ground cover, and a convenient edger for a bed or border. It also looks fine spilling over the rim of a tub or hanging basket.

CULTURE Unlike most other annuals, creeping zinnia thrives in hot and humid conditions; it is extremely tolerant of poor, dry soil as well. Indeed, this plant flourishes in almost any soil, except one that is constantly wet or very fertile. It prefers a spot in full sun, but it will grow in partial shade, though it may form a looser, more sprawling plant there.

Because sanvitalia sends a taproot down into the soil, it does not take well to transplanting. The easiest and safest way to grow creeping zinnia is to wait until the soil has warmed and the danger of frost is past. Then sow the seeds right into the garden.

If you do decide to start the plants indoors, sow the seeds no earlier than 4 to 6 weeks before the last frost date. Keeping sanvitalia seedlings in a pot for a longer time will stunt their root systems, and the plants will never grow well.

GARDENER'S CHOICE 'Gold Braid' is an old but still-popular cultivar with rays of a paler yellow than those of the species type. 'Mandarin Orange' is by far the most common cultivar at local garden centers. It reaches 8 in. high and 12 in. to 16 in. across. Unlike other sanvitalias, its flowers are orange rather than yellow. They measure a full inch across and are semidouble.

PESTS AND DISEASES Usually pest free, but stem rot may attack plants grown in wet soils.

Sanvitalia procumbens
creeping zinnia

Asteraceae—**daisy family**
height: 6 in. to 8 in.; spread: 8 in. to 16 in.

Creeping zinnia thrives in poor, dry soils and in humidity and heat. (Photo by Michael A. Ruggiero.)

Scaevola x *aemula*
scaveola, blue fan flower

Goodeniaceae—**goodenia family**
height and spread: prostrate or
upward-reaching stems to 15 in. long

Its tolerance for a wide range of soils, generous bloom, and easy maintenance have made scaveola an annual star. (Photo by Michael A. Ruggiero.)

Relatively new to the market, blue fan flower hit the ground running about a decade ago when it was "discovered" by the nursery industry. Within a few years, it had become one of the most sought-after flowers on the market. What is the secret of the blue fan flower's success? The flowers are unusual and appealing, and the plant thrives with little care. In addition, it is remarkably versatile, for it shines in any situation that will support a sun-loving annual. It performs as well in Florida as it does in New York and California, and gardeners continue to find new uses for it all the time.

It is the only horticultural success story in a large genus. Scaevola x aemula is the scaevola to most gardeners, yet there are about 100 more species found in Australia and the Pacific Islands, and even one, Scaevola plumeri, that is native to the Florida dunes. These other scaevolas may be used for erosion control or as windscreens, but little else.

The name scaevola derives from the Latin word scaeva, which means "left-handed" or "one-sided," and it refers to the fan-shaped or handlike spread of the petals. The unusual flowers are unlike those of any other annual.

START Purchase plants from a nursery or garden center. Thereafter, take stem cuttings from overwintered plants in early spring, and root them in sand or a mixture of peat and sand; bottom heat hastens rooting.

GARDEN USES Scaevola shines in hanging baskets, containers, and beds, and it works well as a ground cover.

CULTURE Blue fan flower is happiest in moist, well-drained soil that is rich in organic matter. However, it tolerates a wide range of soils, including those that are very sandy. If you grow this plant in a dryish, sandy soil, however, take care to keep the area around the roots moist. Scaevolas wilt when they dehydrate, and after a few such episodes, they may not recover.

Maintenance is easy. Pinch back the growing tips of young plants or rooted cuttings before transplanting them into the garden, to promote bushiness. Feed the plants on a regular basis with a balanced fertilizer.

Deadheading is not necessary—blue fan flower doesn't set seed, and it keeps on blooming until killed by autumn frosts. When fall frosts threaten your scaevolas, dig up a plant or two, cut them back, pot them up, and bring them into the house to overwinter indoors. Place them in a sunny window, and they'll flower most of the winter. In very early spring, you can root cuttings taken from the new growth on your windowsill survivors. You may find it simpler, however, to purchase new plants and start fresh.

GARDENER´S CHOICE 'Blue Wonder' is the most popular cultivar. It bears deep, sky blue flowers marked with a white eye, and it is sold in baskets and pots. 'Petite Wonder' has smaller flowers and is not as vigorous a grower as some other cultivars. 'Outback Purple Fan' bears bluish purple flowers with a yellow eye, and it is especially well suited to use as a ground cover.

There are also white-flowered cultivars, but they usually produce undersized flowers and aren't as showy as the blue- and purple-flowered cultivars.

PESTS AND DISEASES None serious.

Schizanthus spp.
poor man's orchid, butterfly flower
Solanaceae—**nightshade family**
height: 10 in. to 4 ft.; spread: 8 in.
to 15 in.

The distinctive charm of its blossoms and the ease with which it is raised from seed make poor man's orchid a garden standby in cool, moist seasons. (Photo by Michael A. Ruggiero.)

In coastal areas of the Northwest and the upper Northeast, this unique annual has long been a staple of late spring to early summer gardens. The two common names indicate the reason for its enduring popularity: The colorful winged flowers may take only a matter of weeks to raise from seed, but they have the exotic delicacy of orchid blossoms or even a butterfly come down to roost. These floral curiosities are borne profusely on plants that range from the 10-in. to 15-in. height of the modern cultivars to the towering 4 ft. of some of the species types.

All the schizanthus species are native to Chile. Their botanical name comes from the Greek roots schizo, "to divide," and anthos, "flower," and it refers to the flowers' deeply cut mouths.

SOW For early bedding (in late April or early May), sow indoors 14 weeks before transplants are needed. Sow again in midsummer for fall use. Do not cover seed, but place pots in the dark for best germination, which occurs in 8 to 14 days at 60° to 65°F. Grow seedlings at 55° to 60°F.

GARDEN USES The more compact forms are the easiest to integrate into the garden, where they serve equally well as container or bedding plants. As you might expect, poor man's orchid also makes an outstanding cut flower.

CULTURE This annual requires cool temperatures to flourish but cannot tolerate frost. In the Deep South, plant it in mid fall to bloom in winter or early spring; farther north, it is reserved for either spring or fall.

In especially temperate climates, where winters are frost free and summers cool, such as the coastal regions of northern California, Washington, and Oregon, poor man's orchid may be sown right into the garden in early spring, and the seedlings thinned to a spacing of 12 in. between plants. Elsewhere, start plants indoors, 14 weeks before the seedlings are wanted for transplanting into the garden.

Do not cover the seeds when sowing, and take care that the seedlings do not become potbound before you are ready to plant them out. When the plants feel their roots to be confined, they begin to bloom and will no longer grow larger. Pinch the young seedlings to encourage them to branch, and when you plant them out in the garden, give them a well-drained, humusy soil and a sunny, sheltered location. The taller-growing cultivars may need staking.

GARDENER'S CHOICE Schizanthus pinnatus is a 4-ft.-tall species that is the parent of the many newer purple- to violet-flowered cultivars. It is also a parent of Schizanthus x wisetonensis, a race of hybrids that have expanded the color range from purples to reds, whites, and pinks.

'Hit Parade', one of the most popular cultivars, is vigorous but compact, reaching a height of 12 in., and it bears flowers in a wide range of colors. Like the 15-in.-tall 'Disco', 'Hit Parade' is an excellent container plant. 'Star Parade' is even more compact, growing to just 6 in. to 8 in.; it makes an excellent edging or bedding plant. 'Angel Wings', the tallest of the hybrid cultivars, grows to 18 in. and bears $1^{1}/_{2}$-in.-wide flowers in a broad range of colors.

PESTS AND DISEASES Overwatering may cause the plants to rot; aphids are the most common insect pest.

Senecio cineraria
dusty miller

Asteraceae—daisy family
height: 8 in. to 30 in.; spread: 8 in.
to 10 in.

White-leaved dusty miller (upper right) makes a
strong contrast to red-leaved coleus and a white-
flowered zinnia in this container garden. (Photo
by Michael A. Ruggiero.)

❧ **Few names are as evocative as "dusty miller,"** for it summons up so clearly an image of the flour-dusted white foliage of these plants. Unfortunately, this is also an outstanding example of the pitfall of common names. Under the label of dusty miller, you may be sold a miscellaneous collection of plants—artemisias, lychnis, centaureas, or chrysanthemums, as well as the senecio we are describing here—and these plants have little in common other than their whitened foliage. On the other hand, the botanical name, once you get to know it, is every bit as descriptive and much less confusing. Senecio derives from the Latin word senex, which means "old man," a reference to the fluffy white hair of the seedheads. Cineraria means "ash," and is a reference to the whitened foliage.

Senecio cineraria, a native of the Mediterranean region, is the most common of the dusty millers, and you'll find it sold under cultivar names such as 'Silver Dust', 'Cirrus', and 'New Look'. All are primarily foliage plants, whose silvered leaves are cut into a variety of characteristic patterns.

SOW Indoors, 10 to 15 weeks before last frost. Do not cover seed. Germination occurs in 10 to 15 days at 72° to 75°F. Or propagate by stem cuttings taken in late spring or early summer from overwintered plants.

GARDEN USES Dusty millers are excellent choices for containers, beds, and borders, of either informal or formal design. The white foliage makes a good foil for the colors of intermingled flowers: It can tone down loud reds and oranges, and it works equally well to complement the softness of whites, blues, and pinks.

CULTURE These plants thrive in any average soil that is not habitually wet. The reflective, silvered surface of the leaves gives these plants the ability to withstand fierce sunlight, and they are exceptionally drought tolerant.

A situation with full sun is best for these plants, but some light or partial shade during the hottest part of the day won't hurt. Should the shade be any denser, though, your dusty millers are likely to grow tall and weak, and the leaves may lose their silvered appearance, reverting to ordinary green.

Pinch young plants lightly to promote bushiness. Later on, snip off any flowers as they appear, to encourage the plants to focus their energy on leaf growth. The flowers are small and not particularly ornamental, and in fact they rarely appear except on overwintered plants or plants in regions with exceptionally long growing seasons.

GARDENER´S CHOICE Senecio cineraria 'Silver Dust' is the old garden standby, a cultivar whose steel gray leaves are deeply cut, though not as deeply cut as 'Silver Lace'. Plants grow 10 in. to 12 in. tall, tolerate extremely wet and dry weather, and will often winter over outdoors in mild climates. 'Cirrus' and 'New Look' are relatively new cultivars, and both produce leaves that are broader and whiter than those of 'Silver Dust' and not as deeply cut. 'Cirrus' grows to 8 in., while 'New Look' reaches 8 in. to 10 in. and bears slightly larger leaves. 'Silver Queen' serves as a compromise between other Senecio cineraria cultivars. Its leaves aren't as finely cut as those of 'Silver Dust' but are more deeply cut than those of either 'Cirrus' or 'New

Look'. Another dusty miller that deserves mention is Chrysanthemum ptarmiciflorum 'Silver Lace', which has elegant, lacy, almost fernlike leaves borne on 6-in. to 8-in. stems.

PESTS AND DISEASES Plants growing in wet soils are likely to succumb to root and stem rots.

✤ **Although the sky blue flowers** of the Persian shield are not unattractive, they pale in comparison to the flamboyant foliage. The 8-in.-long leaves are as iridescent as a butterfly's wing, and the colors change as the light shifts, slipping from silver, to purple, to green on the upper leaf surface, while remaining deep maroon on the underside. It is this feature that makes this plant so outstanding in summer bedding designs and container plantings.

Anyway, when Persian shield is grown as a summertime annual, as it must be throughout most of North America, the foliage is likely to be its only attraction. Because the emergence of the flowers is keyed to shortening days, this frost-sensitive plant doesn't flower except in winter.

START Start with plants from the nursery. Thereafter, take stem cuttings in early spring. Pinch young plants to promote bushy growth.

GARDEN USES This plant's dark, richly colored foliage makes an exciting contrast to yellow flowers, and an elegant complement to red ones.

CULTURE Give Persian shield rich soil that is well drained but that stays evenly moist; adding a healthy dose of compost or leaf mold to the soil at planting time will ensure the right conditions. In regions with cool summers, this plant will thrive in full sun or partial shade, but in the South, it needs the protection of partial to full shade in summer.

Pinch back the growing tips of young plants to promote bushiness. Take care, though, not to continue pinching as the plants grow up, or they will produce weak branches with undersized leaves.

Persian shield is not normally grown from seed, but you can secure a supply of homegrown plants by digging a specimen or two, potting them up, and moving them indoors before the arrival of the first fall frost. Overwinter the plants on a sunny windowsill, where you may get to enjoy the elusive flowers, and move them back outdoors the following spring. Alternatively, you can take stem cuttings (see p. 119) in early fall and root them indoors in a mix of peat and sand, sand and perlite, or pure perlite. Overwinter the rooted cuttings indoors and then plant them out in springtime.

In either case, wait until the soil and weather have warmed before moving overwintered plants outside. As a native of tropical Myanmar, Persian shield is a tropical native that loves heat and humidity, and it will suffer if planted into cold soil or subjected to cold weather.

PESTS AND DISEASES Plants grown in soggy soil are likely to suffer from root rot. Slugs may attack plants grown in the shade.

Strobilanthes dyerianus
Persian shield

Acanthaceae—**acanthus family**
height: 2 ft. to 3 ft.; spread: 15 in. to 24 in.

Iridescent as a butterfly's wing, Persian shield foliage changes color with the shift of light. (Photo by Michael A. Ruggiero.)

Tagetes spp.
marigold

Asteraceae—daisy family
height: 8 in. to 60 in.; spread: 12 in. to 36 in.

'Snowball' is the newest generation of white African marigold. (Photo by Michael A. Ruggiero.)

❧ **Tough, self-sufficient, and irrepressibly cheerful,** these natives of Mexico are also surprisingly diverse. This is a matter of parentage. The popular garden types, and there are dozens, descend from three different species, each of which has its own distinct character.

The African marigolds (so called because they arrived in our gardens via Africa) are the offspring of *Tagetes erecta*, and their distinguishing characteristic is their imposing double blossoms. These range in size from relatively compact 2-in. to 3-in. pompoms, all the way up to giant blossoms fully 5 in. across that rival the garden mums and dahlias for visual impact. The plants that bear these tend to be husky—there are dwarf African marigolds that grow to a height of only 8 in. to 10 in., but many others reach a height of 3 ft. Their range of flower color is limited—only yellow, gold, and orange, with an occasional white. The African marigolds are also unusually tolerant of heat, and they thrive in poorish soils.

The French marigolds, which were bred in France from the species T. patula, are, as a rule, more compact than their "African" relatives, but they generally bloom more heavily. The flowers come in a wider range of colors, too, ranging from the familiar marigold yellows and oranges up through the reds and maroons. An additional virtue of the French marigolds is their natural tendency to branch: They form dense, bushy plants without the encouragement of pinching back.

Many gardeners who appreciate the look of marigolds dislike the pungent odor characteristic of the African and French types; for them, the signet marigold (T. tenuifolia) is the obvious choice. The attractive, fernlike foliage of this species has a fresh, citrus odor, and the yellow or orange flowers, though measuring just 2 in. across, are borne in quantity. The natural tendency of this species is to form a mound 2 ft. high and wide, but the specimens found at nurseries and garden centers usually belong to the Pumila strain, which is more compact, reaching a height of no more than 12 in.

SOW Indoors, 4 to 6 weeks before last frost date. Germination is in 5 to 7 days at 70°F. Grow at 60° to 65°F. Or sow outdoors after all danger of frost is past.

GARDEN USES The African marigolds work well in bedding and container displays. The long stems and outsized blossoms of the taller cultivars make them a good choice for cut flowers, or for the back of a border. French marigolds can also be used with good effect as individual plants, but their compact, consistent size makes them especially effective as an edging for a bed or border, and they are ideal for carpet bedding designs. The signet marigolds look most at home spilling out and over the top of a wall or the edge of a border or container. This species' fresh-scented flowers may be tossed into salads, so this marigold is an obvious choice for a potager.

CULTURE As a group, the marigolds are sun lovers, though the signet marigold also grows well in light shade. The African and French marigolds are particularly successful on well-drained, average to dryish soils; the signet marigold prefers an evenly moist one, though it must be well drained. One of the most useful characteristics of all these marigolds is their tolerance for poor soils. Indeed, a rich soil is likely to provoke them into soft, floppy growth with few flowers.

Regular deadheading keeps marigolds in bloom and enhances the plants' naturally neat appearance. The blossoms of the larger-flowered African cultivars soak up rain like sponges, and the weight of the water often causes flower stems to split off the plant at the base. This is a problem especially with the taller cultivars, whose long stems act like levers. One way to protect plants against this sort of damage is to plant seedlings $^1/_2$ in. to $^3/_4$ in. deeper in the garden soil than they have stood in their pots or cell packs. Roots will sprout from the buried parts of the stems, helping to anchor them more firmly.

GARDENER'S CHOICE Among the most outstanding of the African marigolds are the Lady series—3-in. to $3^1/_2$-in., fully double flowers, borne prolifically on strong 15-in. to 18-in. plants that never need staking: 'Gold Lady', golden yellow flowers; 'Deep Orange Lady', orange flowers; 'First Lady', clear yellow flowers; 'Primrose Lady', soft primrose yellow. The Crush series, $3^1/_2$-in. to 4-in. flowers on compact 10-in. to 12-in. plants: 'Papaya', gold flowers; 'Pumpkin', orange flowers; 'Pineapple', yellow flowers. The Discovery hybrids, compact, heat-resistant 8-in. to 10-in. plants that bear 2-in. to $2^1/_2$-in. orange or yellow flowers: Cultivars in this series are self-cleaning and do not need deadheading. The Inca series, heat-resistant, 14-in.-tall plants that bear up in rainy weather unusually well for a large-flowered cultivar, with orange, yellow, or gold flowers 4 in. to 5 in. across. 'Snowball' is a Burpee Seed Introduction that bears near white flowers on strong, healthy, 24-in. tall plants. 'French Vanilla' is a bushy plant, whose handsome white blossoms make outstanding cut flowers.

Outstanding French marigolds include the Bonanza series, early flowering, double 2-in. blooms on 10-in.-tall plants; the Bolero series, 'Yellow', 'Orange', and 'Gold Bolero', solid-colored semidouble flowers; 'Flame Bolero', red flowers with golden-orange centers; the Disco series, densely branched, 12-in.-tall plants with $2^1/_2$-in., single yellow, golden, orange, red, or bicolored flowers; the Bounty series, disease resistant, excellent in hot, humid locales, with 2-in. flowers on well-branched, 10-in.-tall plants; 'Mr. Majestic', bushy plants, normally 12 in. tall, but to 24-in. in hot climates, with single yellow flowers striped with mahogany red; 'Red Cherry', compact, 12-in. plants, $1^1/_2$-in. bright red, fully double flowers; 'Striped Marvel', one of the tallest, with plants 24 in. to 30 in., single flowers with red- and yellow-striped petals.

Excellent signet marigolds include the Gem series, plants to 24 in.: 'Lemon Gem', bright yellow flowers; 'Tangerine Gem', orange flowers. 'Lulu' is 12 in. tall with wide, bright yellow flowers.

PESTS AND DISEASES African and French marigolds are susceptible to spider mites, Japanese beetles, plant bugs, and slugs; botrytis blight, aster yellows, stem rot, and leaf spots are the most common diseases. Signet marigolds are generally trouble free.

❧ **In frost-free regions,** this tropical vine from Africa is a perennial, but in most of the United States it must be grown as an annual. Because it grows fairly quickly, it can climb to a height of 6 ft. to 8 ft. in the course of a summer, although 3 ft. to 5 ft. is a more realistic expectation in average conditions.

The plant's botanical name honors an eighteenth-century Swedish botanist, but the common name is more revealing, for it alludes to the dark "eye" that marks the centers of the flowers borne by the original species type vine and many, though not all, of the cultivated types.

Thunbergia alata
black-eyed Susan vine

Acanthaceae—**acanthus family**
height and spread: vine, to 6 ft.

Black-eyed Susan vine never looks better than when spilling over the edges of a hanging basket. (Photo by Michael A. Ruggiero.)

SOW Indoors, 6 to 8 weeks before last frost, or sooner. Use fresh seeds, as old seed doesn't store well; soak seeds 7 to 10 days before sowing. Germination occurs in 10 to 15 days at 70° to 75°F. Alternatively, propagate by stem cuttings rooted in a medium of peat and perlite at 70°F in early spring.

GARDEN USES Use this vine to fill baskets and containers, or let it sprawl over the soil as a ground cover. To grow it as a climber, you can train the vine up a trellis. Better yet, do as most nurseries do and provide a cylinder of wire mesh packed with sphagnum moss—the vine will root into this as it climbs.

Grow your black-eyed Susan vine in a container and you can easily overwinter it in a greenhouse. Then, in spring, propagate it by taking cuttings from the stem tips.

CULTURE The black-eyed Susan vine tolerates a wide range of well-drained soils, but it grows best in soil that is evenly moist and rich in organic matter. In cooler regions, plant it in full sun; in the hottest parts of the South, give it the protection of partial shade. Regular but light feedings of a balanced fertilizer will keep the plant in a vigorous condition.

GARDENER'S CHOICE Cultivars marked with dark eyes include 'Aurantiaca', with orange flowers; 'Alba', white; and 'Lutea', yellow. 'Bakeri' bears pure white flowers without the darker eye. The Susie series features cultivars that bear yellow, orange, or white flowers, with or without the eyes. Seeds of the different types may be purchased separately or in mixed packs.

PESTS AND DISEASES Mealybugs are likely to infest plants overwintered indoors.

Tibouchina urvilleana
glory bush

Melastomataceae—**melastoma family**
height and spread: small shrub to tree

❧ **Glory bush is the common name** of this tropical tree, and it's no exaggeration: The vibrant blossoms are the highlight of any garden fortunate enough to include them.

In frost-free regions, Tibouchina may be treated like any other ornamental tree or shrub, and in fact, this plant has escaped from gardens to become a part of the local flora in Hawaii. Where frost is a fact of life, the Tibouchina must be brought indoors during the cold months. For this reason, it is often grown in containers. Northern gardeners can also plant Tibouchina right into the soil of a garden bed, but if they do so, they must dig up the plant in the fall, prune the stems and branches back by half, and then pot it up so that it can be moved to a sheltered location.

A historical footnote: The botanical name Tibouchina is adapted from the vernacular name given this plant in its native Brazil. The specific name urvilleana honors a French explorer and naval officer Jules Sebastian Cesar Dumont d'Urville.

START Propagate by cuttings taken in the spring, summer, or fall. Root in peat/sand mix or pure sand, in a humid, shaded environment.

GARDEN USES As ground cover, shrub, or tree, this plant provides an exotic feast of velvety tropical foliage, rose-red buds, and rich purple blossoms. This versatile plant may be cultivated singly as a small shrub, massed as a 1-ft.- to 2-ft.-tall ground cover, or even trained into a standard, or tree form.

CULTURE Tibouchina takes its time in bearing flowers: Specimens planted out in spring commonly do not come into bloom until late summer or early fall. The plant requires a well-drained, neutral to slightly acid soil full of organic material so that it holds moisture. Any potting soil used for Tibouchina should also contain a good deal of organic material, and it should be mixed with coarse sand or perlite to ensure good drainage. In the pot or in the ground, the soil must not be overly rich. In particular, an abundance of nitrogen will cause overwintering plants to indulge in a splurge of weak growth. It's better not to encourage the growth of over-wintering plants until early spring. Then, the branch tips should be pinched back, to shape the plant and prompt new budding, and a biweekly schedule of fertilization begun. Use a balanced, water-soluble fertilizer with a formula such as 20-20-20 for this, but apply in a dilute form, mixing it at half the strength called for on the product label.

If you haven't room to overwinter a whole plant, you can perpetuate this year's Tibouchina with cuttings taken in the late summer or early fall. Select short (2 in. to 4 in.), firm shoots and slice them off beneath a node. Dip their bases in rooting hormone and stick them in a mix of 70 percent peat and 30 percent sand or perlite. Keep the cuttings in the shade and cover them with an upended glass jar or clear plastic bag to keep the humidity high around their leaves.

Patient gardeners can also grow Tibouchina from seed. For best results, the seed must be fresh and should be sown soon after it is collected from the parent. Sow the seeds in a sandy, peat-enriched soil, and keep the pots at 70°F until germination occurs. To promote bushiness, pinch out the growing tips of the seedlings after they sprout their third set of leaves.

PESTS AND DISEASES Whiteflies, mealybugs, and spider mites.

Velvety foliage and rich purple blossoms make *Tibouchina* a real "glory bush." (Photo by Michael A. Ruggiero.)

❧ **A hot, dry garden may be death to many annuals,** but it won't faze this southwestern relative of the common sunflower. The Mexican sunflower thrives in the strongest sun and blooms continuously, if deadheaded in a timely fashion.

Tithonia's daisylike blossoms measure 3 in. to 3¹/₂ in. in diameter, and they come in hot colors ranging from strong orange-scarlet to yellow, depending on the cultivar. Adding to the impact of this flower is its height: The plant may grow 6 ft. tall, though most of the cultivated types are smaller.

Although this plant might seem to deserve a name of Mexican origin, the botanist who first labeled it drew instead from ancient Roman mythology. His choice, however, was apt: He named the plant for a king of Troy, Tithonus, who was beloved of the dawn goddess Aurora. With a bit of imagination, you can indeed see the sun rise in the Tithonia's large and fiery discs.

SOW Indoors, 6 to 8 weeks before last frost date. Germination takes place in 5 to 10 days at 70° to 75°F. Outdoors, sow seeds after all danger of frost has passed.

GARDEN USES Grow Mexican sunflower in the middle to back of a bed or border. Butterflies find the flowers irresistible, and hummingbirds are attracted to the darker, orange-scarlet blossoms. Mexican sunflowers also make wonderful cut flowers, though the blossoms must be

Tithonia rotundifolia
Mexican sunflower

Asteraceae—**daisy family**
height: 2 ft. to 6 ft.; spread: 18 in. to 30 in.

Butterflies flock to Mexican sunflowers; hummingbirds are attracted to the dark-flowered, orange-scarlet cultivars. (Photo by Michael A. Ruggiero.)

conditioned after you bring them in from the garden. Recut the stems with a sharp pair of shears and then stand them in a bucket of warm water for several hours before arranging the flowers in a vase.

CULTURE Not fussy about soils, the Mexican sunflower adapts to even poor soils, as long as they are well drained. It does not like a rich loam; when exposed to an excess of nutrients, the Mexican sunflower is likely to shoot up to great heights, bearing masses of foliage but few flowers.

Aside from needing deadheading and a well-drained soil, this plant's only special cultural requirement is support for its tall stems. Plant the taller-growing cultivars in a spot where they will be sheltered from the wind, or stake the plants when they are halfway grown.

GARDENER'S CHOICE The most popular cultivar is 'Torch', which grows 4 ft. to 6 ft. tall and bears 3-in. to 3½-in. orange-scarlet flowers. 'Goldfinger' and 'Sundance' are more compact, reaching 2 ft. to 4 ft. 'Yellow Torch' bears golden yellow flowers on a 4-ft. to 6-ft. plant; the flowers of 'Aztec Sun' are a similar color but the plants stand only 4 ft. tall. 'Goldfinch' is a relatively new cultivar bearing 3-in.-wide, butterscotch yellow blossoms on compact, 3-ft. to 4-ft. plants.

PESTS AND DISEASES Whiteflies are a major pest, especially on plants started in greenhouses. Inspect nursery-grown seedlings carefully for infestations before bringing them home.

Tropaeolum majus
nasturtium or Indian cress

Tropaeolaceae—nasturtium family
height: 12 in. or more; spread: 6 in. to 9 in.

Nasturtiums furnish edible leaves, buds, and flowers, as well as color. (Photo by Michael A. Ruggiero.)

❧ **The latin name of this plant** is most descriptive, for it derives from the Latin word for trophy, and the nasturtium leaves and blossoms do resemble tiny shields and helmets just like those that Roman soldiers brought home as spoils of battle. Lest this sound stiff and classical, it should be noted that nasturtium flowers strike a cheerful, unpretentious note, and that the foliage is appealingly lush.

SOW Outdoors in late spring or indoors 5 weeks before planting out. Soak seed for 5 days prior to sowing. Indoors, sow in individual pots, covering seed with ⅛ in. to ½ in. of soil. Place in a black plastic bag and keep out of the light. Germination should occur in 7 to 14 days at 65° to 70°F.

GARDEN USES These easy-to-grow, mound-forming or climbing plants have long been favorites for window boxes, baskets, and containers of all types. They also make a good show as bedding plants. In addition, nasturtiums are the ideal plant for brightening a vegetable garden or potager, as the flowers and the foliage are both edible. Indeed, the flowers are often used as garnishes or in salads at restaurants, and the buds and seeds may be pickled as a substitute for capers.

CULTURE Nasturtiums are sun lovers and need a site with full sun, though a bit of shade during the hottest part of the day can be welcome, especially in the South. Without this protection, the plants may stop flowering during the height of the summer. Certainly, nasturtiums do best where the air remains cool and breezy.

They also require a very well drained soil of rather average to poor fertility. Rich soil or frequent fertilization encourages the plants to put all their energy into leaf production, and such overfed specimens may flower little or not at all. This, actually, may be what you want if you are growing cultivars with variegated foliage, for the effect of the striped or splashed leaves in a mixed container planting is quite spectacular, and all the more dramatic without the distraction of blossoms.

Nasturtium roots are sensitive to disturbance, so it is best to sow the seed directly where the plants are to grow, or to start them in individual peat pots.

GARDENER'S CHOICE 'Jewel Mix', semidouble flowers of mixed colors on 12-in. plants; 'Glorious Gleam Mix', mixed colors on trailing plants that are useful in baskets; 'Whirlybird Mix', spurless single flowers that face upward and are more noticeable than those of other cultivars; 'Flore-pleno', a double form that doesn't produce seed and is propagated from cuttings; 'Empress of India', a very popular cultivar that has vermilion flowers on a 12-in.-high, mound-forming plant; 'Alaska', bearing blossoms in a wide range of colors including apricot, pink, and cream, with variegated leaves; 'Jewel of Africa', a recent cultivar similar to 'Alaska' but with a climbing habit of growth.

PESTS AND DISEASES Leaf spot, cabbage loopers, aphids, and thrips.

⚘ **This South American native** has long been popular among European gardeners, but it is only now coming into its own in the United States. Crucial to the tall vervain's success is that we are finally learning how to use the plant. Because of its leggy, open habit of growth, it needs to be surrounded by a retinue of other, less lofty annuals. Not only is this more visually attractive, the bushier companions help to suppress the weeds that might otherwise invade the open space around the vervain's base.

A related species, the one for which the whole genus is named, is the European wildflower Verbena officinalis. This vervain has been believed since ancient times to have curative powers and was named for its supposed ability to expel bladder stones: Fer is the Celtic verb "to remove" and faen signifies "stones."

SOW Indoors, 10 to 12 weeks before last frost date. Keep pots at 70° to 75°F and in the dark. Germination should begin in 12 to 18 days. Outdoors, sow in late spring after the soil has warmed.

GARDEN USES In a proper combination, the vervain's airy texture is quite attractive and a decided asset in a container or in massed bedding displays. The long stalks on which the tall vervain bears its flowers also make it an elegant cut flower.

CULTURE Verbena bonariensis prefers full sun and rich, well-drained soil. You should pinch the seedlings twice before planting them out. Make the first pinch, removing the growing tip, when the seedlings have just three sets of leaves. This treatment will force out side branches and make the seedlings bushier. When these side branches have each sprouted three sets of leaves, pinch back their growing tips. This will help to keep the plants compact, with a dense structure and a well-filled center.

Verbena bonariensis
tall vervain, purple top

Verbenaceae—**vervain family**
height: 4 ft. to 5 ft.; spread: 16 in. to 24 in.

Butterflies find vervain irresistible. (Photo by Michael A. Ruggiero.)

When planting vervain in the garden, set the plants slightly deeper into the soil than they were growing in the pots, to encourage fuller root systems and stronger growth.

Once in bloom, your tall vervains will continue to flower even if you do not deadhead them. You may want to practice this sort of finger pruning anyway, as tall vervain has a tendency to self-sow, filling the bed with volunteer seedlings the next year. In some areas of North America, this plant has escaped from the garden to establish itself as a wildflower.

GARDENER'S CHOICE Verbena rigida is a related and similar species that offers slightly larger leaves and a more modest stature: It grows to a height of only 1 ft. to 2 ft.

PESTS AND DISEASES Powdery mildew and damping off can be troublesome.

Verbena x *hybrida* (*Glandularia* x *hybrida*)
garden vervain

Verbenaceae—vervain family
height: 6 in. to 10 in.; spread: 12 in. to 18in.

A creeping plant, garden vervain fits best at the edge of a bed or border or spilling over the edge of a container. (Photo by Michael A. Ruggiero.)

❧ **This is one of those flowers** that never existed in nature but instead originated in the garden through forced mating of different wild species. Unlike the preceding verbena, which provides a vertical accent, the garden verbena is a creeping plant, and as such it is invaluable as an edging for the front of a bed or border, or cascading over the lip of a container or window box. Over the years, gardeners found these plants too colorful and useful to resist, even though the older cultivars have an annoying tendency to stop blooming during hot weather and are magnets for whiteflies. The susceptibility to whiteflies remains (always check plants thoroughly for infestation before bringing them home from the nursery), but the newer cultivars are much more heat tolerant and, outside of the Deep South and the desert Southwest, they bloom all summer long. What's more, the flower colors of the new verbenas are among the most vibrant and clear of any summer-blooming annual, and the onset of fall's cooler weather only enhances their hues. If you tire of the hybrid garden verbenas, you can try one of the other creeping species types described under Gardener's Choice.

SOW Indoors, 12 to 14 weeks before the last frost. Prechill seed for 5 days prior to sowing and use sterilized soil, for verbena are prone to damping off. Place in the dark until germination, which occurs in 12 to 18 days at 70° to 75°F.

GARDEN USES Use the plants anywhere you want a bright sheet of color.

CULTURE Like other verbenas, the garden hybrids prefer a well-drained soil of average fertility, and they flourish in full sun, though they will tolerate partial shade during the early afternoon. If, after a period of heavy flowering, they show signs of flagging, shear them back lightly and fertilize them, and your garden verbenas will soon be in full bloom once again.

GARDENER'S CHOICE Verbena x hybrida offers many series of cultivars, as well as individual types. Novalis series has early-blooming, upright but compact, 10-in.-tall plants that resist heat and rainy weather. Romance series cultivars produce dense flower clusters in a wide range of colors on 6-in., spreading plants. Quartz hybrids are exceptionally resistant to mildew. 'Peaches and Cream' bears a blend of salmon and apricot flowers on 8-in.-high, 10-in.- to 12-in.-wide, weather-resistant plants.

Verbena canadensis, an American native with a creeping habit, has several cultivars. 'Apple Blossom' bears light pink flowers with ruffled petals. 'Silver Anne' has flowers of medium pink with a touch of white. 'Homestead Purple' flowers through the hottest of summers.

Verbena tenuisecta 'Imagination' has exceptionally attractive foliage, which is lacier and more finely cut than that of other species. It tolerates all types of weather conditions, including heat and drought, and it bears small clusters of deep purple flowers continuously from early summer into fall. The species is native to South America. Use both tenuisecta and canadensis cultivars in baskets and other containers, and as a ground cover.

PESTS AND DISEASES Seedlings are prone to damping off. Powdery mildew and whiteflies are the principal problems of mature plants.

The periwinkle includes two notable species of cold-sensitive perennials that can do valuable service as annuals in North American gardens. The greater periwinkle, Vinca major 'Variegata', is a vine whose stems extend to a length of several feet; Madagascar periwinkle (traditionally classified as Vinca rosea but recently reclassified as Catharanthus roseus) is a compact flower that, depending on the cultivar, grows to a height of 4 in. to 18 in., with a spread of 12 in. to 15 in.

The chief attraction of the greater periwinkle is its elegant foliage, which hangs in a variegated curtain of graceful tendrils from window boxes, urns, planters, and baskets. In the milder regions of the country, greater periwinkle also makes a striking semi-evergreen to evergreen ground cover; if planted into a bed after the danger of frost is past, it will cover a surprising area of soil by the end of the growing season.

In contrast, Madagascar periwinkle's most useful feature is its tolerance for heat and humidity. It is an outstanding flower for the southeastern states, continuing to bloom throughout weather that kills outright most of the other plants in the annual garden. For the same reason, Madagascar periwinkle is also excellent for the hot, often muggy conditions of inner-city plantings.

START Start greater periwinkle by taking cuttings any time of year from stem tips or sections of the stems. Cuttings should include three or four nodes; remove lower leaves and root in peat/sand mix. Or layer the stems, burying nodes in the soil until they root. Sow Madagascar periwinkle indoors 10 to 12 weeks before the last frost date. Cover seeds lightly and place container in complete darkness. Germination in 10 to 20 days at 70° to 75°F by day, 60°F by night. Do not overwater.

GARDEN USES An outstanding foliage plant for container designs, greater periwinkle may be dug and potted up and then brought indoors before the first fall frost. Overwintered on a sunny windowsill, the rescued plants will bear star-shaped blue flowers until spring.

Madagascar periwinkle is excellent in mass bedding displays, carpet beds, container plantings, and window boxes. By staking a central stem and pinching off side shoots as they appear, you can also train a Madagascar periwinkle into a handsome standard.

CULTURE Greater periwinkle thrives in light to heavy shade. In addition, it performs well in areas of full sun, except in the Deep South, where it needs some protection. It prefers a rich, organic soil, and when grown as a ground cover, it requires excellent drainage.

Vinca spp.
periwinkle
Apocynaceae—dogbane family
height and spread: varies with species

A swag of greater periwinkle's variegated foliage dresses up a window box, urn, or pot. (Photo by Judi Rutz; © The Taunton Press, Inc.)

Madagascar periwinkle requires full sun and a soil that is warm, well drained, and humusy. Do not set it out into the garden until all danger of frost is past and the soil has warmed sufficiently for planting peppers. Setting this plant out early is likely to stunt it or even cause it to rot and die.

GARDENER'S CHOICE Popular types of Madagascar periwinkle include the Cooler series, compact cultivars that cover themselves with 2-in. to $2^{1}/_{2}$-in. flowers. These include 'Peppermint Cooler', white flowers with a red eye; 'Pink Cooler', rose pink with a white eye; 'Icy Pink Cooler', pastel pink with a white eye; and 'Blush Cooler', light pink with a red eye.

Other interesting new cultivars include the taller growing (18-in. to 20-in.) Pacifica series, which bears 2-in.-wide flowers and includes 'Pacifica Lilac', with light purple flowers; 'Pacifica White', with pure white flowers with a faint pink eye; and 'Pacifica Red', with red flowers with a deeper red eye.

PESTS AND DISEASES Greater periwinkle is generally trouble free, though plants over wintered indoors are susceptible to spider mites and mealybugs. Madagascar periwinkle typically remains pest and disease free.

Viola x *wittrockiana*
garden pansy

Violaceae—violet family
height: 4 in. to 8 in.; spread: 4 in. to 10 in.

Pansies 'Beaconsfield' (center) and 'True Blue' (rear) in an edible combination with lettuces. (Photo by Michael A. Ruggiero.)

❧ **Without question, pansies are the most popular** of all the spring annuals, and it's easy to understand why. The plants are easy to grow and rarely bothered by the sudden frosts that are such a common feature of a northern springtime. On occasion, you'll find your pansies actually encased in ice in the morning, and then thawed, the flowers and buds unharmed, in the afternoon.

Not only are pansies hardy, the cloisonéed blossoms offer an extraordinary range of flower colors. And though they are commonly grown as spring flowers, pansies can be much more. Where summers are cool, as in the Pacific Northwest, they will bloom right through into fall, and in the South they make outstanding annuals for the winter garden.

Most gardeners today opt for convenience, buying nursery-grown pansy plants in early to mid spring and planting them out in the garden immediately. This method of cultivation is easy, and it produces a fine display of flowers. It does, however, limit your choice of pansy cultivars to the handful of best sellers that the nurserymen prefer to stock. Starting your own plants from seed vastly expands your options, putting at your disposal dozens of different cultivars, and pansies of the most unusual, jewellike colors. But it also involves recognizing the pansy for what it really is: a biennial, not a true annual (see later section, Culture).

The name pansy, incidentally, is French; it derives from the word pensée, which means thought, and it alludes to the belief that the violet, and its offspring the pansy, invoked contemplation. Certainly, the "face," the pattern of blotches that marks many pansy flowers, has a thoughtful look to it.

SOW For spring bloom, sow in mid August in a nursery bed and transplant seedlings to the garden in September. Or sow indoors in late October. Cover seeds lightly and place in total darkness; keep seed pots at 65° to 70°F, and germination should occur in 6 to 12 days. Grow seedlings in a cool greenhouse or cold frame to have plants ready for transplanting into the garden in early spring.

GARDEN USES For a resourceful gardener, pansies are a great season-extender. Planting them in a perennial bed or border brings that part of the garden into bloom weeks earlier, and they'll serve as a handsome setting when the early-flowering perennials do start to open.

Pansies can also add another level (literally) of color to a display of spring bulbs. Mass pansies of a contrasting flower color under and among a block of tall hybrid tulips and you'll create a pointillist effect, in which each level of color seems to take energy from the other, and the bed as a whole almost hums.

There is an old-fashioned, formal quality to the exquisite pansy blossoms that makes them perfect for container displays as well. You'll be pleased with their effect in window boxes, pots, urns, or any other kind of planter. If you grow the longer-stemmed pansy cultivars, you'll also find they make fine cut flowers, and you can pick the blossoms from their short-stemmed fellows to use as a garnish on your plat du jour—they are edible.

CULTURE To start your own pansy plants, you should sow the seed outdoors in a shaded nursery bed in mid summer. Transplant the seedlings into the spot where you want them to bloom the following spring, and after the ground freezes, tuck them in with a light mulch of salt hay or evergreen boughs. This protects the plants from the extremes of winter weather and helps to bring them through unharmed to spring, when they will bloom earlier and bear bigger flowers than any plants you find on a nurseryman's shelf.

An alternative method is to sow seeds into the nursery bed in mid summer and then pot up the seedlings into 4-in. plastic pots in September. Store the pots in a cold frame over the winter. In spring, you can use them much as you would nursery-grown transplants. These pot-grown pansies don't offer the same precociousness of the ones you overwinter in the soil, but starting the plants yourself in this fashion does open up all the wonderful options available only to those who grow from seed.

A last option for starting pansies from seed is to grow them in a cool greenhouse. Wait until October to sow the seeds. Keep the greenhouse frost free, but just. Daytime temperatures should stay in the range of 50° to 55°F, while at night the temperature should sink to 45° to 50°F. Keeping the greenhouse warmer than this actually produces smaller plants that will bloom sooner but bear smaller flowers.

In the garden, pansies tolerate a wide range of soils, but they perform best in a moderately fertile, organic-rich, well-drained, and cool soil. Pansies do not cope well with heat or drought, and your plants will fade quickly when the season changes and hot weather settles in. For the same reason, gardeners outside the most temperate regions of the country should consider planting their pansies where they will get some afternoon shade. The usual recommendation is to plant them in full sun or partial shade, and as far as light intensity goes, they will thrive in either setting. As the weather heats up in late spring, however, protection from the sun during the afternoon will keep the plants blooming for several weeks longer. Another simple measure you can take to prolong and enhance the bloom of your pansies is regular deadheading.

GARDENER'S CHOICE The Universal Plus series of 21 cultivars covers all the usual pansy colors except black and orange. The vigorous, weatherproof, early-blooming plants hold their flowers up on strong stems. Antique Shades cultivars bear 3-in.-wide flowers with a silky sheen and pastel colors. 'Crystal Bowl Mix' bears 2^1/$_2$-in.-wide, faceless flowers in clear colors. These plants exhibit an outstanding resistance to heat and cold. 'Padparadja' is named after the famed orange sapphire; it bears 2^1/$_2$-in.-wide, faceless blossoms of deep orange.

'Springtime Black', 'Zorro', and 'Thompson & Morgan Black' are three cultivars whose flowers are all such a deep purple color that they appear to be silky black. They are especially dramatic when mixed with other spring-blooming flowers of white or yellow.

PESTS AND DISEASES You may find aphids clustered on the buds of your pansies or in the crown of the leaves. Slugs also attack pansies.

Zinnia elegans
garden zinnia

Asteraceae—daisy family
height: 6 in. to 40 in.; spread: 6 in. to 18 in.

Zinnia 'Red Sun' makes a colorful and reliable cut or garden flower. (Photo by Michael A. Ruggiero.)

❧ **If garden zinnias were only harder to grow,** they would be much more fashionable. They have all the virtues any gardener could want. Variety—the garden zinnias range from tiny edging and rock garden plants to stalwart bedders and lofty back-of-the-border "mammoths" that stand almost shoulder high. They bear flowers in a bewildering variety of forms, from pompoms, neat puffs of petals, to porcupinelike "cactus-flowered" types with petals rolled into quills. The flower colors are brilliant and cover almost the whole spectrum, and they can also be quite unexpected, like the chartreuse green blossoms of zinnia 'Envy'. If it weren't for the fact that anyone can grow them, zinnias, not orchids, would be the flowers that socialites would be pinning to their gowns.

SOW Indoors, 4 to 5 weeks before last frost date. Germination occurs in 4 to 7 days at 70°F. Sow outdoors after all danger of frost is past.

GARDEN USES Cultivars of various sizes can fill almost any niche in a flower bed or border. Garden zinnias also make outstanding cut flowers, and if sown at 3-week intervals from early spring until late June, they'll keep your vases full from July until frost.

CULTURE Though classified as a distinct species, Z. elegans actually represents a complex intermarriage of Mexican wildflowers. As one might expect of plants with this parentage, garden zinnias prefer well-drained soil, although they also like it to be rich in organic material, and they perform best when the weather is hot and dry. Given full sun and good air circulation, the other basic requirement is a light monthly fertilization.

Pinching back the plants after they produce their third set of leaves encourages branches to sprout or "break" from the base of the stalk, which in turn promotes bushier, more compact growth. Such pinching also promotes the growth of stronger stems and increases the quantity of flowers each plant bears.

Regular deadheading is also important to keep the plants blooming and neat. Otherwise, the only precaution you need observe is that, whenever possible, you do not water late in the day. Doing that is likely to leave the zinnias' foliage wet overnight, which leaves the plants open to infection by the powdery mildew fungus. If possible, water in the morning, so that the sun will have a chance to dry the leaves promptly.

GARDENER'S CHOICE Zinnia cultivars are usually classified by flower type, and small, button, cactus, dahlia, and mammoth are the most common classes. These classifications are of interest mainly to gardeners who grow zinnias for exhibition at flower shows.

Specific cultivars and series of cultivars include 'Thumbelina Mix', bearing $1^{1}/_{2}$-in. flowers in a wide range of colors on 6-in.-tall, mounded plants; the Peter Pan series, offering 2-in.-wide flowers on compact, 10-in.- to 14-in.-tall plants; Dreamland cultivars, bearing fully double 3-in.- to $3^{1}/_{2}$-in.-wide, dahlia-flowered blossoms on 18-in.- to 20-in.-tall plants.

The Radiant series and Cut and Come Again cultivars make 2-ft.- to $2^{1}/_{2}$-ft.-tall plants that bear 3-in.-wide flowers on long, strong stems. These are versatile plants that can hold their own in a bedding display while also being used as a source of cut flowers.

The Sun series includes 'Red Sun', 'Yellow Sun', 'Silver Sun' (which bears pure white flowers), and 'Cherry Sun'. These durable, 18-in.- to 24-in.-tall cultivars bear large (4-in.-diameter) flowers. Their disease and weather resistance is outstanding, and they are a good choice for the middle to back of the border.

'Chippendale' makes a 14-in.- to 16-in.-tall plant that bears 2-in.-wide, semidouble flowers whose mahogany red rays are tipped with yellow. 'Envy' is one of the few annuals to bear chartreuse-green flowers. The 30-in.-tall plants bear 3-in. to $3^{1}/_{2}$-in. flowers that are excellent for cutting.

A related species, the narrow-leaved zinnia (Z. angustifolia), is a simpler, wilder flower with an uncomplicated charm that is easier to fit into a landscape. Because it is several generations closer to the wild, this species is hardier and easier to grow. Naturally compact, the narrow-leaved zinnia forms a low, much-branched plant without any pinching back, and its foliage is much less prone to mildew. The color range is limited to oranges, yellows, and white, but the profusion of flowers makes this plant a very ornamental choice for the front of a border, a container display, or a hanging basket.

Good cultivars include 'White Star' (or 'Star White'), 'Crystal White', 'Gold Star', and 'Orange Star'.

PESTS AND DISEASES Root and stem rots are likely to attack zinnias grown in poorly drained soils. Powdery mildew is a common problem, and these plants are attractive to Japanese beetles.

APPENDIX: ANNUALS FOR SPECIAL USES

Annuals for Cutting

Botanical Name	Common Name	Botanical Name	Common Name
Ageratum 'Blue Horizon'	flossflower	*Dahlia* spp.	dahlia
Amaranthus spp.	tampala, love-lies-bleeding	*Dianthus chinensis*	border pink
Ammi majus	greater ammi	*Gaillardia pulchella*	treasure flower
Ammi visagna	ammi	*Gerbera jamesonii*	Transvaal daisy
Ammobium alatum 'Grandiflorum'	winged everlasting	*Gomphrena globosa*	globe amaranth
Anethum graveolens	dill	*Gypsophila elegans*	annual baby's breath
Antirrhinum majus	snapdragon	*Helianthus annuus*	common sunflower
Browallia speciosa	bush violet	*Heliotropum arborescens*	heliotrope, cherry pie
Bupleurum rotundifolium	roundleaf thorowax	*Hunnemannia fumariaefolia*	Mexican tulip poppy
Calendula officinalis	pot marigold	*Iberis amara*	rocket candytuft
Callistephus chinensis	China aster	*Iberis umbellata*	common candytuft
Carthamus tinctorius	false saffron, safflower	*Lathyrus odoratus*	sweet pea
Celosia argentea var. *cristata*	cockscomb	*Limonium sinuatum*	notched sea-lavender
Centaurea americana	basketflower	*Lisianthus russellianus*	lisianthus
Centaurea cyanus	bachelor's button	*Lupinus* spp.	lupine
Chrysanthemum frutescens	white marguerite	*Matthiola incana*	stock
Chrysanthemum x *grandiflorum*	garden mum	*Moluccella laevis*	bells of Ireland
Clarkia amoena	satin flower	*Nicotiana* x *sanderae*	flowering tobacco
Cleome hasslerana	spider flower	*Nigella damascena*	love-in-a-mist
Consolida ambigua	rocket larkspur	*Penstemon* spp.	annual penstemon
Coreopsis tinctoria	calliopsis	*Phlox drummondii*	annual phlox
Cosmos bipinnatus	cosmos	*Reseda odorata*	common mignonette
Cosmos sulphureus	yellow cosmos	*Salpiglossis sinuata*	painted tongue
Crepis rubra	red hawks-beard	*Salvia coccinea*	red sage

Annuals with Fragrant Flowers

Botanical Name	Common Name
Salvia farinacea	mealy-cup sage
Salvia leucantha	Mexican sage
Scabiosa atropurpurea	pinchusion flower
Schizanthus pinnatus	butterfly flower, poor man's orchid
Tagetes erecta	African marigold
Tagetes patula	French marigold
Tagetes tenuifolia	signet marigold
Trachelium caeruleum	blue throatwort
Trachymene caerulea	blue lace flower
Tropaeolum majus	nasturtium
Verbena bonariensis	vervain
Viola spp.	violet
Viola x *wittrockiana*	garden pansy
Zinnia spp.	zinnia

Botanical Name	Common Name
Ageratum houstonianum	flossflower
Antirrhinum majus	snapdragon
Dianthus barbatus	sweet William
Iberis spp.	candytuft
Ipomoea alba	moonflower
Heliotropium arborescens	heliotrope
Hesperus matronalis	dame's rocket
Lathyrus odoratus	sweet pea
Limnanthes douglasii	meadow foam
Lobularia maritima	sweet alyssum
Lunaria annua	money plant
Matthiola bicolor	night stock
Matthiola incana	stock
Nicotiana alata	flowering tobacco
Reseda odorata	common mignonette
Tagetes spp.	marigold
Verbena x *hybrida*	garden verbena
Viola x *wittrockiana*	garden pansy

Annuals for Semishade to Shade

Botanical Name	Common Name
Alternanthera spp.	Joseph's coat
Antirrhinum majus	snapdragon
Begonia semperflorens-cultorum	wax begonia
Begonia tuberhybrida	tuberous begonia
Bellis perennis	English daisy
Browallia speciosa	bush violet
Caladium x *hortulanum*	fancy-leaved caladium
Calendula officinalis	pot marigold
Campanula medium	Canterbury bells
Centaurea cyanus	bachelor's button
Clarkia spp.	clarkia
Coleus hybrids (syn. *Solenostemon scutellarioides*)	coleus
Consolida ambigua	rocket larkspur
Cynoglossum amabile	Chinese forget-me-not
Eschscholtzia californica	California poppy
Hesperis matronalis	dame's rocket
Iberis umbellata	candytuft
Impatiens spp.	New Guinea impatiens
Impatiens wallerana	garden impatiens
Lobelia erinus	edging lobelia
Lobularia maritima	sweet alyssum
Lunaria annua	money plant
Mimulus ringens	monkey flower
Mirabilis jalapa	four-o'clock
Myosotis sylvatica	forget-me-not
Nemophila menziesii	baby blue eyes
Nicotiana spp.	flowering tobacco
Petunia x *hybrida*	petunia
Phlox drummondii	annual phlox
Salvia coccinea	red sage
Salvia farinacea	mealycup sage
Salvia splendens	scarlet sage
Schizanthus spp.	poor man's orchid
Strobilanthes dyerianus	Persian shield
Torenia fournieri	wishbone flower
Viola x *wittrockiana*	garden pansy

Annuals for Moist Soil

Botanical Name	Common Name
Calendula officinalis	pot marigold
Dianthus chinensis	border pink
Iberis umbellata	candytuft
Kochia scoparia	summer cypress
Lathyrus odoratus	sweet pea
Myosotis sylvatica	forget-me-not
Nemesia spp.	nemesia
Nemophila menziesii	baby blue eyes
Nicotiana spp.	flowering tobacco
Torenia fournieri	wishbone plant
Trachymene caerulea	blue lace flower

Annuals for Sandy Soil

Botanical Name	Common Name
Amaranthus spp.	amaranth
Catharanthus roseus	Madagascar periwinkle
Celosia spp.	cockscomb
Centaurea cyanus	bachelor's button
Clarkia spp.	clarkia
Cleome hasslerana	spider flower
Eschscholtzia californica	California poppy
Euphorbia marginata	snow-on-the-mountain
Gaillardia pulchella	blanket flower
Gazania ringens	treasure flower
Gomphrena spp.	globe amaranth
Gypsophila elegans	annual baby's breath
Helianthus annuus	common sunflower
Ipomoea spp.	morning glory
Kochia scoparius	summer cypress
Limonium sinuatum	statice
Mesembryanthemum spp.	ice plant
Mirabilis jalapa	four-o'clock
Nolana paradoxa	Chilean bellflower
Perilla frutescens	perilla
Portulaca grandiflora	rose moss
Rudbeckia spp.	gloriosa daisy
Salvia spp.	sage
Senecio cineraria	dusty miller
Tropaeolum majus	nasturtium
Verbena spp.	vervain

Annuals Tolerant of Humid Heat

Botanical Name	Common Name
Abelmoschus manihot	sunset hibiscus
Abelmoschus moschatus	musk mallow
Caladium x *hortulanum*	fancy-leaved caladium
Canna x *generalis*	common garden canna
Catharanthus roseus	Madagascar periwinkle
Celosia argentea var. *cristata*	common cockscomb
Cleome hasslerana	spider flower
Coleus x *hybridus*	coleus
Cosmos bipinnatus	cosmos
Dolichos lablab	hyacinth bean
Gomphrena globosa	globe amaranth
Ipomoea alba	moonflower
Ipomoea batatas	ornamental sweet potato
Ipomoea 'Quamoclit'	cypress vine
Ipomoea purpurea	common morning glory
Impatiens balsamina	garden balsam
Impatiens wallerana	garden impatiens
Lantana camara	yellow sage
Portulaca grandiflora	rose moss
Ricinus communis	castor bean
Salvia coccinea	Texas sage
Strobilanthes dyerianus	Persian shield
Thunbergia alata	black-eyed Susan vine
Tibouchina urvilleana	glory bush

Annuals Tolerant of Drought

Botanical Name	Common Name	Botanical Name	Common Name
Ageratum houstonianum	floss flower	*Mirabilis jalapa*	four-o'clock
Amaranthus spp.	tampala, love-lies-bleeding	*Nicotiana* spp.	flowering tobacco
Anagallis monellii	pimpernel	*Nolana paradoxa*	Chilean bellflower
Arctotis grandis	African daisy	*Perilla frutescens*	perilla
Brachycome iberidifolia	Swan River daisy	*Petunia* x *hybrida*	petunia
Briza maxima	quaking grass	*Phlox drummondii*	annual phlox
Calendula officinalis	pot marigold	*Portulaca grandiflora*	rose moss
Callirhoe pedata	poppy mallow	*Rudbeckia* spp.	gloriosa daisy
Catharanthus roseus	Madagascar periwinkle	*Sanvitalia procumbens*	creeping zinnia
Centaurea cyanus	bachelor's button	*Senecio cineraria*	dusty miller
Cleome hasslerana	spider flower	*Tagetes* spp.	marigold
Cosmos bipinnatus	cosmos	*Tithonia rotundifolia*	Mexican sunflower
Cynoglossum amabile	Chinese forget-me-not	*Tropaeolum majus*	nasturtium
Dianthus chinensis	border pink	*Verbena* x *hybrida* (syn. *Glandularia*)	garden verbena
Eschscholtzia californica	California poppy	*Vinca major* 'Variegata'	greater periwinkle
Euphorbia marginata	snow-on-the-mountain	*Zinnia angustifolia*	narrow-leaved zinnia
Gazania ringens	Transvaal daisy		
Gypsophila elegans	annual baby's breath		
Helichrysum bracteatum	strawflower		
Ipomoea spp.	morning glory, moonflower		
Lantana camara	red sage lantana		
Lantana montevidensis	trailing lantana		
Limonium sinuatum	statice		
Melampodium paludosum	blackfoot daisy		

Annual Vines and Plants with a Vinelike Habit

Botanical Name	Common Name
Asarina erubescens (syn. *A. scandens*)	creeping gloxinia
Cardiospermum halicacabum	balloon vine, love-in-a-puff
Cobaea scandens	cathedral bells
Humulus japonicus 'Variegata'	variegated ornamental hops
Humulus lupulus 'Aureus'	golden hops
Ipomoea alba	moonflower
Ipomoea lobata (syn. *Mina lobata*)	Spanish flag
Ipomoea purpurea	common morning glory
Ipomoea quamoclit (syn. *Quamoclit pennata*)	star glory
Ipomoea x multifida (syn. *Quamoclit sloteri*)	cardinal climber
Lab-lab purpurea (syn. *Dolichos lablab*)	hyacinth bean
Lathyrus odoratus	sweet pea
Phaseolus coccineus	scarlet runner bean
Thunbergia alata	black-eyed Susan vine
Rhodochiton atrosanguineus	purple bellvine
Tropaeolum peregrinum	canary creeper
Vinca major 'Variegata'	greater periwinkle

Annuals for Hanging Baskets

Botanical Name	Common Name
Alternanthera dentata 'Rubriginosa'	alternanthera
Brachycombe iberidifolia	Swan River daisy
Browallia speciosa	bush violet
Cobaea scandens	cup and saucer vine
Convolvulus spp.	dwarf morning glory
Fuchsia x hybrida	fuchsia
Impatiens wallerana	garden impatiens
Lantana camara	red sage lantana
Lantana montevidensis	trailing lantana
Lobelia erinus	edging lobelia
Lobularia maritima	sweet alyssum
Nierembergia rivulus	cup plant
Pelargonium peltatum	ivy-leaved geranium
Petunia spp.	petunia
Portulaca grandiflora	rose moss
Thunbergia alata	black-eyed Susan vine
Torenia fournieri	wishbone plant
Tropaeolum majus	nasturtium
Verbena x hybrida	garden verbena
Vinca major 'Variegata'	greater periwinkle

Annuals for Edging

Botanical Name	Common Name	Botanical Name	Common Name
Ageratum houstonianum	floss flower	*Nemophila menziesii*	baby blue eyes
Anagallis monellii	pimpernel	*Petunia* spp.	petunia
Antirrhinum majus	snapdragon	*Phacelia campanularia*	California bluebell
Begonia semperflorens-cultorum	wax begonia	*Phlox drummondii*	annual phlox
Begonia x tuberhybrida	tuberous begonia	*Portulaca grandiflora*	rose moss
Bellis perennis	English daisy	*Salvia splendens*	scarlet sage
Briza maxima	quaking grass	*Sanvitalia procumbens*	creeping zinnia
Catharanthus roseus	Madagascar periwinkle	*Senecio maritima*	dusty miller
Celosia spp.	cockscomb	*Tagetes patula*	French marigold
Cheiranthus cheri	wallflower	*Tagetes tenuifolia*	signet marigold
Coleus hybrids		*Tropaeolum majus*	nasturtium
(syn. *Solostemon scutellarioides*)	coleus	*Verbena x hybrida* (syn. *Glandularia*)	garden verbena
Dianthus chinensis	border pink	*Viola x wittrockiana*	garden pansy
Felicia amellioides	felicia	*Zinnia angustifolia*	narrow-leaved zinnia
Gazania ringens	Transvaal daisy	*Zinnia elegans* (dwarf)	zinnia
Iberis umbellata	candytuft		
Impatiens wallerana	garden impatiens		
Lobelia erinus	edging lobelia		
Lobularia maritima	sweet alyssum		
Limnanthus douglasii	meadow foam		
Matricaria matricarioides	dames rocket		
Mesembryanthemum spp.	ice plant		

INDEX

Note: references in bold indicate an entry in The Essential Annuals.